Macroeconomics Workbook: Principles and Practice

ISBN 978-1-60904-835-8

Kari L. Battaglia & Susan L. Dadres

Published by

Stipes Publishing L.L.C.
www.stipes.com

Table of Contents
Macroeconomics Workbook
Principles and Practice
2019

This Workbook belongs to ____

If found, please return to the Economics Department or call ____________________

Course Information:

____

____

____

Instructor Information:

____

____

____

Important Dates and Assignments:

____

____

____

____

____

____

____

____

____

CHAPTER 1 Introduction to Macroeconomics: Basic Definitions and the Fundamentals of Graphing

The **economy** refers to the sum of all the decisions, or choices, made and actions taken by individuals and groups, including households, businesses, and government, that involve the use of any kind of resource. **Economics** is a social science that studies the choices individuals and societies make regarding the use of resources. Economics is divided into microeconomics and macroeconomics. **Microeconomics** studies the decisions of individuals, households, and firms and focuses on the interaction of buyers and sellers in specific markets and the production decisions of firms. **Macroeconomics** is the study of the economy as a whole; it uses economic aggregates, such as the national unemployment rate, the rate of inflation, and the economy's growth rate, to measure economic activity and to evaluate the performance of the economy. Macroeconomics also studies policies designed to promote full employment, price stability, and a healthy rate of economic growth.

The study of economics can be approached from both a positive and a normative perspective. **Positive economics** deals with statements about what is, which can be tested against facts. **Normative economics** deals with statements of what should be and requires value judgments. For example, *many low-income families do not have health insurance*, is a positive statement about what is, while "government should do something to help low-income families obtain health insurance" is a normative statement. Economists develop and test positive statements and often make normative statements in the form of policy recommendations.

Whether engaged in microeconomic analysis or macroeconomic analysis, positive analysis or normative analysis, economists are concerned with observing behavior, understanding relationships, predicting outcomes, and identifying solutions to economic problems. It is a field of study with enormous practical applications, yet may seem abstract at times as we attempt to develop generalized explanations for why events occur as they do.

The Fundamental Economic Problem

The fundamental economic problem is scarcity. **Scarcity** exists because there are not enough resources available to produce all the goods and services that people want and need. This means resources are limited relative to the desired uses for them. Economists classify **resources** (also referred to as **inputs** or **factors of production)** into four categories:

- Land and other natural resources
- Labor services
- Capital (structures and equipment)
- Entrepreneurial ability

The **land** resource category encompasses all gifts of nature. These natural resources include land as well as timber, water, minerals, and climate. The importance of land as an input into the production of an output depends on the type of output produced. Producing a haircut does not require a significant amount of land, or natural resources, while producing energy does.

Labor services represent the physical and mental talents of people. Labor includes the production efforts of all kinds of workers in every industry—manufacturing, retail, and services. Labor is the most significant input in almost every productive endeavor. For most people, labor is the resource they have available to sell, and payments to labor are the greatest portion of the cost of producing output in the United States.

Capital is the physical plant and equipment used in production and refers to the structures that have been built and the machines, tools, and equipment that have been produced in the past, which can now be used to produce goods and provide services. A business firm invests in capital when it builds a factory or office building, or acquires new machines, tools, or equipment, for its workers to use. The word capital often means money in everyday use, and when people talk about investments, they may be talking about buying stocks and bonds. It is important to distinguish between the everyday use of words and the way economists use these words.

Entrepreneurs are innovators who start or operate a business in the expectation of earning profit. They organize resources to produce the goods or services that are sold by the business. Entrepreneurs take risks; they often see an opportunity before anyone else or offer something new and different. In a market economy, entrepreneurs make many of the decisions about how to allocate scarce resources, and they are motivated to make efficient decisions in order to maximize profits.

All of the above resources are scarce (limited), and decisions must be made about how to use them. Scarcity means that society faces tradeoffs. When a resource is used in one activity, it cannot be used in another activity. For example, the timber cut down and used to make wooden billboards cannot also be used to produce housing; society trades, or gives up, the opportunity to use the wood to build houses in order to create billboards. **Opportunity cost** is the value of the best alternative that must be given up when a choice is made. The opportunity cost of the billboards is the value of the possible housing foregone, or given up, assuming the creation of housing is the next best alternative use of the wood. In order to use resources efficiently, society must consider opportunity cost when making decisions about how to allocate scarce resources among competing uses.

Economic Models and Economic Theory

The fundamental economic problem facing all societies is scarcity, which refers to the fact that we do not have enough resources to produce everything people want and need. Scarcity forces all societies to address the fundamental questions of **what outputs to produce, how to produce the outputs, and who ultimately gets to consume the outputs?** One purpose of economic theory is to develop an understanding of how society deals with this problem. Since there is scarcity and we can't have everything, what is the best way to use available resources? In other words, what should we produce? This also leads to the questions of how to produce and for whom. Economic theories and models are used to simplify and make sense of such broad questions that society is attempting to answer.

Economic **models** are designed to simplify reality in an attempt to explain real-world relationships and predict outcomes. In a basic economics course, the relationships identified and analyzed are generally between two economic variables, such as unemployment and the price level. Building a model begins with identifying the assumptions about what variables are important to the relationship and should be included in the model. The **ceteris paribus assumption** is used to isolate the relationship between two variables by holding other influences on the relationship constant. For example, the positive statement "consumer spending increases when national income increases, ceteris paribus," means that other events that might cause consumer spending to change, such as a decline in consumer confidence regarding job security, are being held constant in order to see how a change in national income affects consumer spending. Once a relationship has been identified and tested, a **theory** can be developed.

Economic theories are not necessarily complex; rather, a good economic theory explains important relationships. Many economic theories that have been widely accepted and applied take on the status of a "law" such as the law of demand, the law of supply, and the law of diminishing returns. One of the most important economic models you will learn about is the supply and demand model, which is based on theories about demand, supply, and market equilibrium.

Cautions and Pitfalls

Building economic models and developing economic theories that may be used to help design economic policy requires a disciplined and analytical approach in order to avoid several common pitfalls, or errors, in economic reasoning. These errors (fallacies) in reasoning can occur and lead to the wrong conclusion; being aware of these fallacies in reasoning can help economists and policy makers avoid them.

The **fallacy of false cause** (**post hoc fallacy or association-causation issue**) occurs when it is incorrectly assumed that if one event follows another, the first event must have caused the second event. In many cases, there may be an association between the two events, but one is not causing the other. An example is the relationship between ice cream sales and criminal activity. In many large cities, an increase in ice cream sales is followed closely by an increase in criminal activity. Concluding that eating ice cream leads to criminal behavior is erroneous. These events are associated because both tend to occur in the summer, but there is no cause-effect relationship. It is important not to confuse **association** (or **correlation**) with **causation**.

The **fallacy of division** occurs when it is incorrectly assumed that what is true for the whole is also true for each part of the whole. An example of the fallacy of division is concluding that because free trade brings benefits to the economy as a whole, it is also beneficial for each segment of society. Some segments of society may be worse off as a result of free trade. The fallacy of division occurs primarily in macroeconomics because it deals with the whole that is made up of many different parts. The opposite may also occur.

The **fallacy of composition** occurs when it is incorrectly assumed that what is true for the parts is also true for the whole. A general example of the fallacy of composition is concluding that because a specific group in the economy benefits from a government policy, the entire economy benefits as well. If government decides to establish a national health care program, all of society will be called upon to help pay for the program. Some groups in the economy may be better off as a result of nationalized health care; but some groups may be worse off, and the economy as a whole will not necessarily be better off. It should not be assumed that just because some groups will be better off as a result of a policy that all groups will be better off.

The Circular Flow Model

The **circular flow model**, which was developed in the mid-eighteenth century in France, was one of the first models used to help explain economic relationships. This model shows the interaction of participants in a market economy and can be used to help explain microeconomic relationships and macroeconomic measures.

In the simplest version of the circular flow model, the economy consists of two sectors: the **business sector (firms)** and the **household sector (consumers),** and two markets: the **product market (output market)** and the **resource market (input market)**. Scarce resources (also called factors of production or inputs) are exchanged in resource markets, and final goods and services, or outputs, are exchanged in product markets.

In a market economy that is based on private property, every person is part of the household sector, acting as consumers in product markets and as suppliers in resource markets. As consumers we **demand** goods and services like food, clothing, housing, medical care, and entertainment. As resource owners, we **supply** our labor services and other factors of production like the drilling rights to land we own or our entrepreneurial ability.

The business sector includes the firms that produce goods and services. Some of these are proprietorships, owned by a single individual; others are partnerships, owned by a group of individuals. Most firms in the U.S. are organized as proprietorships and partnerships but most of the output sold in the United States is produced by corporations. A corporation is considered a separate legal entity and is usually owned by a group of stockholders. Firms **supply** goods and services in the product market and **demand** resources, for example, by hiring workers. It is assumed that the goal of a firm is to maximize profit.

The diagram below shows the interactions that occur between the business sector and the household sector. The outer circle represents a **real** flow and the inner circle a **monetary** flow.

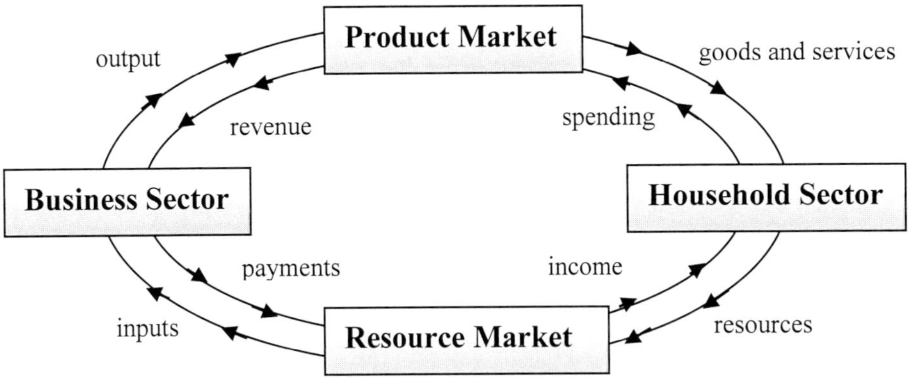

The model illustrates that households exchange resources for income in the resource market, and then spend income on goods and services in the product market. Business firms make payments for the use of inputs in the resource market and use those inputs to produce output, which is sold in the product market. **Microeconomics** studies the flow between the two sectors in a specific market by looking at only one part of the circular flow at a time. **Macroeconomics** studies the total flow of income (monetary flow) and output (real flow) through the economy and looks at the whole model at one time.

The simplest version of the circular flow model implicitly assumes that households spend all their income. In reality, households save part of their income and these savings flow into the financial market. In financial markets, those who have saved money are the suppliers of loanable funds, while those who wish to borrow money are the demanders of loanable funds. The circular flow diagram can be extended to include the financial market, where households are generally on the supply side and business firms on the demand side as they seek to borrow funds to finance capital purchases.

Government levies many kinds of taxes and uses tax revenues to pay for national defense, roads and highways, education, police and fire protection, and many other goods and services. The public sector can be added to the circular flow model to show how government interacts with the household sector and the business sector through product and resource markets.

Some of the goods and services produced in the business sector are **exported** and sold in other countries; some of the goods and services purchased by the household sector are **imported** and purchased from other countries. A country experiences a **trade surplus** when the value of exports exceeds the value of imports. A **trade deficit** occurs when the value of imports exceeds the value of exports; and a **balance of trade** occurs when the value of exports equals the value of imports. The circular flow model can be extended by adding the foreign sector. You can imagine that once you add all the different sectors and markets, the simple diagram shown on the previous page becomes quite complex.

The circular flow model helps illustrate the basic principles of macroeconomics. Macroeconomics looks first at the microeconomic relationships that make up the whole economy. After looking at how the parts work, the parts can be aggregated in order to look at the whole. Macroeconomics measures the circular flow of economic activity by measuring **national income** (total payments to the factors of production in a given period) and **gross domestic product** (market value of all final goods and services produced in the economy in a given period). Once the flow of income and output have been defined and measured, they can be compared to the economy's potential to produce output and generate income. If the flow is not as large as it could potentially be, macroeconomic theory attempts to identify why it is not. Macroeconomic policy based on theory may then be developed to increase the flow of income and output in order to reach the economy's potential.

The Fundamentals of Graphing

A graph is a model of the relationship between two or more variables. Graphs are frequently used in economics to illustrate and analyze the specific relationship that exists between two variables and how that relationship may change when other influences affecting it change. The **independent variable**, usually denoted X, has a value that can change freely. The value of the **dependent variable**, usually denoted Y, changes in response to a change in the independent variable, and its value depends on the value of the independent variable. Basic economic analysis focuses on the relationship between two variables, and the relationship can be graphed on a Cartesian plane. A Cartesian plane is divided into four quadrants; most graphs in economics use only the first quadrant (quadrant I) because negative values of many economic variables do not make sense. In quadrant I, the values of both the independent and dependent variables are positive. However, this does not mean there is necessarily a positive, or direct, relationship between the two variables.

The differing values for the independent variable and corresponding values for the dependent variable can be expressed as a point on a two-dimensional graph. Each point has two coordinates – the X, or horizontal, coordinate, and the Y, or vertical, coordinate – which are given paranthetically as (X,Y). A **direct**, or **positive**, relationship exists when a change in the independent variable causes the dependent variable to change in the same direction. This means that an increase in the value of X leads to an increase in the value of Y and vice-versa, assuming X is the independent variable and Y is the dependent variable. Direct relationships are graphed as curves that slope upward to the right. The Cartesian plane below shows the graph of the line between the two points (2,1) and (5, 4).

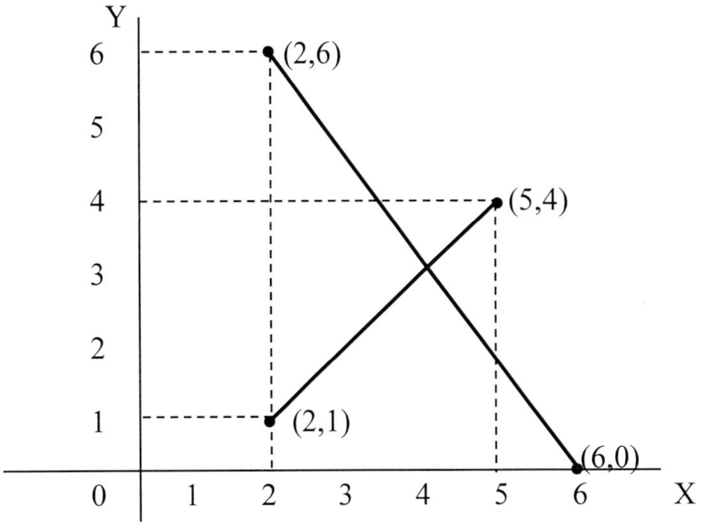

An **inverse**, or **negative**, relationship exists when a change in the independent variable causes the dependent variable to change in the opposite direction. This means that an increase in the value of X leads to a decrease in the value of Y and vice-versa, assuming X is the independent variable and Y is the dependent variable. Inverse relationships are graphed as curves that slope downward to the right. The line between the two points (2, 6) and (6, 0) is graphed on the Cartesian plane above.

The direction of the line between any two points indicates the type of relationship that exists between the two variables. If a direct relationship exists, the curve will slope upward to the right, indicating that an increase in the independent variable leads to an increase in the dependent variable. Frequently, this relationship needs to be quantified. In other words, by how much will the dependent variable increase as a result of the increase in the independent variable? The **slope** of the line between the two points provides this information. Slope measures the change in the variable on the vertical axis in response to a one unit change in the variable on the horizontal axis. Slope is usually denoted as 'm' and can be expressed as:

$$\text{Slope} = m = \frac{\text{vertical change}}{\text{horizontal change}} = \frac{\text{rise}}{\text{run}} = \frac{\Delta Y}{\Delta X} = \frac{Y_2 - Y_1}{X_2 - X_1}$$

Slope is constant along a straight line but varies from point to point along a curve. The slope of a horizontal line is zero while the slope of a vertical line is undefined, or infinity. The graph below shows a direct relationship between the quantity of ice cream cones sold and the total revenue received by the ice cream seller. In this instance, the quantity of ice cream cones sold is the independent variable, and total revenue is the dependent variable. Total revenue is found by multiplying the number of ice cream cones sold by the price* of each cone.

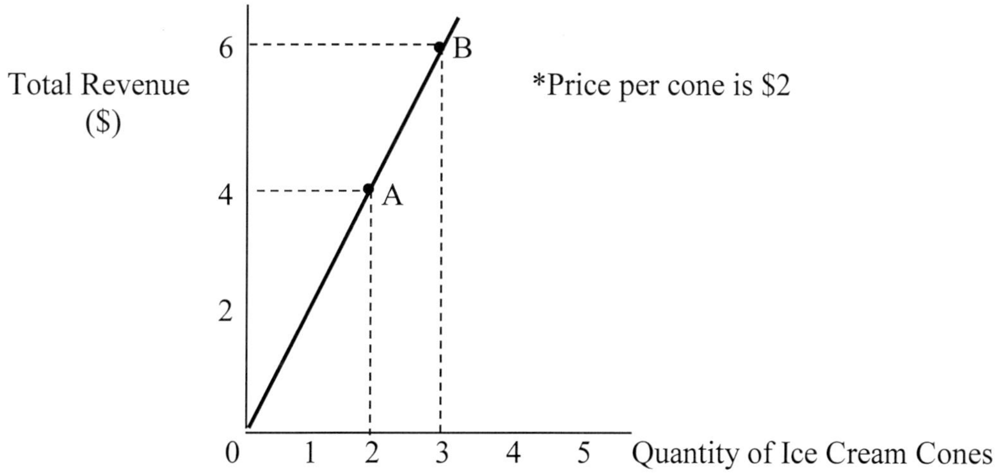

The slope of this line is found by dividing the vertical change by the horizontal change between any two points on the line. The coordinates for point A are (2,4) and the coordinates for point B are (3, 6). Using the formula above, $m = Y_2 - Y_1/X_2 - X_1 = (6-4)/(3-2) = 2$. The slope of this line is positive 2. This means that for every 1 unit increase in the quantity of ice cream cones sold, total revenue will increase by 2 units. If the quantity of ice cream cones sold decreases, total revenue received by the ice cream parlor will decrease. A line that slopes downward to the right has a negative slope, indicating that an increase in the independent variable leads to a decrease in the dependent variable, and vice-versa.

The basic relationship illustrated by a graphed line can also be expressed algebraically as the **equation of a line**. The general form of the equation of a line is **Y = mX + b**, where Y is the dependent variable, X is the independent variable, m is the slope, and b is the **Y-intercept**. The Y-intercept is the value of Y when X is zero and is given by the point at which the line intersects the vertical axis. The equation of the line graphed above is $Y = 2X + 0$, or $Y = 2X$.

Simple mathematical models are useful for analyzing economic relationships and predicting outcomes in the real world. One basic economic model is the supply and demand model used to help explain how a market economy works. In particular, it shows how the quantity of output bought and sold in a market responds to changes in the market price of the output. Chapter 3 develops the graphic model of supply and demand, and a principles of economics course usually relies on the graphic model to illustrate the relationship between price and quantity. The relationship between price and quantity demanded and price and quantity supplied can also be given algebraically. The example below simplifies the relationships by assuming they are linear. In reality, both demand and supply curves are not usually straight lines. Once the relationships have been expressed as mathematical equations, the equations can be used to predict the price and quantity that are likely to prevail in the market.

Suppose the following equations represent the supply and demand curves for jackets. The price, P, is dollars per jacket, and the quantity, Q, is the number of jackets per time period.

Supply: $P = Q_S + 20$ where Q_S is quantity supplied
Demand: $P = 100 - Q_D$ where Q_D is quantity demanded

The market for jackets is in equilibrium at the price where the quantity supplied of jackets is equal to the quantity demanded of jackets. In equilibrium, the market will have one unique equilibrium price (P_E). At P_E, buyers will desire to purchase the exact number of jackets that suppliers desire to offer for sale and $Q_S = Q_D$; this is the equilibrium quantity (Q_E). If the price and quantity are the same for both supply and demand, then the two equations can be set equal to each other in order to solve for the equilibrium quantity and price.

$$Q + 20 = 100 - Q$$
$$2Q = 80$$
$$Q = 40$$

Equilibrium quantity, Q_E, is 40 jackets per time period. To solve for equilibrium price, plug $Q = 40$ into either the supply or demand equation and solve for price. Equilibrium price, P_E, is $60 per jacket, as calculated below.

Supply: $P = 40 + 20 = 60$
Demand: $P = 100 - 40 = 60$

These equations can also be used to show what will occur in the market at different prices. For example, if price is $80, then the quantity supplied and quantity demanded in the market at a price of $80 per jacket can be determined simply by plugging in $80 for P in each equation.

Supply: $80 = Q_S + 20$ and $Q_S = 80 - 20 = 60$
Demand: $80 = 100 - Q_D$ and $Q_D = 100 - 80 = 20$

At price equal to $80 per jacket, quantity supplied is 60 jackets but quantity demanded is only 20 jackets. At P = $80, sellers will have 40 jackets that will not be sold.

NAME____ SECTION#________________

Print Last Name, First Name

BASIC DEFINITIONS

1. "Economics" is ***best*** defined as:
   a. a social science that studies how individuals and societies make choices regarding how to allocate scarce resources among competing uses.
   b. a branch of sociology that analyzes how government uses its unlimited resources to satisfy the unlimited wants of society.
   c. the study of how to maximize the benefits received by the majority of an economy's citizens.
   d. the study of how large corporations can make the greatest amount of profit.

2. Macroeconomics:
   a. studies the decisions and behaviors of individual businesses and markets.
   b. uses economic aggregates to measure activity in the economy as a whole.
   c. focuses on the individual components of the economy.
   d. concentrates on activity in specific markets and industries.

3. Positive economics:
   a. takes an optimistic approach to identifying what should be.
   b. is not appropriate for the study of market economies.
   c. explains what is and can be tested against the facts.
   d. attempts to identify what should be, which requires a value judgment.

4. Capital as a factor of production is best represented by:
   a. a robot used on the assembly line of an automobile manufacturing facility.
   b. a U.S. government savings bond.
   c. a fresh water lake used by households for recreational swimming and boating.
   d. a registered nurse that works in the emergency room of a hospital.

5. Which of the following represents a ***normative*** macroeconomic statement?
   a. No one should be unemployed in a country as large as the United States.
   b. Historically, the national unemployment rate is higher during severe economic downturns than during periods of substantial economic growth.
   c. Wealthy people don't mind paying high prices for food and clothing.
   d. A firm operating in a perfectly competitive market will maximize profit by producing where marginal revenue equals marginal cost.

6. The fundamental economic problem society faces, forcing it to decide how to allocate resources and distribute output, is:
   a. unemployment.
   b. recession.
   c. scarcity.
   d. scarce wants and needs.

7. All of the following are examples of factors of production, or resources, ***except***:
   a. an office building.
   b. members of a labor union.
   c. deposits in a company's bank account.
   d. cash registers in a grocery store.

8. Opportunity cost is:
   a. the value of the best alternative that must be foregone when a choice is made.
   b. the value of all alternatives that must be foregone when a choice is made.
   c. not as important to microeconomic decisions as it is to macroeconomic decisions.
   d. not useful when evaluating economic alternatives.

9. Stan earned an "A" on an economics exam after eating oatmeal and toast for breakfast. Stan's friend, Steve, decided to eat oatmeal and toast for breakfast on the day of his exam because he believed that what Stan had for breakfast was the main reason Stan earned an "A." Steve's conclusion that eating oatmeal and toast resulted in Stan earning an "A" is likely to be an example of:
   a. the fallacy of composition.
   b. the fallacy of division.
   c. the ceteris paribus assumption.
   d. the fallacy of false cause (post hoc fallacy).

10. Which of the following statements is most likely to reflect the fallacy of division?
   a. The entire economy will benefit from a national health care plan, therefore each group in the economy must benefit from such a plan.
   b. Some groups in the economy will benefit from a national health care plan, therefore the entire economy must benefit from such a plan.
   c. Increasing government provision of health care to the nation's poor will lead to an increase in the demand for health care.
   d. The government should increase its provision of health care to the nation's poor.

NAME____ SECTION#_______________
Print Last Name, First Name

BASIC DEFINITIONS

1. Which of the following topics is most likely to be studied in a macroeconomics course?
   a. The impact of a federal government policy change on the national unemployment rate
   b. The reaction of regular customers to an increase in the price of menu items at a local restaurant
   c. The pricing policy of a small firm selling output in a highly competitive market
   d. The reasons why one taxi service is more profitable than another taxi service

2. Jenny left her job as a production engineer to start her own consulting business. She took $40,000 out of savings to rent an office and buy a computer and office furniture. As factors of production, Jenny is ***best*** described as ___________ and the computer and office furniture are ***best*** described as ______________.
   a. labor; an entrepreneur
   b. an entrepreneur; capital
   c. capital; labor
   d. an entrepreneur; labor

3. "It is not fair that students have to pay to park on campus" is an example of a:
   a. macro statement.
   b. positive statement.
   c. normative statement.
   d. negative statement.

4. The purpose of a good theory or model is to:
   a. predict the future with perfect accuracy.
   b. explain real world relationships.
   c. determine what society should do to maximize happiness.
   d. make relationships more complicated than they are in reality.

5. Microeconomics focuses primarily on:
   a. economic growth and price stability within a country.
   b. the decisions and behaviors of individuals and firms.
   c. economic aggregates, such as unemployment, inflation, and economic growth.
   d. how government policy should be used to decide what and how to produce.

6. The term ***ceteris paribus*** means:
   a. "certain restrictions pertain" and is one reason why consumers cannot be completely sovereign in the United States.
   b. "let the buyer beware" and is the main focus of a microeconomics course.
   c. "all is a parable" and uses stories to explain the invisible hand of the market.
   d. "all other things held constant" and is used to isolate the relationship between two variables.

7. "Gross Domestic Product increases during periods of economic growth" is an example of a:
   a. normative macroeconomic statement.
   b. positive macroeconomic statement.
   c. normative microeconomic statement.
   d. positive microeconomic statement.

8. Scarcity exists because:
   a. there are not enough resources available to satisfy all of society's wants and needs.
   b. most people do not use their own personal resources as efficiently as possible.
   c. the government taxes income away from some sectors of the economy and transfers it to other sectors, leaving those that have been taxed with fewer resources.
   d. consumers want to pay the lowest price possible and producers want to make the highest profit possible.

9. Sally plans to go to the movie during the afternoon in order to pay the matinee ticket price of $6 rather than the prime time ticket price of $8. The opportunity cost of the movie to Sally is:
   a. the next best use of her $6 plus the next best use of the time she will spend going to the movie.
   b. the next best use of the time she will spend going to the movie minus $2 because she will save $2 by going to the matinee.
   c. zero if going to movies in the afternoon is her favorite pastime.
   d. not important because her decision will not impact anyone except her.

10. The fallacy of composition may occur because:
   a. something that is beneficial to society as a whole is not necessarily beneficial to each part of society.
   b. microeconomic issues are more important than macroeconomic issues because the economy is divided into microeconomic units.
   c. because two events are associated does not always mean that one event caused the other event.
   d. something that is beneficial to some groups in the economy is not necessarily beneficial to the economy as a whole.

NAME____ SECTION#______________
Print Last Name, First Name

BASIC DEFINITIONS

INSTRUCTIONS: Fill in the following ten blanks with the correct word or phrase.

1. ____________________________ studies the behaviors of individuals and specific markets.

2. ____________________________ studies the economy as a whole.

Classify 3. – 5. as a ***positive*** *economic statement* or a ***normative*** *economic statement.*

3. "Everyone should have to learn something about economics in order to make more informed choices as consumers and voters." ________________________________

4. "If a government tax on gasoline causes the price of gasoline to increase, people are likely to decrease the amount of gasoline they buy." ______________________________

5. "Individuals should be able to decide whether their social security contributions are kept in less risky government bonds or more risky stocks."______________________________

6. ______________________ refers to the physical plant and equipment used in production.

7. _______________________________ are the innovators and risk-takers who combine resources to produce an output.

Identify which *fallacy in reasoning* is potentially represented by examples 8. – 10. and fill in the blank with one of the following: **false cause, composition, or division.**

8. John bought stock after his favorite team made the playoffs because the value of his stock portfolio increased the last time his team made the playoffs. ________________________

9. Anne works in the technical support industry and argues that since policies designed to discourage outsourcing would protect her job and make her better off, society as a whole would benefit from policies that discourage outsourcing. _______________________

10. If the economy as a whole is better off due to free trade, then each member of the economy must also be better off as a result of free trade. ______________________________

NAME____ SECTION#______________

Print Last Name, First Name

THE CIRCULAR FLOW MODEL

Use the simple two-sector circular flow model illustrated below to respond to items 1 – 5.

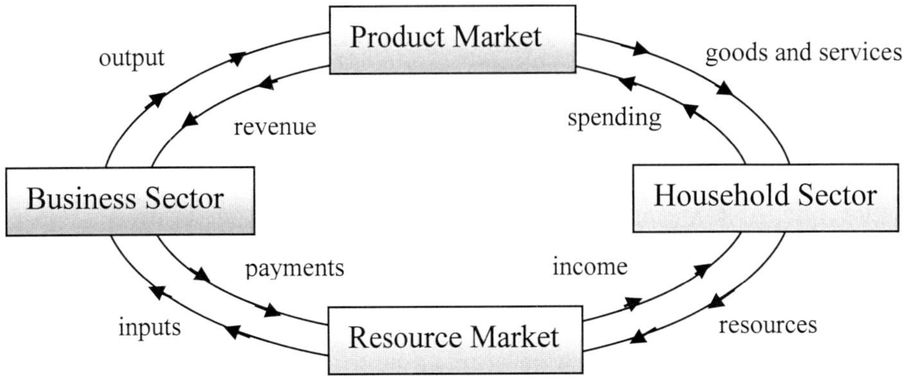

1. Business firms ________________ goods and services in the Product Market.
   supply/demand

2. Business firms ________________ factors of production in the Resource Market.
   supply/demand

3. Households ____________________ goods and services in the Product Market.
   supply/demand

4. Households ____________________ factors of production in the Resource Market.
   supply/demand

5. The simplest version of the circular flow model assumes that households spend all of their income. In reality, is this true? Adding the Financial Market to the model would make it more realistic. Describe how households and businesses would participate in the Financial Market.

NAME____ SECTION#______________

Print Last Name, First Name

THE CIRCULAR FLOW MODEL

1. The simple two-sector circular flow model of economic activity:
   a. shows that people cannot be both suppliers and demanders.
   b. shows the trade-off between the law of supply and the law of demand.
   c. illustrates government's role as the main supplier of resources in a market economy.
   d. illustrates the relationship between households and business firms in a market economy.

2. Households supply inputs, or factors of production, in:
   a. product markets.
   b. resource markets.
   c. super markets.
   d. money markets.

3. Goods and services are exchanged in:
   a. product markets.
   b. resource markets.
   c. the household sector.
   d. the business sector.

4. Demand decisions are made by:
   a. households in product markets and business firms in resource markets.
   b. households in resource markets and business firms in product markets.
   c. households and business firms in product markets.
   d. households and business firms in resource markets.

5. Supply decisions are made by:
   a. households in product markets and business firms in resource markets.
   b. households in resource markets and business firms in product markets.
   c. households and business firms in product markets.
   d. households and business firms in resource markets.

6. In the circular flow of economic activity, business firms:
   a. demand labor in product markets.
   b. supply labor in resource markets.
   c. demand goods and services in product markets.
   d. supply goods and services in product markets.

7. In the two-sector circular flow model of the economy:
   a. households supply goods and services and demand factors of production.
   b. households demand and supply goods and services.
   c. business firms supply goods and services and demand factors of production.
   d. business firms demand and supply factors of production.

NAME____ SECTION#__________

Print Last Name, First Name

8. The circular flow model depicts:
   a. the inter-relationships of market participants in a capitalist economy.
   b. the maximum amount of output that an economy can produce in a given time period.
   c. an inverse relationship between the price of a product and the quantity demanded of the product.
   d. a direct relationship between prices and output in a market economy.

9. In a market, or capitalist, economy most payments for inputs or factors of production are made by:
   a. households (consumers).
   b. business firms.
   c. the government.
   d. foreigners.

10. In a market, or capitalist, economy most payments for goods and services are made by:
   a. the government.
   b. foreigners.
   c. households (consumers).
   d. business firms.

NAME____ SECTION#______________

Print Last Name, First Name

MATH AND GRAPHS

1. A positive, or direct, relationship between two variables is illustrated by:
   a. a horizontal line.
   b. a vertical line.
   c. a line that slopes upward to the right.
   d. a line that slopes downward to the right.

2. The slope of a line can be calculated by dividing the:
   a. horizontal change by the vertical change between any two points on the line.
   b. vertical change by the horizontal change between any two points on the line.
   c. horizontal distance from the origin to the point by the vertical distance from the origin to the point.
   d. vertical distance from the origin to the point by the horizontal distance from the origin to the point.

3. The slope of a line through the coordinates (6, 1) and (2, 3):
   a. is -2.
   b. is -½.
   c. is ½.
   d. cannot be determined from the information given.

4. If the equation of a line is $Y = 10 - 2X$, then:
   a. the slope of this line is 10 and the Y-intercept is 2.
   b. the slope of this line is 2 and the Y-intercept is 10.
   c. X and Y are inversely, or negatively, related.
   d. X and Y are not related.

5. If a function has a slope of 5 and a Y-intercept of 2, the equation for this function is:
   a. $Y = 5 + 2X$.
   b. $X = 2Y + 5$.
   c. $X = 2 + 5Y$.
   d. $Y = 5X + 2$.

6. If a decrease in the price of airline tickets leads to a decrease in the quantity supplied of airline tickets, then the graph of the relationship between the price of airline tickets and the quantity supplied of airline tickets will be a curve that slopes:
   a. downward to the right indicating an inverse, or negative, relationship between the price and quantity supplied of airline tickets.
   b. upward to the right indicating an inverse, or negative, relationship between the price and quantity supplied of airline tickets.
   c. downward to the right indicating a direct, or positive, relationship between the price and quantity supplied of airline tickets.
   d. upward to the right indicating a direct, or positive, relationship between the price and quantity supplied of airline tickets.

7. If a line representing the relationship between two variables has a negative slope, then:
   a. an increase in the independent variable leads to a decrease in the dependent variable.
   b. an increase in the independent variable leads to an increase in the dependent variable.
   c. an increase in the dependent variable leads to a decrease in the independent variable.
   d. the independent and dependent variables are unrelated.

8. If the equation of a line is Y = 50 + 0.8X, then:
   a. Y is equal to 50 when X is equal to zero.
   b. if X is 100, then Y is 130.
   c. a graph depicting this relationship would slope upward to the right.
   d. all of the above are true.

Use the graph below to answer questions 9 and 10:

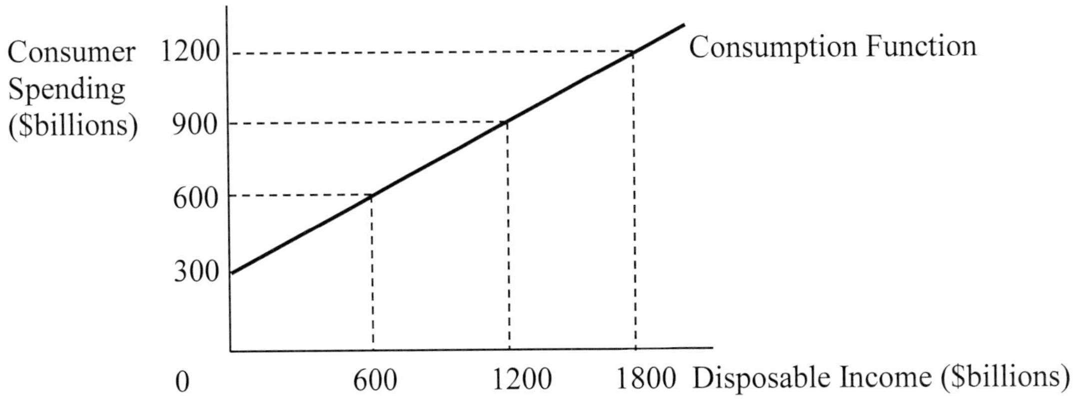

9. The graph above indicates that ______________ is the independent variable and that consumer spending and disposable income are ______________ related.
   a. disposable income; directly (positively)
   b. disposable income; inversely (negatively)
   c. consumer spending; directly (positively)
   d. consumer spending; inversely (negatively)

10. The graph above shows that a $600 increase in disposable income results in a ___________ in consumer spending, meaning that the slope of this line is _______.
   a. $600 increase; 1
   b. $300 increase; ½
   c. $600 decrease; -1
   d. $300 decrease; -½

NAME____ SECTION#______________
Print Last Name, First Name

THE EQUATION OF A LINE

Y = mX + b represents the general form of an equation of a line. Answer questions 1-5 with respect to a specific line represented by the equation **Y = 0.8X + 500.**

1. The slope of this line is __________.

2. When X = 2,000, the value of Y is __________.

3. When X = 2,500, the value of Y is __________.

4. The "Y-intercept" is ____________.

5. The relationship between X and Y is direct/inverse (circle the correct answer).

Use the following coordinates to answer questions 6 – 8:

X	Y
0	**20**
1	**18**
2	**16**

6. The slope of a line with these coordinates is __________.

7. The "Y-intercept" of this line is __________.

8. The equation of this line is _________________________.

Use the following equations to answer questions 9 and 10.

$$Q_S = 5P \text{ and } Q_D = 150 - 5P$$

9. What value for P satisfies the condition $Q_D = Q_S$? _____________

10. Given the value for P found in number 9, what will be the value of $Q_D = Q_S$? __________

NAME____ **SECTION#**________________

Print Last Name, First Name

PRACTICE GRAPHING

Use the following information to respond to items 1 – 10:
An empirical macroeconomic study revealed the following relationship between after-tax income (the X-axis variable) and consumer spending (the Y-axis variable).

After-tax Income (X)	Spending (Y)
$10,000	**$10,000**
$20,000	**$18,000**
$30,000	**$26,000**

1. Plot the relationship in the grid provided.

2. Is this relationship direct (positive) or inverse (negative)? ____________________

3. The independent variable is ______________________________________

4. The dependent variable is ______________________________________

5. The slope of this line is ________________

6. The "Y-intercept" is ________________

7. The equation for this line is ______________________________________

8. Consumers are expected to spend ____________________ if after-tax income is $40,000.

9. Consumers are expected to save ____________________ if after-tax income is $40,000.

10. At what after-tax income level will savings = $0 (or at what income level will consumer spending be equal to after-tax income)? ______________________________

CHAPTER 2 Production Possibilities and Economic Systems

Scarcity forces all societies to make decisions about what to produce from available resources. Before the question of what to produce can be addressed, we have to know what can be produced. The production possibilities model is a simple way of portraying what outputs can be produced using an economy's current resources and technology. The model is usually presented as a graph called a production possibilities frontier (PPF), or production possibilities curve. The PPF represents the limits to what a society can produce at a given point in time. A **production possibilities frontier**, or curve, is a graph illustrating the combinations of two types of output that can be produced by a society using the available resources and technology. In order to identify what the possible combinations are, assumptions regarding resources and technology must be made. Drawing a PPF for two outputs in a given time period assumes that:

1) the types and amounts of available resources are fixed
2) the technology used to produce the outputs is constant
3) available resources are fully employed
4) production is efficient.

The model addresses the question of what combinations of two types of output can be produced. The answer to the question depends on the amount of resources, technology, and time available.

A Straight-Line PPF: Constant Opportunity Cost

Suppose an economy produces two outputs, jeans and denim skirts, and that it has 40 yards of fabric, 4 huge spools of thread, 2 sewing machines, 2 workers and 1 week for production. The table below is a **production possibilities schedule** and shows some of the combinations of jeans and skirts that can be produced from the above resources and current level of technology, assuming that the resources are fully employed and that production is efficient. If all of the fabric is used to produce skirts, then 40 can be produced but 0 jeans can be produced. The combination of 40 skirts and 0 jeans is combination A. If this economy uses all of its resources to produce jeans, it can produce 20 jeans, but then 0 skirts can be produced. Combination E with 20 jeans and 0 skirts is another possibility for production. The table below identifies several different combinations of skirts and jeans that can be produced under the original assumptions of the model.

Combination	Jeans	Skirts
A	0	40
B	5	30
C	10	20
D	15	10
E	20	0

If the economy chooses to produce 5 jeans, then it can produce only 30 skirts. A combination of 5 jeans and 40 skirts is not possible. Combinations A through E represent the maximum amounts of the two outputs that can be produced from the available resources and technology.

The different combinations can be plotted as points on a graph and connected to form a production possibilities frontier (PPF). The graph below shows the different combinations of jeans and skirts that can be produced using currently available resources and technology. Combinations A through E are only some of the possible combinations; all combinations on or inside the PPF are possible. Points on the curve represent attainable combinations that fully employ available resources and technology and are efficient, such as combinations A through E. Points inside the curve represent attainable combinations that are inefficient, such as point F. At point F, 10 skirts and 5 jeans are produced but the economy has the resources and technology to produce 10 skirts and 15 jeans, or 30 skirts and 5 jeans. Producing at combination F is inefficient because the economy has the ability to produce more output.

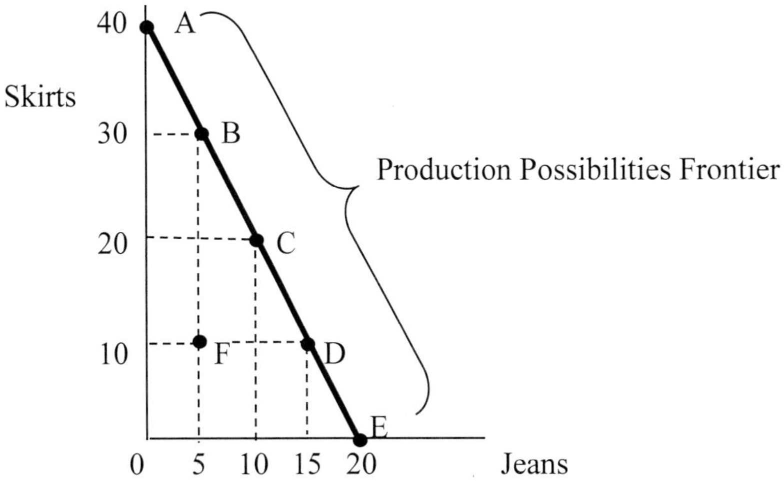

The above PPF is a straight-line, indicating that the opportunity cost of continuing to increase the production of jeans is constant. Moving from combination B to combination C entails giving up 10 skirts to gain 5 jeans; moving from combination C to combination D entails giving up 10 skirts to gain 5 jeans. The slope of the PPF is constant meaning there is **constant opportunity cost** associated with increasing the production of one output. In this case, the slope is –2; the opportunity cost of one pair of jeans is 2 skirts. This occurs because the resources can be used to produce both jeans and skirts and are equally well-suited to producing both types of output. In reality, most resources are better at some types of production than others so PPFs are not usually straight lines.

A Bowed PPF: Increasing Opportunity Cost

Increasing opportunity costs are encountered when resources are not well suited to all types of production. This means that continuing to increase the production of one output entails giving up increasingly larger amounts of the other output. When opportunity cost is increasing, the production possibilities frontier will bow outward and be concave to the origin. Land is a good example of a resource that is not well-suited to producing all outputs. Some land is very fertile and can yield high amounts of agricultural outputs; some land is not as good for growing crops but may be fine for productive activities, such as grazing cows. Corn may not grow well on all of the available land but cows may graze equally well on all of the available land.

In the following example, the available land is used for growing corn and grazing cows.

Combination	Corn	Cows
A	14	0
B	12	1
C	9	2
D	5	3
E	0	4

If all the land is planted in corn, the economy can produce 14 units of corn but will have no cows, as represented by combination A. To have one unit of cows, land has to be taken away from corn production, which occurs when moving from combination A to combination B. Combination B is 1 cow unit and 12 corn units; cows increased by 1 unit but corn decreased by 2 units (from 14 to 12) when moving from combination A to combination B. The opportunity cost of the first unit of cows is 2 units of corn because that land will not be available for corn production if cows are put on it. The land least suited to corn production will be the first land given to the cows (remember, the cows can graze equally well on all of the land that is available). Moving to combination C means devoting more land to cows and less to corn. The land given to the cows could have produced 3 units of corn so the opportunity cost of the second unit of cows is 3 units of corn.

Continuing to add cows means yet more land is taken away from the production of corn. The last unit of land given over to cow grazing is the best suited to corn production so the opportunity cost of the fourth unit of cows is 5 units of corn. Notice that cows are increasing by equal increments (one cow unit each time), but the opportunity cost of continuing to increase the number of cows is increasing: the number of corn units that must be given up to gain 1 additional cow unit increases as we move from point A to point B to point C to point D to point E. The above production possibilities schedule illustrates **increasing opportunity cost**; graphing this data will yield a PPF that bows outward, as shown below.

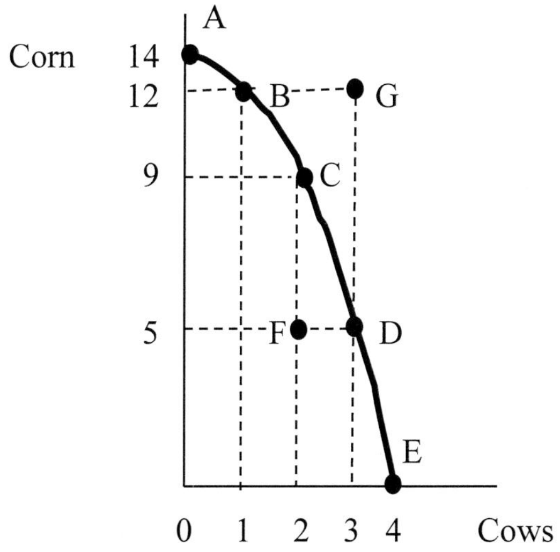

When an economy is producing at a point on its production possibilities curve, such as points A through E in the cow and corn example, the economy is using its resources fully and efficiently. A movement from point A to point B, for example, could be accomplished by shifting resources from the production of corn to the production of cows. Each point on the frontier is possible, but we cannot know which point society prefers without additional information about what society considers to be most desirable.

Point F lies inside the production possibilities curve and corresponds to a combination of corn and cows less than what the economy is capable of producing. Producing a combination that lies inside the curve indicates that resources are idle (not being used) or being used inefficiently (producing less than they can), which keeps society from producing at its potential. Idle labor resources mean unemployed labor resources, so an economy may be producing at a point inside its production possibilities because of high unemployment. If the problem is unemployment, then reducing unemployment can result in a movement from a point inside the production possibilities curve to a point on the curve (for example, from F to C). Similarly, if the problem is inefficiency, then improving efficiency can cause a movement from a point inside the curve to a point on the curve.

Points outside of the frontier, such as point G, represent combinations of output that are unattainable because the economy cannot produce combinations outside of the PPF given the current level of resources and technology. Moving to a combination that is outside the current PPF means the original assumptions regarding the level of resources and technology available for production must change. When this happens, the economy's ability to produce changes and the PPF shifts.

<u>The Production Possibilities Model and Economic Growth</u>

Points outside the production possibilities frontier are currently unattainable because production at a point on the production possibilities frontier requires using all resources fully and efficiently. Over a period of time, it is very likely that the quantity or quality of resources will change, or that technology will improve, making the economy capable of producing more. This process is known as **economic growth**, and is shown as an outward shift of the production possibilities curve. Economic growth is a long-term process that permits increased production of goods and services and improved material standards of living. In the production possibilities model, economic growth requires an increase in the resources available for production, an increase in the technology used in production, or a combination of the two.

An increase in a country's population leads to an increase in its labor force. The quality of workers can also improve over time, as investment in human capital (education and training) makes them more productive. When a country has more workers or has more productive workers, the country's ability to produce goods and services increases, ceteris paribus. Similarly, when firms invest in capital, there are more factories, machines, and tools with which to produce goods and services. An increase in the capital stock is another way a country can achieve economic growth. Spending on research and development (R&D) promotes invention, resulting in improved technology. Technological improvements can result in economic growth by making workers more productive or by making it possible to produce and use more advanced machines and tools.

Whether caused by an increase in the quantity or quality of resources or an improvement in technology, economic growth shifts the production possibilities frontier outward. If the production possibilities frontier shifts outward from PPF_1 to PPF_2, the economy is able to produce more of both types of output. This shift indicates that if the source of economic growth is, for example, more resources, then these additional resources can be used either to produce wheat or to produce automobiles.

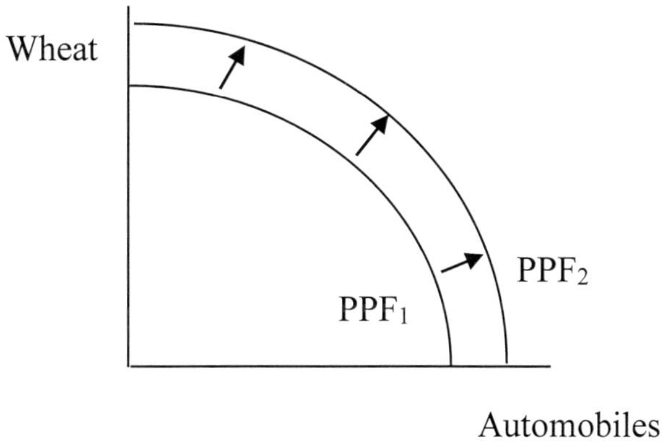

In other cases, growth may be industry-specific, as shown below. The production possibilities frontier may rotate outward from one of the axes, as demonstrated below.

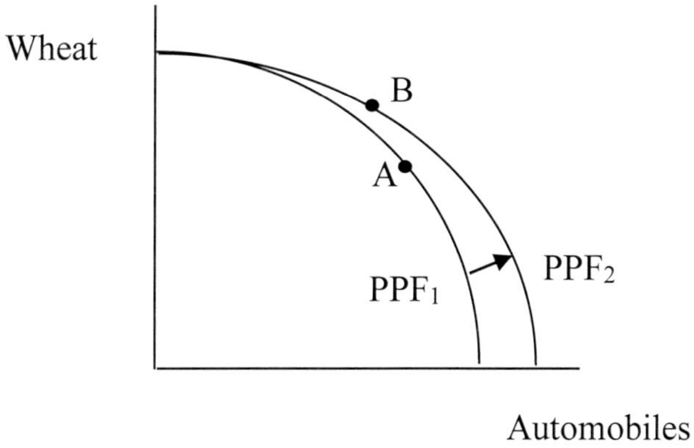

This type of shift would occur, for example, if technological progress occurred only in the automobile industry or if we had more machines specifically designed for automobile production. However, technological progress in the automobile industry can lead to increased output of wheat if we move from point A to point B in the above graph, for example. This occurs because when resources are more productive in the automobile industry, a given level of production requires fewer resources, so some resources are free to move to the production of other goods.

Economic growth is one of the primary macroeconomic goals and we will focus on how the economy's rate of growth is measured, how government can use economic policy to promote growth, and the relationship between economic growth and living standards in later chapters.

The PPF, Opportunity Cost, and the Marginal Rate of Transformation

On the graph below, the points on the curve represent full employment and efficient production. Points B, C, and D are combinations of guns and butter that are possible. If this society is at a point on its PPF, increasing the production of guns can be accomplished only by decreasing the production of butter. Moving from point B to point C, for example, means giving up 2 units of butter to produce the third gun (or one additional gun). The number of units of one good that must be given up in order to gain one more unit of the other good represents the **opportunity cost** of moving from one point to another along the curve. The opportunity cost of moving from point B to point C is the 2 units of butter that are given up to gain 1 gun.

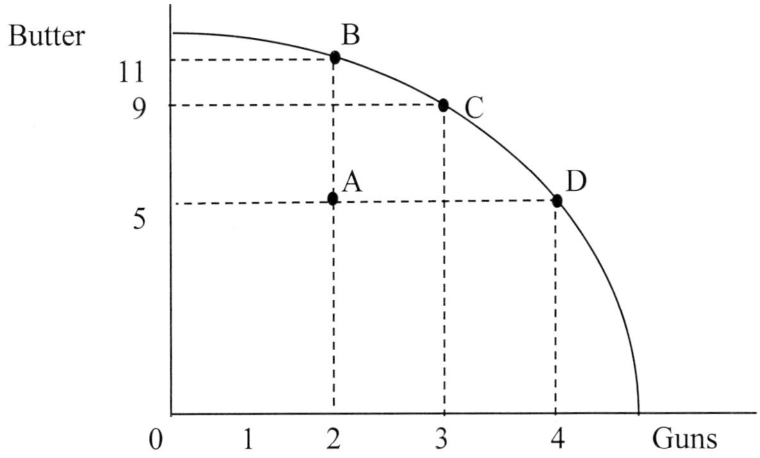

The **marginal rate of transformation** (**MRT**) is the slope of the PPF and is a measure of the opportunity cost of moving from one point to another along the curve. For PPFs that bow outward, the MRT increases from point to point moving down along the PPF because of the **law of increasing opportunity costs**. On the graph above, the opportunity cost of moving from point B to point C is 2 units of butter, while the opportunity cost of moving from point C to point D is 4 units of butter. Therefore, opportunity cost increases as society moves down and to the right along its PPF. Increasing opportunity costs are encountered because resources are not equally well-suited to all types of production. Increasing the production of one output by equal increments requires giving up increasing amounts of the other output. In other words, the opportunity cost of one good in terms of the other is increasing, leading to PPFs that bow outward (concave to the origin). For linear PPFs, the MRT is constant because opportunity cost is constant. This occurs only if resources are equally well-suited to both types of production.

Production possibilities frontiers identify the combinations of two types of outputs an economy can produce; the model does not identify which combination is best, or most desirable, for society. Society must rely on some type of allocative mechanism to decide what outputs and how much of each output to produce. The fundamental questions of what outputs to produce, how to produce outputs, and who gets to consume the outputs produced are addressed by the type of economic system society chooses. There are many options available, but economic systems in general can be divided into the two main types of capitalism and socialism.

Economic Systems

An economic system is comprised of many elements that direct resources and behaviors in a society. It is the laws, traditions, institutions, and mechanisms that are combined to allocate resources and distribute outputs. For example, several mechanisms are used to answer the question of "who gets a seat in your economics class?" To begin with, society had to deem education desirable and to have chosen to devote resources to the production of higher education. Once the education is available, who gets to consume it must be addressed. Many decision-making mechanisms are employed to answer this question. There is a set of criteria that must be met before a student is admitted to college, such as completing high school and taking college entrance exams. Once satisfactorily met, a student must enroll for classes. Enrolling may be based on a priority system, such as graduating seniors first, and then some queuing mechanism may be used that allows students to enroll on a first-come, first-served basis. The student then must have a way to pay for the class in order to keep the seat.

The process of allocating just one seat in an economics class has several layers and can be complicated. Attempting to allocate resources and distribute output efficiently in an economy as large as the United States can seem impossible. The U.S. produces and consumes more than twenty percent of world output but comprises only about five percent of the world's population. Society has to have some way of directing production and consumption on a large scale to achieve the **macroeconomic goals of full employment, price stability, and economic growth** as efficiently as possible. The primary mechanism used in the U.S. is markets, which are the basis for a capitalistic economy.

Writing his *Inquiry into the Nature and Causes of the Wealth of Nations* in 1776, Adam Smith proposed that a free market economy is capable of achieving an efficient allocation of resources without the need for government intervention. He wanted to replace the very visible hand of government officials with an **invisible hand** that would guide resources to their best use and generate the best living standards possible given scarcity. Smith argued that a system in which transactions are voluntary, resources are privately owned, and markets are competitive, would lead to efficient outcomes. Smith believed that people left alone to pursue their own self-interest would unintentionally promote the best interests of society as well, as if guided by "an invisible hand." There would be no need for government to direct resources and economic activity. Smith advocated a policy of ***laissez-faire***, arguing that a free market economy would self-correct. Many of Smith's arguments were directed at Mercantilists, who advocated government policies that limited imports and restricted trade. The purpose of the protectionist policies advocated by Mercantilists was to accumulate gold, which they used to judge the wealth of a nation. By contrast, Smith argued that the wealth of a nation could best be judged by the living standards of its citizens and that a free market economy would lead to an increase in the wealth of the nation.

Capitalism is an economic system in which resources are privately owned and decisions about how to use those resources are made by individuals and firms. In a capitalist, or market, economy, there is **private property** and **decentralized decision-making**. Those who own resources make decisions in pursuit of their own self interest. A market system is based on the existence of **incentives**, which means that people are motivated through self-interest to make efficient choices.

In a **planned, or command,** economy, government owns or controls most resources and uses central planning to decide how to allocate resources. Rather than relying on incentives, central planners direct resources to certain lines of production and decide who gets the output. In theory, government planners seek to use society's resources to produce the goods and services that members of society need most. **Socialism and communism** are types of planned economies. Many of the specific objectives of a socialist or communist economy were outlined in *The Communist Manifesto*, written by Karl Marx and published in 1848. Currently, many formerly communist nations (often referred to as transitional economies) are moving from government ownership of resources and centralized decision-making to economies characterized by private ownership of resources and decentralized decision-making.

In even the most extreme cases of pure capitalism or free-market economies, it is necessary for government to provide a legal framework, so a market economy does not imply anarchy. Market-based incentives rely on government to define and protect property rights at the very least. There is very little incentive for someone to work hard to purchase a nice car if another can steal the car without penalty. In the U.S., most agree that the government does more than provide the legal framework necessary for capitalism to function, and we will be analyzing how and why governments intervene in a market economy throughout this course.

The U.S. has an economic system that is commonly referred to as a **mixed** system because it has elements of both market and planned economies. Although markets play a dominant role and most resources are privately owned, the government has some control over resource allocation. Our choice of a mixed economy reflects a desire to protect some members of society from poverty and starvation. In addition, government frequently gets involved in economic decisions because of microeconomic **market failures**, which are discussed at length in a microeconomics course. Government enacts regulations to protect the environment, it provides for the national defense, it subsidizes health care and education, and uses antitrust legislation to promote and protect competition.

Government also plays a role in helping to smooth the ups and downs in macroeconomic activity. Congress may intervene in the macroeconomy by using its ability to tax and spend in order to influence economic outcomes. The use of the federal government's budget for the purpose of altering economic outcomes is referred to as **fiscal policy**. Congress may design spending bills with the intention of reducing unemployment, or tax laws with the intention of promoting research and development in order to foster economic growth. The Federal Reserve is the central bank of the U.S. and conducts **monetary policy**. The Federal Reserve, or the Fed, uses its ability to influence the money supply and credit conditions in order to achieve its primary objective of price level stability.

NAME____ SECTION#______________

Print Last Name, First Name

PRODUCTION POSSIBILITIES

1. A production possibilities frontier is drawn assuming all of the following ***except***:
   a. available resources are fully employed.
   b. the technology used in production is constant.
   c. resources are interchangeable in production.
   d. the amount of resources is fixed.

2. Production possibilities frontiers (curves):
   a. illustrate the optimal way a society can distribute its wealth.
   b. illustrate the limits to what can be produced from current resources and technology.
   c. eliminate the dilemma of resource scarcity by providing a positive approach to dealing with opportunity cost.
   d. are drawn assuming inefficiency and unemployment.

Use the data in the production possibilities schedule below to answer questions 3 – 6:

Combination	Apples	Peaches
A	0	400
B	100	300
C	200	200
D	300	100
E	400	0

3. The opportunity cost of moving from combination C to combination D is:
   a. 100 peaches.
   b. 100 apples.
   c. 200 peaches.
   d. 200 apples.

4. A combination of 200 apples and 100 peaches is:
   a. unattainable given current resources and technology.
   b. inefficient in the use of current resources and technology.
   c. unattainable in the use of future resources and technology.
   d. inefficient in the use of current resources but efficient in the use of technology.

5. The production possibilities frontier drawn from the above schedule will be:
   a. a straight line indicating constant opportunity cost.
   b. a straight line indicating increasing opportunity cost.
   c. bowed outward indicating increasing opportunity cost.
   d. bowed outward indicating constant opportunity cost.

6. The above data indicate that the resources and technology available:
   a. should be used to produce something other than apples and peaches.
   b. are better suited to growing apples than to growing peaches.
   c. are better suited to growing peaches than to growing apples.
   d. are equally well suited to growing both apples and peaches.

NAME____ SECTION#________________
Print Last Name, First Name

Use the graph below to answer questions 7 – 9:

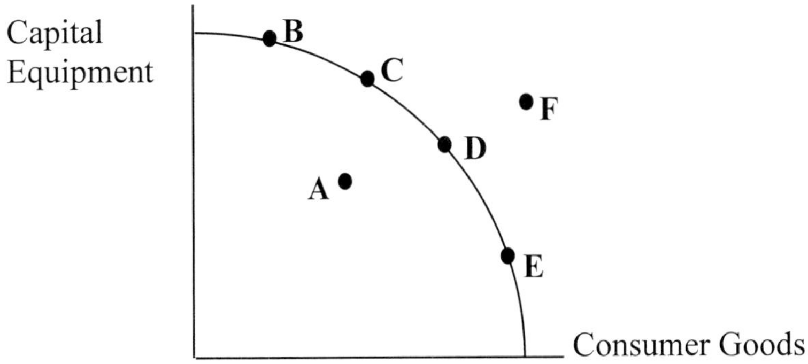

7. Efficient use of resources and technology is represented by point ______, and inefficient use is represented by point ______.
   a. **A; F**
   b. **B; A**
   c. **E; F**
   d. **C; E**

8. The shape of the above production possibilities frontier reflects:
   a. increasing opportunity cost.
   b. decreasing opportunity cost.
   c. constant opportunity cost.
   d. economic growth.

9. Producing combination **F** requires:
   a. an increase in the resources and technology this economy uses in production.
   b. an increase in the desirability of consumer goods.
   c. a shift from increasing opportunity cost to constant opportunity cost.
   d. None of the above will enable this economy to produce combination **F**.

10. In the production possibilities model, economic growth is illustrated by:
   a. a straight-line PPF.
   b. the downward slope of the PPF.
   c. a bowed outward PPF.
   d. an outward shift of the PPF.

NAME____ SECTION#______________

Print Last Name, First Name

PRODUCTION POSSIBILITIES

1. In the production possibilities model, the opportunity cost of a good is:
   a. not related to the production of other goods.
   b. the amount of money that must be spent to produce it.
   c. the amount of other goods that must be given up in order to produce it.
   d. the amount by which any point on the curve deviates from the optimal point.

Use the data below to answer questions 2 – 4:

Production Possibilities Schedule

Combination	Cars	Bicycles
A	0	180
B	1	165
C	2	135
D	3	90
E	4	0

2. The opportunity cost of the third car is _______ bicycles.
   a. 15 b. 30 c. 45 d. 90

3. The above production possibilities schedule illustrates:
   a. decreasing opportunity cost.
   b. increasing opportunity cost.
   c. constant opportunity cost.
   d. a direct relationship between the production of cars and bicycles.

4. Producing a combination of 2 cars and 180 bicycles:
   a. is not possible given current resources and technology.
   b. is currently possible but indicates that resources are not being used efficiently.
   c. is currently possible but is an undesirable combination of cars and bicycles.
   d. indicates that this economy cannot experience economic growth.

5. Points inside a production possibilities frontier imply that:
   a. the economy is producing the maximum possible amount of output.
   b. production is inefficient or resources are unemployed.
   c. resources are efficiently allocated and fully employed.
   d. technology is continually changing.

6. Which of the following will cause a movement from a point inside an economy's production possibilities frontier (PPF) to a point on its PPF?
   a. An increase in the unemployment rate
   b. An increase in the efficiency with which resources are used
   c. A government ban on production techniques that cause pollution
   d. A government tax on capital but not labor

NAME____ SECTION#______________
Print Last Name, First Name

Use the graph below to answer questions 7 – 9:

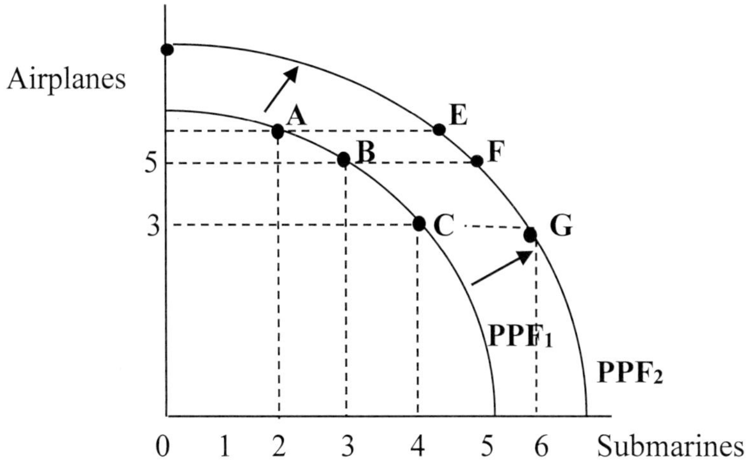

7. The opportunity cost of moving from combination B to combination C on PPF_1 is:
   a. 1 submarine.
   b. 3 submarines.
   c. 2 airplanes.
   d. 4 airplanes.

8. If this economy's ability to produce is represented by PPF_1, then a combination of 3 airplanes and 4 submarines:
   a. is unattainable given current resources and technology.
   b. represents full employment and efficient production.
   c. is the optimal way of using current resources and technology.
   d. represents the optimal amount of submarines for society.

9. On PPF_2, the combination of submarines and airplanes that society values most highly is:
   a. combination E.
   b. combination F.
   c. combination G.
   d. impossible to determine from the information given.

Use the graph below to answer question 10.

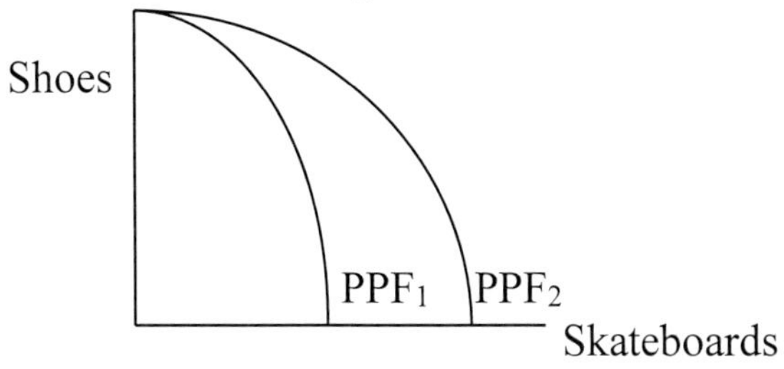

10. The shift from PPF_1 to PPF_2 could occur in response to:
   a. increased unemployment in the shoe industry.
   b. increased unemployment in the skateboard industry.
   c. technological improvements in the shoe industry.
   d. technological improvements in the skateboard industry.

NAME____ SECTION#_______________
Print Last Name, First Name

PRODUCTION POSSIBILITIES
SHORT-ANSWER QUESTIONS

Fill in the blanks based on the Production Possibilities Model and the graph below.

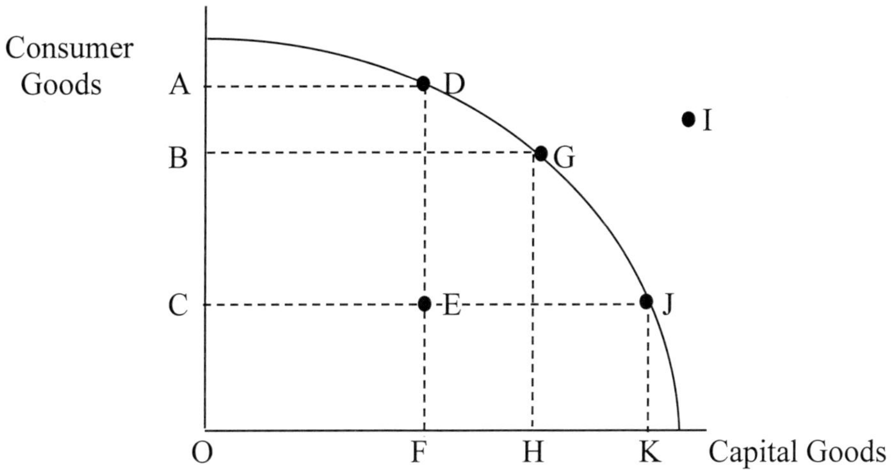

Inefficient production or unemployed resources is represented by point (1) __________.

Production is efficient and available resources are fully employed at point (2) __________,

point (3) __________, and point (4) __________.

The opportunity cost of moving from point D to point G is the distance (5) ______________.

The opportunity cost of moving from point G to point J is the distance (6) _______________.

The shape of the PPF is (7) ____________________________________, which illustrates

(8) ________________________________ opportunity cost.

The combination of consumer goods and capital goods represented by point I is

(9) ________________________________ given current resources and technology.

This economy needs more resources and/or an increase in technology, or must experience

(10) ________________________________, to produce at point I.

NAME____ SECTION#______________

Print Last Name, First Name

PRODUCTION POSSIBILITIES

INSTRUCTIONS: Fill in the blanks below with the appropriate term or phrase from the production possibilities model.

Three of the assumptions employed when drawing a given production possibilities frontier are:

1.____

2.____

3.____

4. A straight-line production possibilities frontier implies that opportunity cost is

   ______________________________.

5. Production possibilities frontiers that bow outward illustrate ________________________

   opportunity cost.

6. Points on a production possibilities frontier indicate ______________________________

7. Points inside a production possibilities frontier indicate ___________________________

8. An outward shift of the production possibilities frontier illustrates

   ____.

9. In the production possibilities model, economic growth can result from

   ____.

10. In the production possibilities model, economic growth can also result from

    ____.

NAME____ SECTION#______________

Print Last Name, First Name

COMPARATIVE ECONOMIC SYSTEMS

1. Scarcity forces a society to address all of the following fundamental economic questions ***except***:
   a. for whom should output be produced?
   b. what outputs should be produced?
   c. what is the best way to maintain full employment?
   d. how should output be produced?

2. The major macroeconomic policy goals of most industrialized nations are:
   a. an equal distribution of income, full employment, and price stability.
   b. economic growth, price stability, and an equal distribution of income.
   c. full employment, price stability, and economic growth.
   d. price stability, economic growth, and market equilibriums.

3. All of the following are essential elements of capitalism ***except***:
   a. private property.
   b. government-owned resources.
   c. competition.
   d. a market or price system.

4. A mixed economy:
   a. has elements of both a planned and a market system.
   b. relies primarily on government to determine what outputs should be produced.
   c. is characterized by centralized decision-making and government control of most resources.
   d. is another term for a command economy.

5. A laissez-faire approach to policy involves:
   a. active management of the economy by government.
   b. government allowing economic problems to self correct.
   c. sacrificing economic growth in order to ensure price stability.
   d. centralized planning.

6. In a market economy, ________ motivates producers to choose the most efficient means of production.
   a. a central planning board
   b. profit
   c. government
   d. altruism

NAME____ SECTION#______________

Print Last Name, First Name

7. A decentralized system comprised of many buyers and sellers each attempting to maximize their own gain under competitive conditions best describes:
   a. socialism.
   b. central planning.
   c. a mixed economy.
   d. the market system.

8. Which of the following statements is ***false***?
   a. In a socialist system, government attempts to make decisions that are in the best interest of society.
   b. The institution of private property is essential to a market system.
   c. In a command economy, the role of government is small or even nonexistent.
   d. In a market system, producers are free to pursue maximum profit.

9. In a command, or socialist, system:
   a. most resources are owned by individuals.
   b. decision-making is very decentralized.
   c. government planning boards may set output targets.
   d. All of the above are true

10. Most economic systems address the issues of what to produce, how to produce, and who gets to consume output with:
   a. the market mechanism only.
   b. central planning only.
   c. a laissez-faire approach.
   d. a combination of market and government decisions.

CHAPTER 3 Demand and Supply

In a capitalistic economy, market forces answer the three fundamental economic questions of what to produce, how to produce, and for whom to produce. A market is comprised of all of the buyers and sellers interacting to satisfy a goal. The basic market model of demand and supply assumes that the goal of sellers in their market interactions is to maximize profit and the goal of buyers is to maximize their satisfaction. Demand and supply analysis is a useful tool for explaining and understanding economic events.

A market for a particular good or service, or item, exists when there is both a demand and a supply for that item. There is a **demand** when potential buyers are both willing and able to purchase the item. There is a **supply** when potential sellers are both willing and able to make the item available for sale. Demand can exist without supply: for example, people can be willing and able to pay for luxury trips to the moon, but there is no supply of such trips. Supply can exist without demand: for example, people can be willing and able to sell their specialized labor services, but there may not be someone willing and able to hire them. When demand and supply occur simultaneously, a market emerges. To understand how markets work, it helps to look at demand and supply separately first.

Demand

Demand models the behavior of buyers in markets. The decision to buy any item is made by taking a lot of information into account, such as the price asked, the amount the buyer has to spend, and the availability of substitutes for an item. Assuming that the main factors that influence buying decisions are held constant except price, the model starts by showing how buyers respond to a change in the price of an item. A demand function gives the relationship between **price** and **quantity demanded,** ceteris paribus (holding everything else constant).

The relationship between the price of a particular product and the quantity demanded of that product may be shown graphically, in equation form, or as selected points displayed in a table. The following table is a **demand schedule** that shows the quantity demanded of pizzas in a hypothetical college town, at different prices per pizza, assuming all factors that influence the decision of how many pizzas to buy are held constant except price.

Price $ Per Pizza	Quantity Demanded 1,000s Pizzas per year
$12	0
10	20
8	40
6	60
4	80
2	100

Notice that as the price per pizza falls, the quantity demanded of pizzas increases, and vice-versa. This relationship is stated in the **Law of Demand**, which says that a greater quantity will be demanded at lower relative prices than at higher relative prices, ceteris paribus. In other words, if nothing changes except price, buyers respond to an increase in price by decreasing quantity demanded and to a decrease in price by increasing quantity demanded. There is an **inverse**, or **negative**, relationship between **price** and **quantity demanded**, ceteris paribus.

When the demand function is plotted on a graph, the quantity demanded is on the horizontal axis, and the price is on the vertical axis. The resulting curve will slope downward to the right, as indicated by the Law of Demand. The graph below shows the demand curve for pizza in the hypothetical college town. If price is $8, the demand curve shows that quantity demanded is 40,000 pizzas per year. This combination is point A on the demand curve. If price is $6, quantity demanded is 60,000 pizzas per year, given by point B. Decreasing price from $8 to $6 is shown by a movement along the demand curve from point A to point B, and quantity demanded increases from 40,000 to 60,000 pizzas per year.

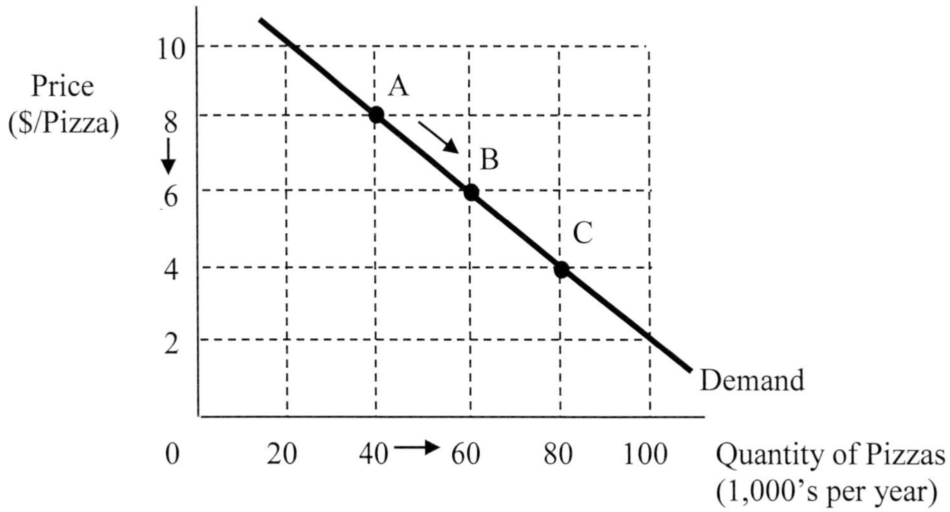

Supply

Supply models the behavior of sellers in markets. In a perfectly competitive market, each individual seller takes the market price as given. Sellers take into account many factors other than price, including the cost of producing the item and the number of other sellers in the market, when deciding how much output to supply. Assuming that the main factors that influence selling decisions are held constant except price, the model starts by showing how sellers respond to a change in the price of an item. Remember, the assumed goal of the seller is to maximize profit. If the cost of producing output is held constant, then an increase in the price of the product means the seller earns a greater profit and will be willing to make a greater amount of output available. A supply function gives the relationship between **price** and **quantity supplied,** ceteris paribus (holding everything else constant).

The following **supply schedule** shows the quantity supplied of pizzas in our hypothetical college town at different prices per pizza, assuming all factors that influence the decision of how many pizzas to sell are held constant, except price.

Price $ Per Pizza	Quantity Supplied 1,000s Pizzas per year
$12	120
10	100
8	80
6	60
4	40
2	20
0	0

Notice that as the price per pizza falls, the quantity supplied of pizzas decreases, and vice-versa. This relationship is stated in the **Law of Supply**, which says that a greater quantity will be supplied at higher relative prices than at lower relative prices, ceteris paribus. In other words, if nothing changes except price, sellers respond to an increase in price by increasing quantity supplied and to a decrease in price by decreasing quantity supplied. There is a **direct**, or **positive**, relationship between **price** and **quantity supplied**, ceteris paribus.

The graph below shows the supply curve for pizza in the hypothetical college town. It slopes upward to the right, as indicated by the Law of Supply. At a price of $8, quantity supplied is 80,000 pizzas per year, given by point E; at a price of $6, quantity supplied is 60,000 pizzas per year, given by point B. Decreasing price from $8 to $6 is shown by a movement along the supply curve from point E to point B, and quantity supplied decreases from 80,000 to 60,000 pizzas per year.

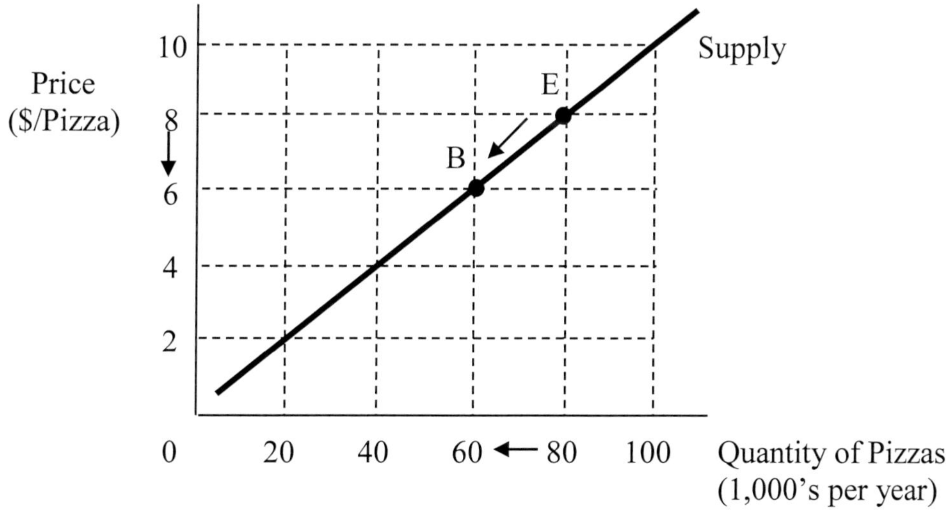

Market Equilibrium

A market is in equilibrium when the plans of buyers and sellers coincide. Specifically, a market is in equilibrium at the price for which quantity demanded is equal to quantity supplied. There is one unique combination of price and quantity that lies on both the demand and supply curves; this point is at the intersection of the two curves.

The demand curve and supply curve can be combined in a single diagram with price on the vertical axis and quantity on the horizontal axis to identify market equilibrium (where supply and demand intersect).

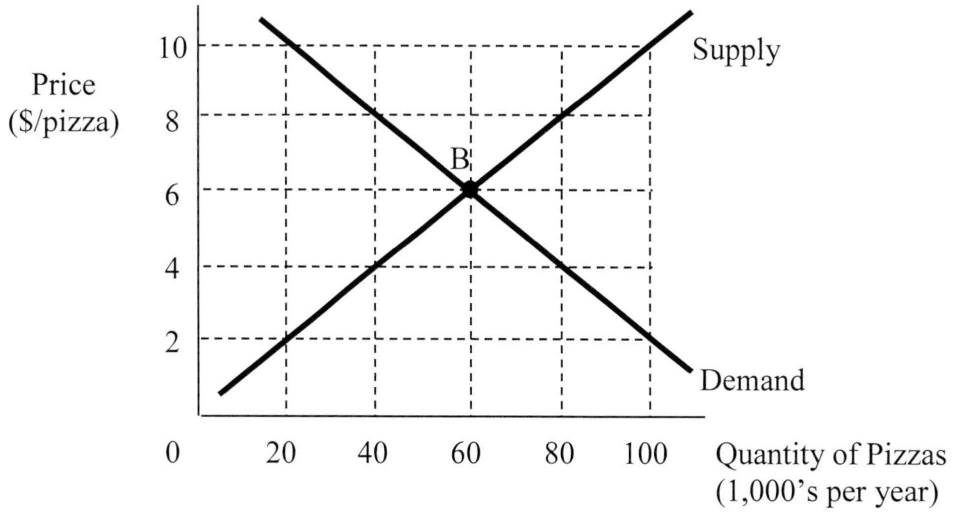

Point B, which corresponds to a price of $6, is the only point that lies on both the demand curve and the supply curve. At a price of $6, quantity demanded is 60,000 pizzas and quantity supplied is 60,000 pizzas. The price at which quantity demanded equals quantity supplied is referred to as the **market-clearing**, or **equilibrium, price**. In the market for pizzas, $6 is the **equilibrium price** and 60,000 pizzas is the **equilibrium quantity**.

When quantity supplied exceeds quantity demanded, there is a **market surplus**. The size of the surplus is measured by subtracting the quantity demanded from the quantity supplied. At a price of $8, which is above the equilibrium price, the quantity supplied is 80,000 pizzas and the quantity demanded is 40,000 pizzas, resulting in a surplus of 40,000 pizzas.

When quantity demanded exceeds quantity supplied, there is a **market shortage**. The size of the shortage is found by subtracting quantity supplied from quantity demanded. At a price of $2, which is below the equilibrium price, quantity demanded is 100,000 pizzas and quantity supplied is 20,000 pizzas. There is a shortage of 80,000 pizzas.

In summary, any price above equilibrium is associated with a surplus, and any price below equilibrium is associated with a shortage. When the price is at the equilibrium value (where supply and demand intersect), the quantity demanded equals the quantity supplied, and there is neither a surplus nor a shortage. Notice that it is not true that demand is equal to supply. Demand is the entire downward-sloping curve, and quantity demanded is one amount associated with a particular price, shown by one point on the demand curve. Likewise, supply means the entire function, and quantity supplied means a particular number of units that firms are willing and able to sell at a particular price.

Observation of real-world markets reveals that there is a strong tendency for price to fall when a surplus exists and for price to rise when a shortage exists, provided there are no legal restrictions preventing price changes. Given these tendencies, it is reasonable to expect the price to gravitate toward the market-clearing or equilibrium value, where the supply curve and the demand curve intersect.

Factors that Shift Demand

The law of demand specifies an inverse relationship between price and quantity demanded, ceteris paribus, and a demand curve shows this relationship. The demand curve on the left shows that the quantity demanded is Q_1 when the price is P_1, and that the quantity demanded increases to Q_2 when the price falls to P_2. The change in price causes a **movement along** the demand curve from point A to point B. The only factor that causes a movement from point A to point B along D_1 is a decrease in the price of this product from P_1 to P_2. Furthermore, a change in the price of this product cannot cause the demand for this product to change or shift, assuming all other factors are held constant.

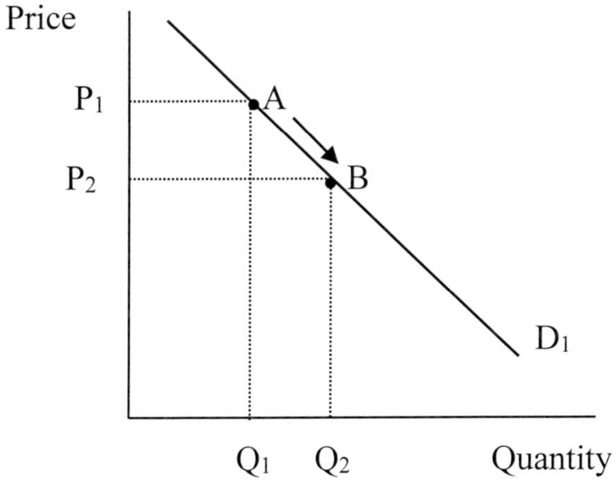

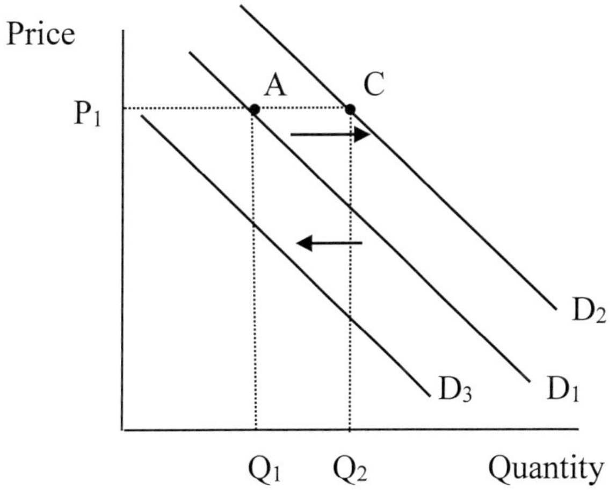

A change in demand occurs when a non-price factor that influences demand changes. The non-price factors are held constant when the demand curve is drawn. A change in demand is graphed as a shift of the demand curve. The graph on the right shows changes in demand. The rightward shift from D_1 to D_2 illustrates an **increase in demand.** As demand increases, or shifts to the right, consumers are willing and able to purchase more of this product at every price. For example, if the price is P_1, consumers want to buy Q_2 units rather than Q_1 (this is shown as a movement from point A to point C in the graph). A **decrease in demand** is shown by a leftward shift of the entire demand curve, such as from D_1 to D_3, in the graph on the right.

There are many events that cause demand curves to shift. Some events cause demand to increase and shift to the right. Other events cause demand to decrease and shift to the left. We will look at some events that frequently explain demand shifts, but keep in mind that a change in the price of the product represented in the graph cannot be responsible for a shift.

Generally, a market demand curve shifts as a result of a change in:

- Tastes and Preferences
- Income
- The price of related goods
- The number of buyers
- Expectations (of buyers)

Fashion trends, diet fads, and reports linking certain products to cancer or other serious side effects can affect consumer **tastes and preferences**. For example, if you read a report that drinking more milk improves your metabolism and helps you lose weight, you might purchase more milk. Changes in tastes and preferences can cause the demand for some products to increase because they are healthier or more fashionable, while causing the demand for other products to decrease. For example, when skirts are fashionable, the demand for pants might fall. Often, we can attribute known changes in demand to changes in tastes and preferences, if no other explanation presents itself.

Income is another major factor that influences buying decisions. The relationship between income and demand depends on the type of good being considered. For **normal goods**, increases in income lead to increases in demand, and decreases in income lead to decreases in demand. Most goods are normal goods. For example, if your income increases, you may purchase more meals in restaurants. Your demand for restaurant meals increases as a result of the increase in your income; the price of restaurant meals did not change – your income changed, and that is why your demand changed. For **inferior goods,** demand decreases when income increases, and demand increases when income decreases. You can probably think of at least one item that you will never buy once you become wealthy; you will not stop buying it because its price went up; you stop buying it because your income went up. The increase in income led to a decrease in demand. Such an item is called an inferior good, because people buy less of it following an increase in income or wealth.

There are four possible shifts due to a change in income or wealth.

- Demand shifts to the right (increases) following an increase in income for a normal good
- Demand shifts to the right (increases) following a decrease in income for an inferior good
- Demand shifts to the left (decreases) following a decrease in income for a normal good
- Demand shifts to the left (decreases) following an increase in income for an inferior good

The demand for a product may change, or shift, as a result of a change in the **price of a related good**. **Substitutes** are two things that perform the same basic function. If corn and beans are **substitutes**, then an increase in the price of corn causes an increase in the demand for beans; consumers buy more beans, not because the price of beans fell, but because the price of corn increased, so the demand for beans increased. **Complements** are two things used together, such as hotdogs and hotdog buns. A decrease in the price of hotdogs might cause people to buy more hotdog buns. The price of hotdogs buns did not fall; people are buying more buns for a reason other than a decrease in the price of buns, so the demand for hotdog buns increased.

Demand may change if the **number of buyers** in a market changes. A market demand curve is derived by adding the quantity demanded (Q^D) of each buyer at each price. For example, if the market consists of two consumers, Lara and Jesse, market demand is obtained by adding, at each price, the amount demanded by both buyers.

Price	Lara's Q^D	Jesse's Q^D	Total Q^D
\$3.00	10	15	25
\$2.00	14	22	36

The market demand curve can be drawn by plotting total Q^D at each price. Graphically, a market demand curve is derived by horizontally adding the individual demand curves of the consumers in the market, as shown below.

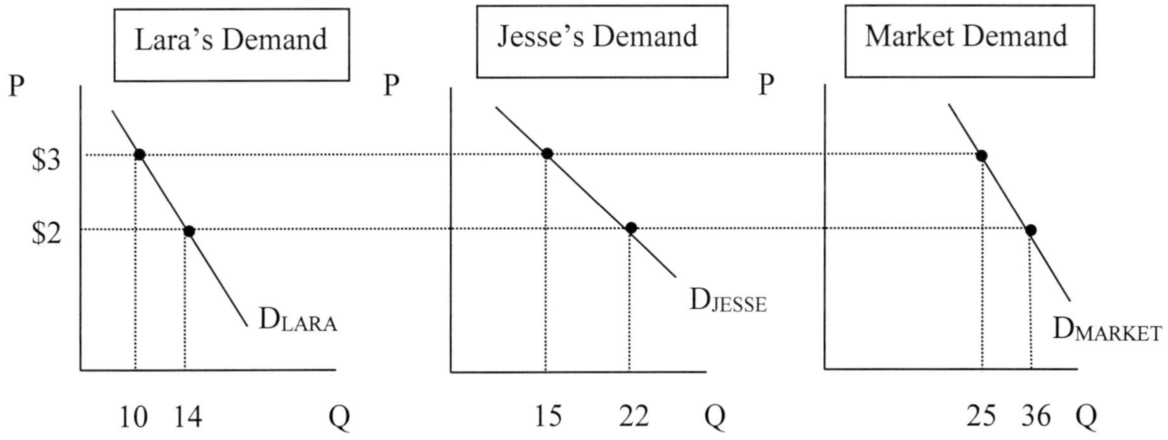

If another consumer is added to this market (assuming the third consumer has a positive Q^D at prices of \$2.00 and \$3.00), total Q^D will be larger at each price. Graphing market demand with three consumers gives a market demand curve that is to the right of the market demand curve generated assuming two consumers, and so on. Therefore, each time another consumer is added to the market, the market demand curve will typically shift rightward, or increase.

Expectations can influence buying decisions in different ways. For example, a consumer's demand for normal goods would likely fall today if the consumer expects a drop in income or wealth in the near future. Similarly, the expectation of higher product prices in the future can motivate consumers to buy now, causing the demand for those products to increase and shift to the right.

Once you learn the distinction between a shift and a movement, you can rely on your common sense to help you determine the direction of a shift when you are asked to analyze a specific event. Remember, only a change in the price of X will cause a movement along the demand curve for X, so do not confuse price with the other variables that influence buying choices.

Factors that Shift Supply

The law of supply specifies a direct relationship between price and quantity supplied, ceteris paribus, and a supply curve shows this relationship. The supply curve on the left shows that the quantity supplied is Q_1 when the price is P_1 and that the quantity supplied increases to Q_2 when the price increases to P_2. The increase in price causes a **movement along** the supply curve from point A to point B, and quantity supplied increases from Q_1 to Q_2. The movement along the curve as a result of the price change is not a change in supply because the supply curve for an item does not shift when the price of the item changes.

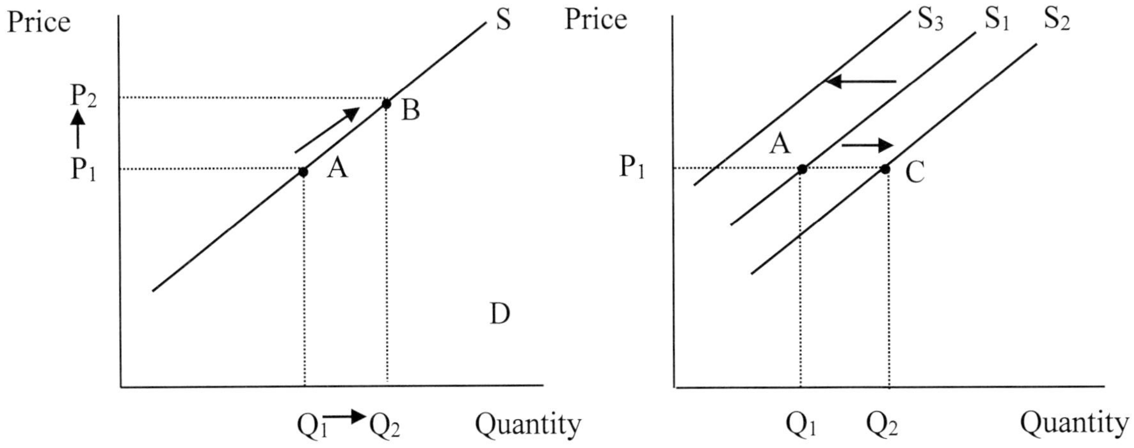

Sellers may change the quantity offered for sale at every price when a non-price influence on supply changes. A change in supply is graphed as a shift of the supply curve. An **increase in supply** is represented by a rightward shift of the supply curve, such as the shift from S_1 to S_2 in the graph on the right. As supply increases, or shifts to the right, firms are willing and able to sell more of this product at every price. For example, if the price is P_1, firms want to sell Q_2 units rather than Q_1. A **decrease in supply** is illustrated by a leftward shift of the supply curve, such as the shift from S_1 to S_3 in the graph on the right. There are many events that can cause supply to shift. Some events cause supply to increase and shift to the right. Other events cause supply to decrease and shift to the left.

Generally, a market supply curve shifts as a result of a change in:

- Costs of production
- Production technology
- The price of other producible goods
- The number of sellers
- Expectations (of sellers)
- Taxes and Subsidies
- Acts of nature

Changes in **costs of production** affect supply decisions. When suppliers can produce their product at a lower cost, the result is an increase in supply. Holding product price the same, lower production costs mean higher profits, and higher profits motivate firms to sell more at each price. Cheaper raw materials or lower wage rates cause costs of production to fall and supply to increase and shift to the right, while more expensive inputs cause supply to decrease, or shift to the left.

Improved **technology** used to produce the output causes supply to increase, or shift to the right. Technological advance has the effect of making it cheaper to produce, or provide, a good or service. For example, advances in telecommunications have made it cheaper to provide cellular service, and the development of microchips made personal computers smaller and cheaper to produce. Advances in technology are assumed to increase supply. If a given technology made it more expensive to produce the same product, a firm would not adopt it.

Changes in the **price of other producible goods** can also affect the supply curve. If there is more than one possible product that the seller can make with available resources, then a change in one product price can affect the supply of the other product. For example, if the price of wheat increases, the supply of corn can fall if farmers plant wheat instead of corn. The change in the price of wheat will cause a movement along the supply curve of wheat and a shift of the supply curve of corn.

Just as a market demand curve is derived by adding the quantity demanded of each consumer at different possible prices, a market supply curve is derived by adding the quantity supplied of each seller at different possible prices. An increase in **the number of sellers** causes the market supply curve to increase, or shift to the right, while a decrease in the number of sellers causes the market supply curve to decrease, or shift to the left.

If **sellers' expectations** change, the supply curve may shift as a result. For example, if sellers expect the price of their product to rise in the future, they may hoard the product, hoping to sell it later at a higher price. This behavior causes supply to decrease in the present period.

Supply functions may change in response to changes in **taxes and subsidies**. Taxes effectively make selling a product more expensive if it is the seller's duty to collect taxes on each sale and then send the money to the government. A subsidy is the opposite of a tax, with the government paying the seller and making it cheaper for sellers to provide the product. Thus, a tax, or an increase in a tax, causes supply to decrease and shift to the left, while a subsidy, or an increase in a subsidy, causes supply to increase and shift to the right.

Acts of nature may also be responsible for supply shifts in some cases, especially in agricultural markets. Floods or droughts can reduce supply by destroying crops. Unusually good weather can cause a bumper crop, resulting in increased supply.

Once again, common sense is the best guide when analyzing events to determine whether supply shifts or demand shifts, and the direction of the shifts. This allows you to move from a real-world event to a prediction about how that event will likely affect product prices, production levels, and consumption levels. This final step reveals the purpose and value of demand and supply analysis to anyone who has ever asked a question like "why is the price of gasoline so high?" or "why are cell phones so cheap?"

Changes in Equilibrium Price and Quantity: Shifts in Demand and Supply

To analyze a single event, such as a change in income or a change in technology, first determine whether the event shifts demand or supply, and then determine the direction of the shift. A single shift in demand or supply will generate a new intersection point of the demand and supply curves and a new equilibrium price and quantity in the market. The best way to understand how equilibrium price and quantity change, given a demand shift or a supply shift, is to sketch the graphs. The four graphs below show the four possible single shifts. In each case, the initial equilibrium is given by point A, and the new equilibrium (after the shift) is given by point B.

Increase in Demand

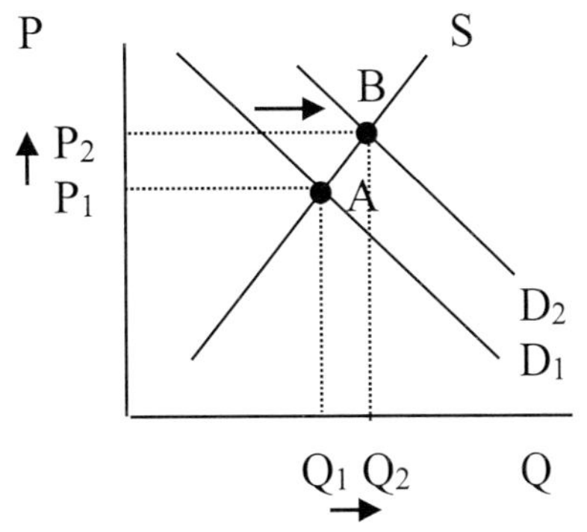

An increase in demand leads to an increase in both equilibrium price and quantity.

Decrease in Demand

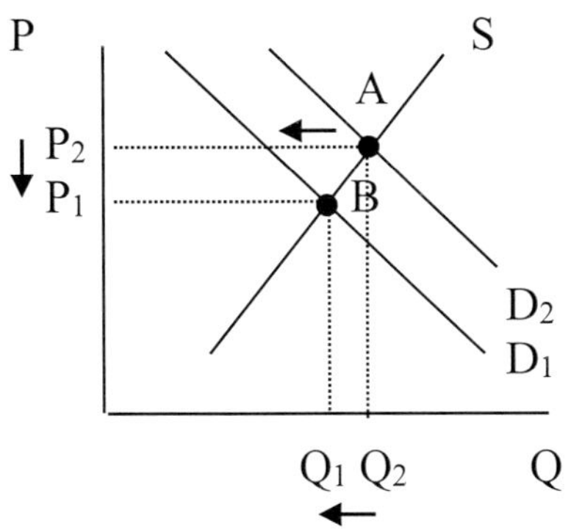

A decrease in demand leads to a decrease in both equilibrium price and quantity.

Increase in Supply

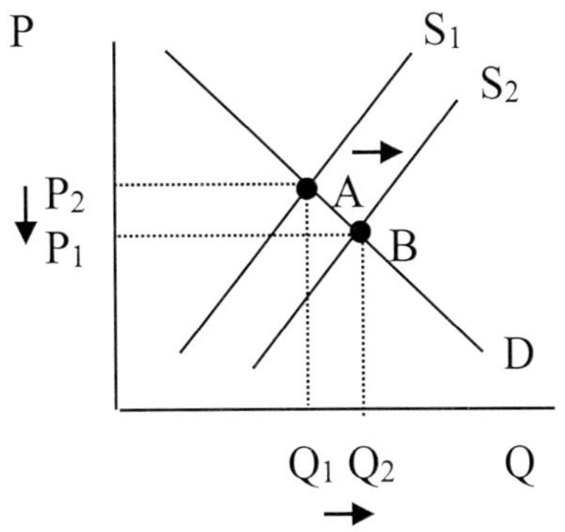

An increase in supply leads to a decrease in equilibrium price and an increase in equilibrium quantity.

Decrease in Supply

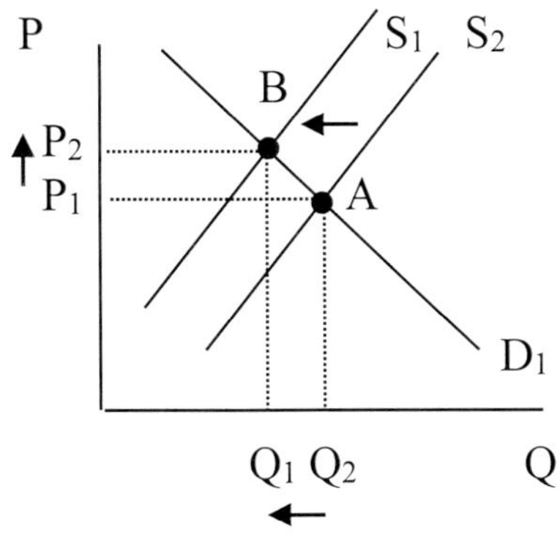

A decrease in supply leads to an increase in equilibrium price and a decrease in equilibrium quantity.

The four diagrams above show what happens when one curve shifts and the other stays the same. In reality, there may be several factors changing at once in a particular market and the analysis becomes more complicated.

The impact of a double shift depends on the magnitude of each shift. For example, what happens if production technology improves, causing supply to increase, and at the same time, a change in consumer preferences causes an increase in demand? Both changes cause equilibrium quantity to increase, as shown in the graphs on the previous page. However, the increase in demand causes price to go up, but the increase in supply causes price to go down. Which direction price moves depends on which shift is bigger – and a principles of economics course generally just deals with the direction of a change, not the size of a change.

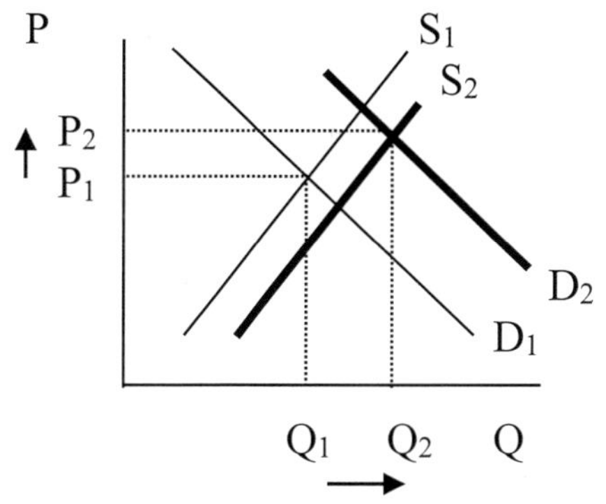

When demand and supply are both shifting to the right, the effect on equilibrium price depends on the size of the two shifts.

If the demand shift is larger, as shown to the left, then equilibrium price rises.

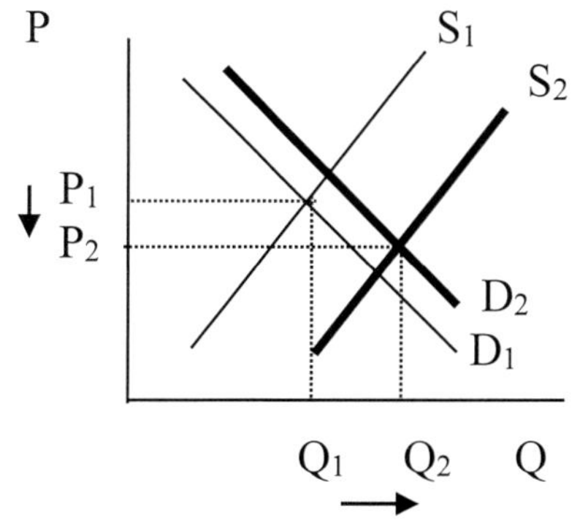

If the supply shift is larger, as shown to the left, then equilibrium price falls.

In either case, equilibrium quantity rises because both shifts cause an increase in quantity.

When demand and supply shift simultaneously, it may be best to draw two graphs: one with demand shifting and another with supply shifting. The direction of the change in P and Q in each graph can then be compared.

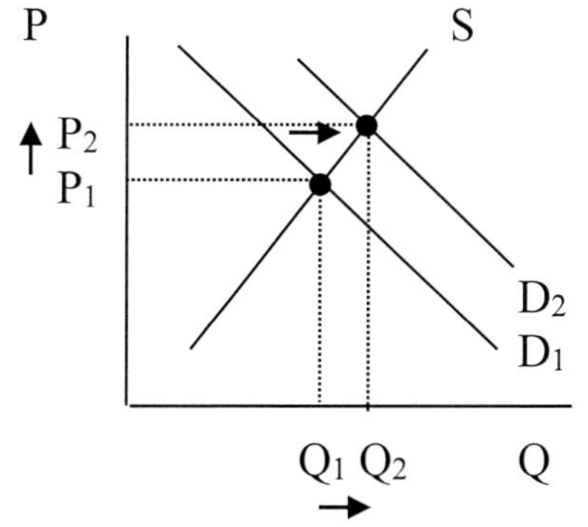

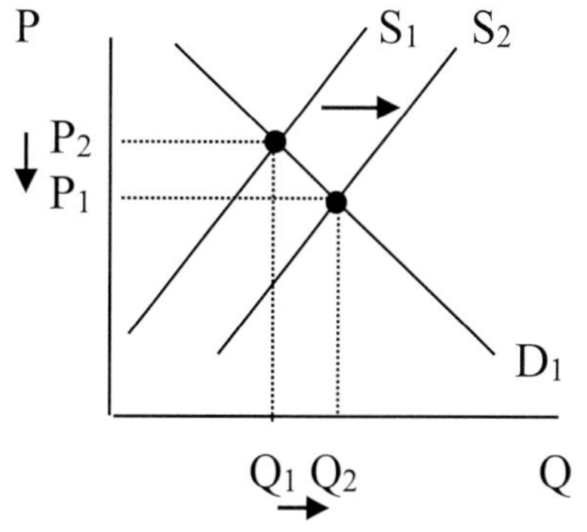

If both demand and supply increase, demand and supply analysis predicts that equilibrium quantity will increase, but equilibrium price could increase, decrease, or stay the same. The change in equilibrium price cannot be determined from the information given.

Price Ceilings and Price Floors

Policymakers might decide to set a maximum legal price, or a **price ceiling,** to protect buyers from prices that are thought to be too high. A binding price ceiling is one that is established below the equilibrium price. A price ceiling set above the equilibrium price is not binding because it does not prevent equilibrium from being attained. An example of a price ceiling is rent controls in an urban area; price ceilings for gasoline have been proposed recently.

Government policymakers might decide to set a minimum legal price, or a **price floor,** in an effort to protect sellers in a particular market. A binding price floor is one that is established above the equilibrium price. A price floor set below the equilibrium price is not binding because it does not prevent equilibrium from being attained. One important example of a price floor is the minimum wage.

The graph below summarizes the basic impact of a price ceiling and a price floor on a market.

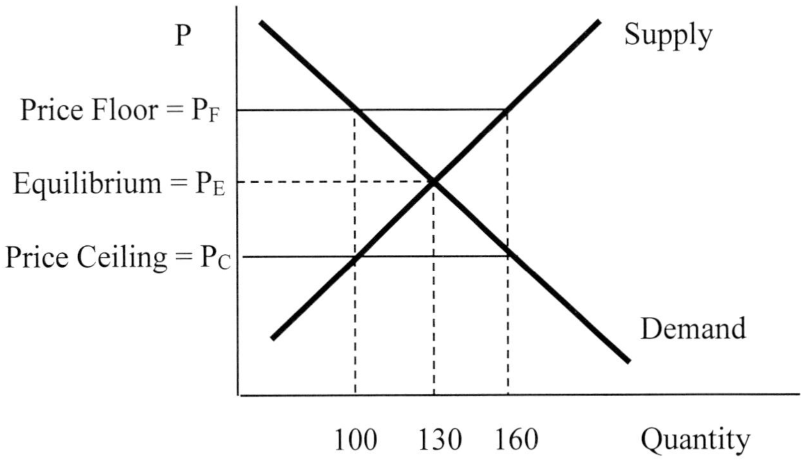

The price ceiling is below equilibrium; the ceiling limits the price that a seller can legally charge in this market to P_C. Price cannot go above the price ceiling, which means it cannot move up to equilibrium. The impact is a shortage: quantity demanded is 160 units but quantity supplied is only 100 units, and there is a shortage of 60 units at the price ceiling. If the ceiling were placed on something such as the fee a doctor could charge, the short-run impact may be a shortage of doctors' office visits. It may also become more difficult to get an appointment, waiting times at doctors' offices may increase, and visits may become shorter. The quality of each visit could also decline. In the long run, qualified individuals may choose NOT to enter the profession, and the shortage may become worse.

The price floor is above equilibrium; it supports the price sellers receive for an input or output. Buyers must pay a minimum of the price floor in this market. Price cannot fall below the price floor, which means it cannot move down to equilibrium. The result is a surplus: quantity supplied is 160 units and quantity demanded is 100 units, and there is a surplus of 60 units at the price floor of P_F. If the price floor is the minimum wage, the result may be a surplus in the labor market which means there is unemployment.

NAME____ SECTION#______________
Print Last Name, First Name

DEMAND AND SUPPLY

Use the graph below to answer questions 1 – 3:

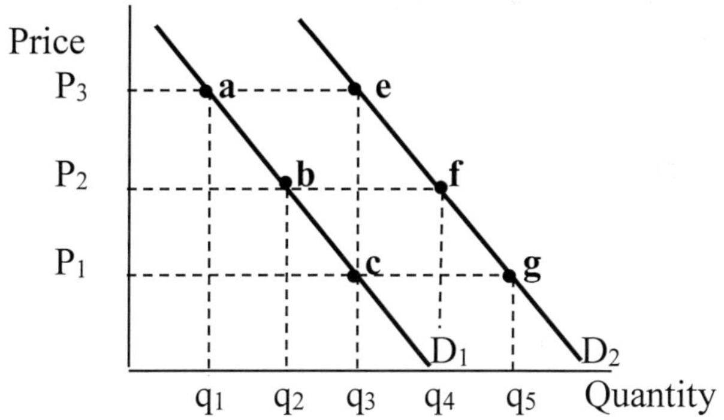

1. An increase in demand would be shown by a movement:
   a. along D_1 from point **b** to point **c**.
   b. along D_1 from point **b** to point **a**.
   c. from point **c** on D_1 to point **g** on D_2.
   d. from point **f** on D_2 to point **b** on D_1.

2. A movement from point **b** to point **a** along D_1 is caused by:
   a. an increase in consumer income.
   b. an increase in the price of a substitute product.
   c. an increase in the price of the product.
   d. a decrease in the price of the product.

3. On D_2, a decrease in price from P_2 to P_1 results in a:
   a. movement along D_2 from point **f** to point **e** and a decrease in quantity demanded from q_4 to q_3.
   b. movement along D_2 from point **f** to point **g** and an increase in quantity demanded from q_4 to q_5.
   c. shift from D_1 to D_2.
   d. shift from D_2 to D_1.

4. The relationship between price and the amount of a good or service consumers are willing and able to buy is given by:
   a. a demand curve.
   b. a production possibilities frontier.
   c. the circular flow model.
   d. a supply curve.

5. The law of demand illustrates the:
   a. direct (positive) relationship between price and demand.
   b. inverse (negative) relationship between price and demand.
   c. direct (positive) relationship between price and quantity demanded.
   d. inverse (negative) relationship between price and quantity demanded.

NAME____ SECTION#______________
Print Last Name, First Name

6. Which of the following would be expected to cause the demand for fish to decrease?
   a. An increase in the number of people that live near oceans and lakes
   b. An increase in the price of fish
   c. An increase in the price of chicken, assuming chicken and fish are substitutes
   d. A study claiming that fish contain a high level of contaminants that may cause cancer

7. The law of supply states that, everything else constant:
   a. price and quantity supplied are inversely related.
   b. quantity demanded and quantity supplied are directly related.
   c. price and quantity supplied move in opposite directions.
   d. price and quantity supplied move in the same direction.

8. Ceteris paribus, a decrease in the price of coats leads to:
   a. a decrease in the quantity supplied of coats.
   b. a decrease in the supply of coats.
   c. a decrease in the quantity demanded of coats.
   d. a decrease in the demand for coats.

9. Ceteris paribus, a decrease in the number of camera manufacturers leads to:
   a. a decrease in the supply of cameras.
   b. an increase in the supply of cameras.
   c. a decrease in the quantity supplied of cameras.
   d. a decrease in the quantity demanded of cameras.

10. Ceteris paribus, a decrease in the wages paid to autoworkers leads to:
   a. a rightward shift (increase) in the supply of autos.
   b. a leftward shift (decrease) in the supply of autos.
   c. an increase in the price of autos.
   d. an increase in the cost of producing autos.

NAME____ SECTION#______________

Print Last Name, First Name

DEMAND AND SUPPLY

1. According to the law of supply, an increase in the price of smart phones will cause:
   a. the quantity demanded of smart phones to decrease, ceteris paribus.
   b. the quantity supplied of smart phones to increase, ceteris paribus.
   c. the demand for smart phones to decrease, ceteris paribus.
   d. the supply of smart phones to increase, ceteris paribus.

2. The law of demand states that an increase in the price of a haircut, ceteris paribus, leads to:
   a. a decrease in the demand for haircuts.
   b. an increase in the demand for haircuts.
   c. a decrease in the quantity demanded of haircuts.
   d. an increase in the quantity demanded of haircuts.

3. Ceteris paribus, the demand for Dallas area public transportation is likely to increase (shift to the right) if:
   a. the Dallas area population increases.
   b. Dallas area residents are more willing to take the bus to work.
   c. Dallas area consumers experience a decrease in income and public transportation is an inferior good.
   d. the price of owning and operating a car in the Dallas area increases.
   e. All of the above may cause the demand for Dallas area public transportation to increase.

4. Ceteris paribus, advancements (increases) in production technology cause:
   a. the demand curve to shift leftward.
   b. the demand curve to shift rightward.
   c. the supply curve to shift leftward.
   d. the supply curve to shift rightward.

5. Which of the following events would cause the demand for baseball gloves to decrease?
   a. A decrease in the popularity of playing baseball
   b. A decrease in the price of baseball gloves
   c. An increase in the price of baseballs and baseball bats
   d. Both a. and c. are likely to cause a decrease in the demand for baseball gloves.
   e. None of the above are likely to affect the demand for baseball gloves.

6. If suppliers decrease the amount of output they are willing and able to make available for sale at *all* prices, then:
   a. supply increases and the supply curve shifts right.
   b. supply decreases and the supply curve shifts left.
   c. demand increases in response and the demand curve shifts right.
   d. demand decreases in response and the demand curve shifts left.

7. Which of the following best explains a decrease in the supply of video games?
   a. A decrease in the number of video game manufacturers
   b. Higher costs for producing video games
   c. An increase in the wages paid to video game developers
   d. All of the above
   e. Answers a. and b. only

Use the graph below to answer questions 8 – 10:

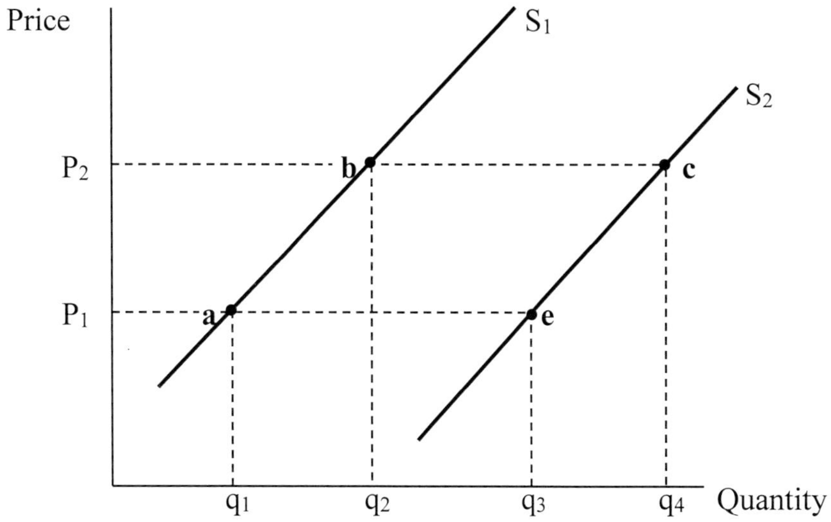

8. A decrease in supply would be shown by moving from point:
   a. **a** to point **b**.
   b. **b** to point **c**.
   c. **c** to point **e**.
   d. **e** to point **a**.

9. A movement from point **c** to point **e** along S_2 is caused by:
   a. an increase in price which will lead to a decrease in quantity supplied.
   b. an increase in price which will lead to an increase in quantity supplied.
   c. a decrease in price which will lead to a decrease in quantity supplied.
   d. a decrease in price which will lead to an increase in quantity supplied.

10. Which of the following is most likely to cause a rightward shift from S_1 to S_2?
   a. An improvement in production technology
   b. An increase in the costs of production
   c. An increase in the price of the product
   d. A decrease in the price of the product

NAME____ SECTION#_______________
Print Last Name, First Name

SUPPLY AND DEMAND GRAPHS

Price per Loaf of Bread	Quantity Demanded Loaves of Bread per Day	Quantity Supplied Loaves of Bread per Day
$5	0	80
$4	20	60
$3	40	40
$2	60	20
$1	80	0
$0	100	0

Graph the demand relationship and the supply relationship for fresh baked bread from a local bakery on the grid below and then fill in blanks 1. – 10.

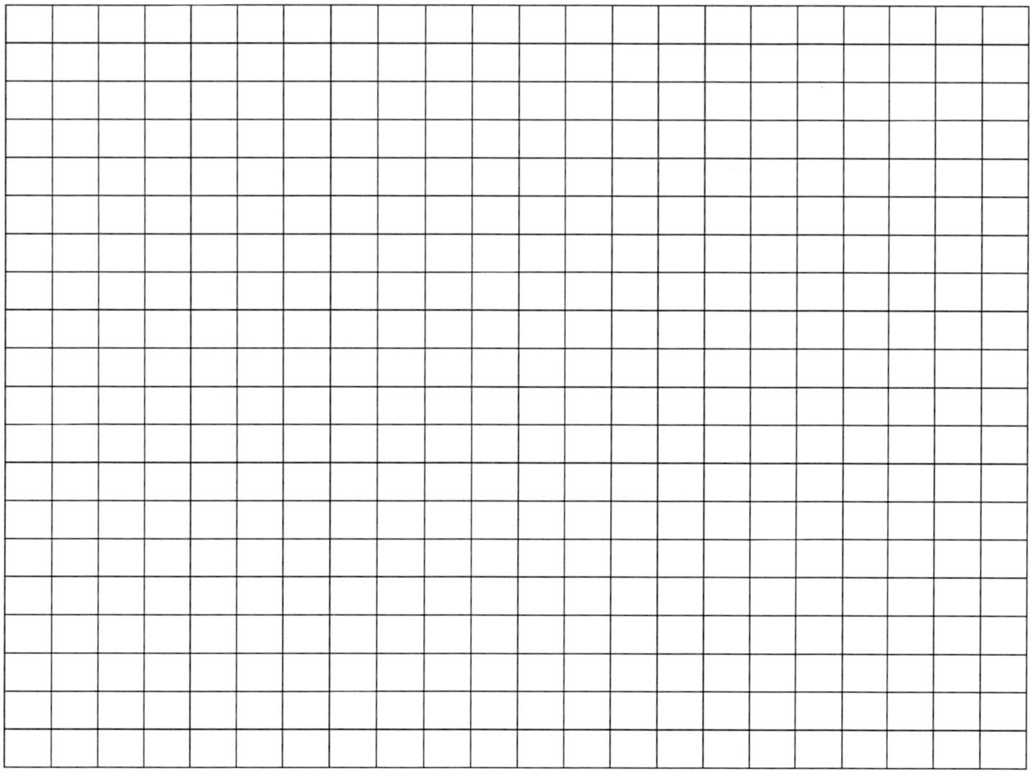

The equilibrium price in this market is (1) $______ per loaf and the equilibrium quantity in this market is (2)______ loaves per day. If price is $4 per loaf, quantity demanded is (3)_______ and quantity supplied is (4) ______. At P = $4, there is a (5)_________________________ of (6)_______ loaves and the price of a loaf of bread is likely to (7)____________________. If price is $2 per loaf, there is a (8)_________________________ of (9)________ loaves of bread and the price of a loaf of bread is likely to (10)__________________________.

NAME____ SECTION#______________
Print Last Name, First Name

SUPPLY AND DEMAND GRAPHS

In the space below, show the effect on equilibrium price and quantity of (a) an increase in demand, (b) a decrease in demand, (c) an increase in supply, and (d) a decrease in supply. Label the new demand curves D_2, the new supply curves S_2, the new equilibrium prices P_2, and the new equilibrium quantities Q_2.

(a)

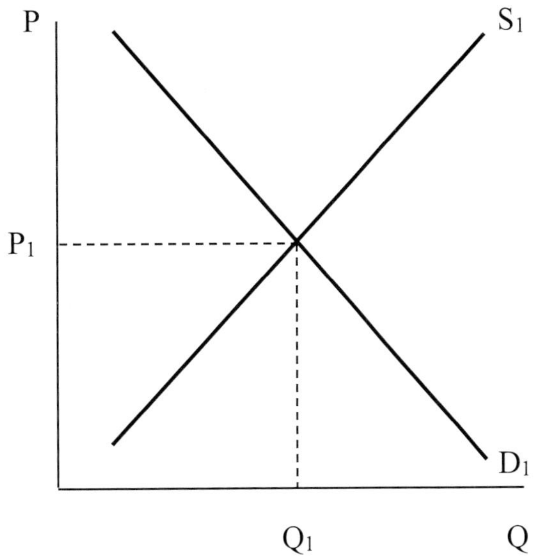

(b)

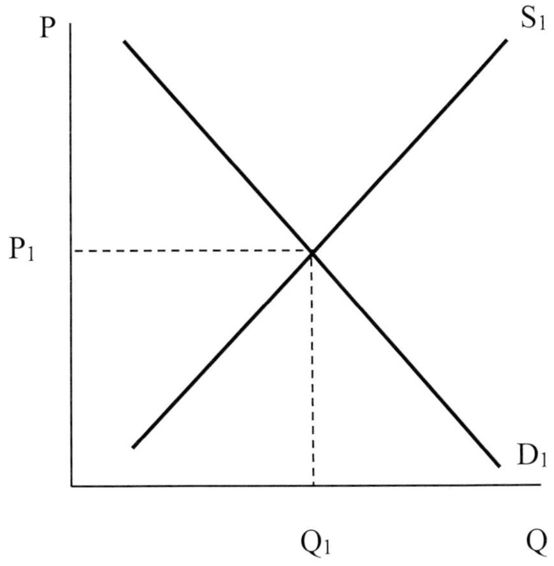

(c)

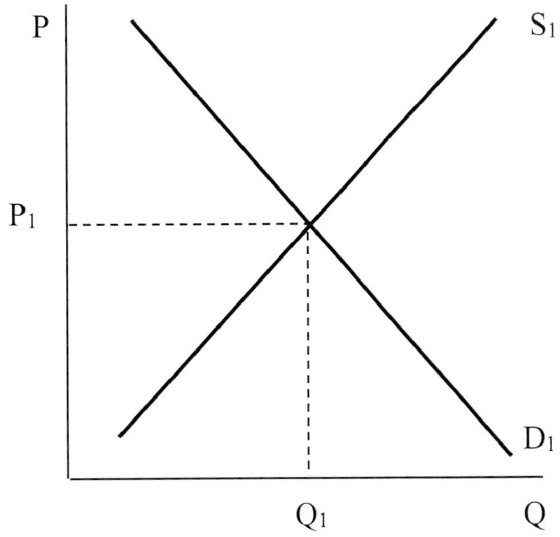

(d)

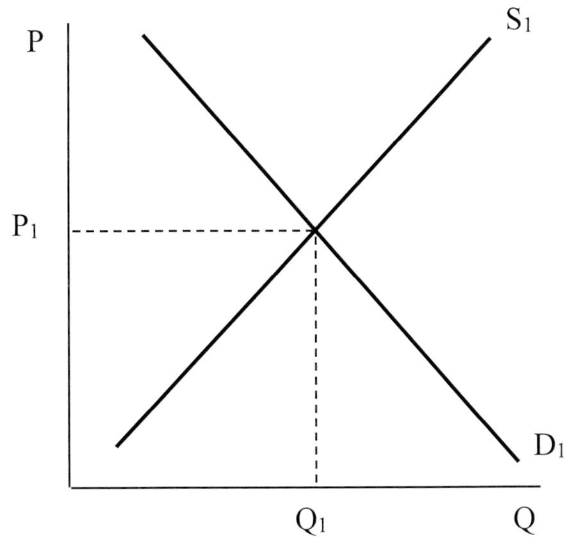

NAME________________________________ SECTION#____________

Print Last Name, First Name

MARKETS: SUPPLY AND DEMAND

1. Ceteris paribus, an increase in the number of suppliers in a market causes:
   a. demand to shift right and equilibrium price and quantity both rise.
   b. demand to shift left and equilibrium price and quantity both fall.
   c. supply to shift left and equilibrium price rises and equilibrium quantity falls.
   d. supply to shift right and equilibrium price falls and equilibrium quantity rises.

2. Ceteris paribus, when a decrease in consumer income causes demand to decrease:
   a. equilibrium price and equilibrium quantity both increase.
   b. equilibrium price and equilibrium quantity both decrease.
   c. equilibrium price increases and equilibrium quantity decreases.
   d. equilibrium price decreases and equilibrium quantity increases.

Use the graph below to answer questions 3 – 5:

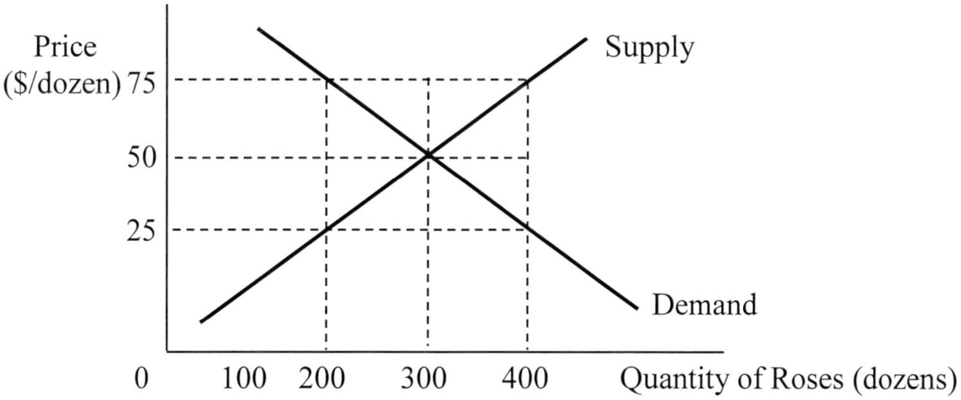

3. The equilibrium price of a dozen roses is _______ and the equilibrium quantity of roses is _______ dozen.
   a. $25; 200
   b. $50; 300
   c. $50; 400
   d. $75; 400

4. A price of $75 per dozen roses results in a _______ of _______ dozen roses.
   a. shortage; 100
   b. shortage; 200
   c. surplus; 100
   d. surplus; 200

5. A price of $25 per dozen roses results in a _______ of _______ dozen roses.
   a. shortage; 100
   b. shortage; 200
   c. surplus; 100
   d. surplus; 200

NAME____ SECTION#__________________
Print Last Name, First Name

Use the data below to answer questions 6 – 8:

Price of X	Quantity of X Demanded	Quantity of X Supplied
$8	200	600
$7	300	500
$6	400	400
$5	500	300
$4	600	200

6. What is the equilibrium price of good X?
   a. $4
   b. $5
   c. $6
   d. $7

7. There will be a surplus of 400 units of X at a price of _________.
   a. $5
   b. $6
   c. $7
   d. $8

8. At a price of $5, there is a ________ of ________ units of X.
   a. surplus; 400
   b. surplus; 200
   c. shortage; 400
   d. shortage; 200

9. If people increase their preferences for dining in restaurants versus dining at home, what will happen to the equilibrium price and quantity of restaurant meals, ceteris paribus?
   a. Price increases and quantity decreases
   b. Price decreases and quantity increases
   c. Price and quantity both decrease
   d. Price and quantity both increase

10. What will happen to the equilibrium price and quantity of widgets if the supply of widgets decreases and the demand for widgets decreases at the same time?
    a. Equilibrium quantity will decrease but the change in equilibrium price cannot be determined from the information given
    b. Equilibrium price will increase but the change in equilibrium quantity cannot be determined from the information given
    c. Both equilibrium price and quantity will increase
    d. Equilibrium price will decrease and equilibrium quantity will increase

NAME____ SECTION#_____________
Print Last Name, First Name

MARKETS: DEMAND AND SUPPLY

1. When the price of a product is above the equilibrium price and prices are flexible:
   a. a shortage exists and price will rise.
   b. a surplus exists and price will fall.
   c. a shortage exists and price will fall.
   d. a surplus exists and price will rise.

2. Ceteris paribus, what will happen to the equilibrium price and quantity of orange juice if a winter freeze destroys half of Florida's orange crop?
   a. Equilibrium price and quantity both rise
   b. Equilibrium price and quantity both fall
   c. Equilibrium price rises and equilibrium quantity falls
   d. Equilibrium price falls and equilibrium quantity rises

Use the graph below to answer questions 3 – 5:

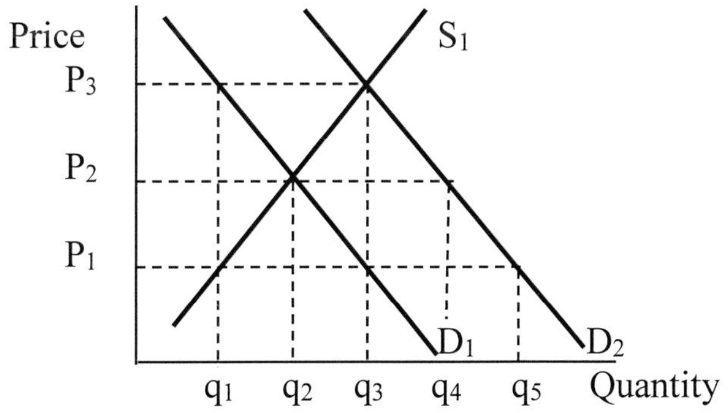

3. If this market is represented by D_1 and S_1, then equilibrium price is _______ and equilibrium quantity is _______.
   a. P_2; q_2
   b. P_1; q_3
   c. P_3; q_3
   d. P_1; q_1

4. If demand increases from D_1 to D_2 but price remains the same as in number 3 above, then there will be a:
   a. surplus equal to the distance $q_3 - q_1$.
   b. surplus equal to the distance $q_4 - q_2$.
   c. shortage equal to the distance $q_3 - q_1$.
   d. shortage equal to the distance $q_4 - q_2$.

5. The shift from D_1 to D_2 might have come about due to:
   a. a decrease in the price of this product.
   b. an increase in the supply of this product.
   c. an increase in consumer income if this good is a normal good.
   d. an increase in consumer income if this good is an inferior good.

6. Markets tend toward equilibrium:
   a. whenever producers attempt to maximize profits.
   b. only if government price setting policies are successful.
   c. if prices are fixed.
   d. if prices are able to fall to clear surpluses and prices are able to rise eliminate shortages.

7. If the supply of housing is fixed (i.e., the supply curve is a vertical line) and the demand for housing increases, then supply and demand analysis predicts that:
   a. the price of housing will also be fixed.
   b. the price of housing will fall.
   c. the housing market will be unable to achieve a new equilibrium.
   d. the price of housing will rise.

8. A decrease in the demand for apples, ceteris paribus, leads to:
   a. an increase in both the equilibrium price and quantity of apples.
   b. a decrease in both the equilibrium price and quantity of apples.
   c. a decrease in the equilibrium price of oranges and an increase in the equilibrium quantity of apples.
   d. an increase in the equilibrium price of oranges and a decrease in the equilibrium quantity of apples.

9. If the cost of producing good Z decreases at the same time good Z becomes more popular, then the graphing model of supply and demand predicts that:
   a. the equilibrium price and quantity of good Z will both increase.
   b. the equilibrium price of good Z will increase and the equilibrium quantity of good Z will decrease.
   c. the equilibrium quantity of good Z will decrease but the equilibrium price of good Z could increase, decrease, or stay the same.
   d. the equilibrium quantity of good Z will increase but the equilibrium price of good Z could increase, decrease, or stay the same.

10. A decrease in the number of sellers in a market that occurs at the same time that there is an increase in the number of buyers in that market will cause:
    a. equilibrium price to increase, but the change in equilibrium quantity cannot be determined without further information.
    b. equilibrium price to decrease, but the change in equilibrium quantity cannot be determined without further information.
    c. equilibrium quantity to decrease, but the change in equilibrium price cannot be determined without further information.
    d. equilibrium quantity to increase, but the change in equilibrium price cannot be determined without further information.

NAME____ SECTION#______________

Print Last Name, First Name

PRICE CEILINGS AND FLOORS

Use the graph below to answer questions 1 – 5:

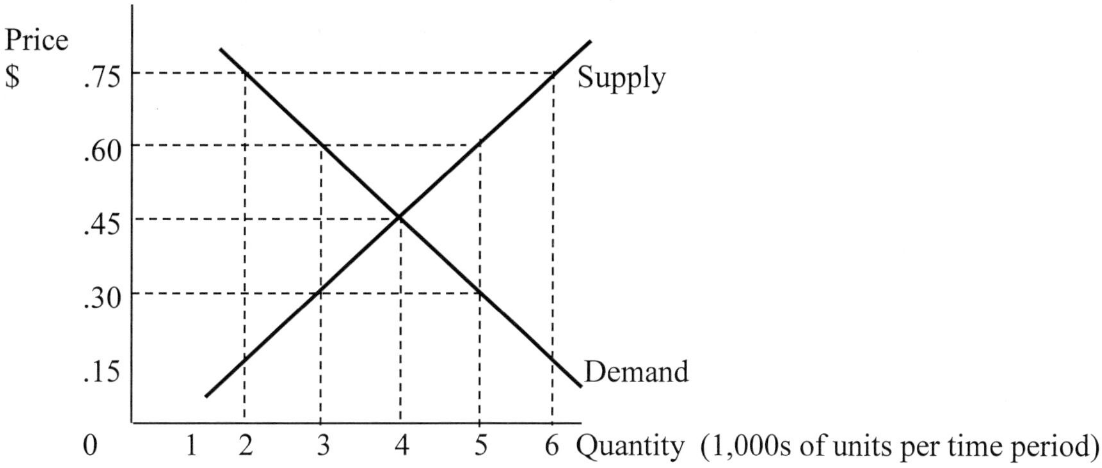

1. Suppose the above graph represents the market for carrots. If government's goal is to keep the price of carrots at $0.60 per unit, then government will likely:
   a. impose a price ceiling at $0.60 per unit.
   b. impose a price floor at $0.60 per unit.
   c. implement a system of rationing carrots to limit consumption per household.
   d. allow market forces to determine the equilibrium price.

2. A market surplus of 2,000 units would occur at a price of:
   a. $.30 per unit.
   b. $.45 per unit.
   c. $.60 per unit.
   d. $.75 per unit.

3. Government could set a price ______at $.30 per unit, which would lead to a ______.
   a. floor; surplus in the amount of 1,000 units
   b. floor; surplus in the amount of 2,000 units
   c. ceiling; shortage in the amount of 1,000 units
   d. ceiling; shortage in the amount of 2,000 units

4. Suppose government has established a price floor at $0.60 per unit. If the demand for this product decreases:
   a. the surplus that existed in this market will be eliminated.
   b. the surplus that existed in this market will become larger.
   c. the shortage that existed in this market will be eliminated.
   d. the shortage that existed in this market will become larger.

5. At a price of $.45 per unit:
   a. the market is in equilibrium.
   b. there is a shortage in the amount of 1,000 units.
   c. there is a surplus in the amount of 2,000 units.
   d. there is a shortage in the amount of 3,000 units.

NAME____ SECTION#______________

Print Last Name, First Name

6. An example of an existing price floor in the U.S. is:
   a. the minimum wage.
   b. a higher tax rate for high income households.
   c. the limit on the fee that can be charged for a visit to a doctor's office.
   d. all of the above are examples of existing price floors.

7. Government may impose a price ceiling in the market for a particular good or service in order to:
   a. prevent firms from leaving that market.
   b. protect some buyers in that market.
   c. ensure that buyers in that market receive the maximum amount of satisfaction from the good or service.
   d. enable firms in that market to earn a maximum profit.

Use the table below to answer questions 8 – 10:

Price	**Quantity Demanded**	**Quantity Supplied**
$100	**700**	**500**
$200	**600**	**600**
$300	**500**	**700**
$400	**400**	**800**
$500	**300**	**900**

8. In the absence of any price controls, the market will reach equilibrium at a price of:
   a. $200 and a quantity of 600.
   b. $300 and a quantity of 1,200.
   c. $400 and a quantity of 800.
   d. $500 and a quantity of 300.

9. If government established a price floor of $200 in this market:
   a. there would be a shortage of 200 units.
   b. there would be a surplus of 200 units.
   c. it would not have an impact on this market.
   d. equilibrium price in this market would decrease.

10. If government established a price ceiling of $100 in this market:
   a. there would be a shortage of 200 units.
   b. there would be a surplus of 200 units.
   c. equilibrium price in this market would increase.
   d. it would not have an impact on this market.

CHAPTER 4 Unemployment and Inflation

Macroeconomic goals include full employment, price stability, and economic growth. When the economy is operating at full employment, the actual rate of unemployment is equal to the "natural" rate, defined as the long-term sustainable rate and estimated to be between 4 and 6 percent. The actual rate of unemployment is estimated each month to see how close the economy is to full employment. The price level and the rate of inflation are estimated each month as well, and the goal is to keep the inflation rate low. The third goal is a healthy rate of growth, measured as the percentage change in real GDP, which is addressed in the next chapter.

Measuring Unemployment

The Bureau of Labor Statistics (BLS) reports data about the U.S. economy, which can be found at www.bls.gov. The data used to calculate the unemployment rate are derived from the Current Population Survey (CPS), which is a monthly survey of households conducted by the Bureau of Census for the BLS. Approximately 60,000 households are surveyed each month to gather information about employment, unemployment, earnings, productivity, and other economic statistics. The civilian non-institutionalized **labor force** includes people over the age of 16 who are working or actively seeking employment, and excludes members of the military and those who have been institutionalized.

Aggregate measures of the economy's performance are based on sample statistics. Since mid-2013, the **labor force participation rate** (LFPR) has been approximately 63 percent. This means 63 percent of those in the survey are participating in the labor force, so it is then estimated that 63 percent of the population participates in the labor force. Valid inferences can be drawn about the population based on a sample as long as the sample is random, or unbiased, and sufficiently large. For example, if you wanted to estimate the percentage of students on your campus who use the campus library, you would want to select a random sample of students, and you would want to survey more than a few. Going to the campus library and asking three students if they use the library would give you a biased statistic of 100 percent.

After selecting a random sample of households, the BLS asks members of the sample a series of questions designed to determine how each respondent should be classified. Each person is classified in only one of the three categories – employed, unemployed, or not in the labor force. The **labor force** consists of the **employed** plus the **unemployed**. The inability of labor force participants to find a job is known as **unemployment**. To be counted as unemployed, the respondent must indicate that she does not have a job, but she has actively looked for work in the prior 4 weeks and is currently available for work. Workers who are waiting to be called back to a job from which they had been temporarily laid off are counted as unemployed even if they are not actively seeking work. The percentage of the labor force that is unemployed is the **unemployment rate**. The unemployment rate was 3.7 percent as of September 2018.

$$\textbf{Unemployment Rate} = \frac{\textbf{Number of unemployed people}}{\textbf{Labor Force}} \times 100$$

Suppose the population is 300 million and the labor force is 165 million. If 157.5 million workers are employed, while 7.5 million are unemployed, the unemployment rate is 4.55 percent.

$$\textbf{Unemployment Rate} = \frac{\textbf{7.5 million}}{\textbf{165 million}} \times 100 = \textbf{4.55 percent}$$

Workers are classified as employed if they worked as little as one hour for pay during the survey week or if they did at least 15 hours of unpaid work in a family-operated enterprise. They are also classified as employed even if they are overqualified for the work they are performing. When workers are **underemployed**, they often continue to search for employment, and the rate of unemployment understates how many workers are engaged in job search. For example, suppose that of the 157.5 million workers who are employed, 2.5 million recently lost full-time jobs and have taken part-time, temporary jobs to provide some income while they conduct job searches. If they were counted as unemployed, then the unemployment rate would be 6.06 percent instead of 4.55 percent. It is a matter of opinion whether the 4.55 percent reported rate is accurate or an underestimate because it requires a judgment about how these workers should be classified. The BLS does not attempt to estimate underemployment, stating that "because of the difficulty of developing an objective set of criteria which could be readily used in a monthly household survey, no official government statistics are available on the total number of persons who might be viewed as underemployed" in their frequently asked questions.

Other measurement problems include "discouraged workers" and the phantom unemployed. **Discouraged workers** are people who are willing and able to work, but have given up actively seeking employment due to lack of success. This problem is especially significant during recession when the economy is weak and jobs are scarce. The existence of discouraged workers causes the reported unemployment rate to understate the true unemployment problem because they are not included in the labor force. For example, suppose that of the 135 million people who are not in the labor force, 1 million reported that they are not currently looking for work due to discouragement over job prospects. If we were to classify these discouraged workers as unemployed, then the labor force would increase from 165 million to 166 million, and the unemployment rate would increase from 4.55 percent to 5.12 percent. The BLS publishes information about persons not in the labor force by desire and availability for work, indicating how many of those not in the labor force are discouraged workers.

There are also people who claim to be unemployed (actively seeking work), when in fact they are not; this is sometimes referred to as **phantom unemployment**. The motivation for making a false claim may be that these individuals are currently receiving unemployment benefits. Unemployment insurance is a program that provides benefits to workers who were laid off. Eligible workers receive a weekly benefit (equal to approximately one-half of lost wages for the average worker) as long as they remain unemployed, up to 26 weeks in most cases. To maintain eligibility, these individuals must be available for work and actively seeking work each week. The phantom unemployed are collecting benefits, but not really seeking work, and so they may provide inaccurate information if included in the BLS survey. This may cause the reported unemployment rate to overstate the true unemployment problem because the phantom unemployed are not actively seeking work, but are being counted as unemployed.

Types of Unemployment

There are many reasons why someone might be currently unemployed: a person who just graduated from college and is looking for a job; a person who left a boring job to find a more challenging one; a person who relocated to a new city; a person who was staying home to care for children and has decided to rejoin the labor force; a person who was fired from their job; or a person who was laid off might be currently unemployed. Unemployment is a temporary state for most people. The average duration of unemployment is about 15 weeks, but this time tends to be significantly longer during economic downturns. Some percentage of the labor force is unemployed every month, but it is not the same people month after month. Instead, each month some unemployed workers are able to find jobs, and some employed workers lose jobs or leave jobs, while some people leave the labor force and retire and others enter the labor force. Those who are unemployed each month can be classified as frictionally, structurally, or cyclically unemployed. Workers can also be classified as seasonally unemployed, but the unemployment rate is seasonally adjusted, so seasonal unemployment is not reflected in reported rates.

Frictional unemployment occurs when there are jobs available, and there are qualified workers who are willing and able to accept those jobs, but the process of looking at job vacancies, applying for positions, interviewing, and being hired takes some time. Frictional unemployment occurs because workers have just left or lost a job, just entered the labor force, or re-entered the labor force and it takes time to become employed again. It also takes time from the employers' perspective to advertise a position, screen applicants, interview candidates, and make a hiring decision. Technology has improved our access to information and probably helped to reduce the job search time, but even with complete information, the job search process takes time because it is an important decision, for both the employee and the employer. Thus, frictional unemployment is not considered to be a sign of economic troubles, but is instead regarded as normal or natural.

Changes in the economy that eliminate jobs, relocate jobs, and create new jobs requiring skills the unemployed do not possess can also result in some people being unemployed. **Structural unemployment** occurs when there is a *mismatch* between the skills or location of people looking for work and the skill requirements or location of available jobs. Technological change may cause some job skills to become obsolete, causing structural unemployment, while creating demand for workers with different skills. For example, many employers use automated telephone service, eliminating the need for telephone receptionists to answer and direct calls. This technological change created some structural unemployment. At the same time, technology caused increased demand for workers familiar with office software or data entry. Structural change tends to eliminate some jobs and create others, but the difference between structural unemployment and frictional unemployment is that the structurally unemployed workers do not have the skills needed to be hired for the available jobs in their location. These workers often need education and training before they can find work because their skills are no longer in demand. As with frictional unemployment, a certain amount of structural unemployment is normal or natural, indicating that the economy is growing and changing due to, for example, technological improvement.

Most economists agree that it is normal, or natural, to have some relatively low unemployment each month due to the existence of frictional and structural unemployment. Recall that **full employment** is one of the macroeconomic goals; if some amount of unemployment is natural, then the full-employment unemployment rate will be greater than zero because there will be some frictional and structural unemployment. Despite the existence of some unemployment, there is a balance between the number of workers seeking jobs and the number of jobs available when the economy is at full employment. The rate of unemployment that occurs when the economy operates at full employment is called the **natural rate of unemployment (NROU);** cyclical unemployment will be 0 percent at the NROU. **Cyclical unemployment** is associated with unemployment above the natural rate and is considered a symptom of economic downturn or **recession**. A recession is a downturn in the overall economy and not in just one sector. Macroeconomic policy is designed to stimulate activity in all sectors of the economy and avoid or eliminate cyclical unemployment. According to the Federal Reserve, which is the central bank of the U.S., the natural rate of unemployment is the rate at which inflation is stable. Exactly what that rate is as a percentage seems to have changed over time due to changes in factors such as technology and demand.

During a recession, the unemployment rate is higher than the natural rate because there are more people who are unemployed. The unemployed may have initially been either frictionally or structurally unemployed, but if labor market conditions are such that there are fewer job vacancies economy-wide, the period of unemployment for the average job-seeker will start to increase. Each month, fewer of the unemployed are able to find new jobs, or more of the employed lose their jobs, which results in a higher rate of unemployment. The most likely explanation for this is that business sales are weak in a number of industries and employers are laying off workers or allowing their work force to shrink through attrition by choosing not to replace workers who have retired or left voluntarily.

When there is **cyclical unemployment,** the number of job-seekers exceeds the number of jobs available. For example, the unemployment rate in the U.S. was about 25 percent in 1933 due to the Great Depression. If discouraged workers had been counted as unemployed, some estimates put the rate of unemployment close to 50 percent in that year. Such high rates of unemployment is clearly not natural, which motivated economists, led by John Maynard Keynes, to study the causes of cyclical unemployment and to propose government policies that might help the economy create more jobs and eliminate cyclical unemployment.

In the most recent economic downturn, which began in December 2007, the U.S. unemployment rate rose from 4.9 percent to 10.1 percent by October 2009 and has since steadily decreased and was 5.8 percent by October 2014; the downward trend continued and the unemployment rate was 3.7 percent by the beginning of October 2018.

The major macroeconomic consequence of excessive unemployment is lost output: output that is not produced but could have been produced. In addition to lost output, high rates of unemployment for prolonged periods can lead to societal problems and political unrest. The microeconomic consequences for individuals include loss of income, loss of benefits such as employer-provided insurance, and declining savings. Prolonged periods of unemployment can also produce negative long-term emotional, psychological, and physical side-effects.

Measuring Inflation

Inflation is a persistent increase in the average level of prices of goods and services. Most people pay attention to inflation, or a rising price level, because it affects them personally. Inflation means that the cost of living is higher, so people need to earn more to maintain their living standards. In other words, an increase in the price level leads to a decrease in the **purchasing power** of a given money income. The Bureau of Labor Statistics (BLS) estimates the Consumer Price Index each month, and this is the basis for the reported rate of inflation that most people hear about and use to approximate the increase in their own cost of living. Inflation as measured by the CPI has been relatively low in the past several decades, and even became negative during the most recent economic downturn. The BLS reports the rate as steadily increasing from 0.1 percent in 2015 to 2.7 percent by August 2018.

The **Consumer Price Index (CPI)** is a measure of changes in the average price of goods and services purchased by consumers. The CPI measures changes over time in the prices of a typical "market basket" of consumer goods and services and is known as a fixed-weight price index. The specific items included in the market basket and their quantities are held constant, and price data are collected each month. For example, suppose the market basket consists of 5 apples and 10 oranges. The table below provides price data and shows the calculation of expenditures on the market basket in the two periods.

Time Period	Price per apple	Price per orange	Expenditures
1	\$0.50	\$0.75	(5)(0.5) + (10)(0.75) = \$10
2	\$0.60	\$1.00	(5)(0.6) + (10)(1) = \$13

Notice that a consumer purchasing this market basket would be getting the same products in the two periods, but would have to spend more in period 2 because of inflation. The necessary expenditure rose from \$10 to \$13, a 30 percent increase, which is a weighted average of the 20 percent increase in the price of apples and the 33 percent increase in the price of oranges. Based on this data, we can conclude that the inflation rate is 30 percent. A price index can be constructed using the following formula:

$$\text{Price Index} = \frac{\text{Expenditure on the market basket in the current period}}{\text{Expenditure on the market basket in the base period}} \times 100$$

The price index for time period 2 in the above table is calculated below. The price index for time period 1 is equal to 100 if we have designated time period 1 as the base period.

$$\text{Price Index} = \frac{\$13}{\$10} \times 100 = 130$$

The CPI is calculated using this approach, except that instead of using a market basket consisting of 5 apples and 10 oranges, the CPI is based on a market basket that includes hundreds of items that consumers purchase—food and beverages, housing, apparel, transportation, medical care, recreation, education, and others. You can find this data online at www.bls.gov.

The CPI reflects **substitution bias** because it is calculated using a fixed market basket. Rational consumers attempt to minimize the impact of inflation on their living standards by substituting away from products that have become relatively more expensive. To the extent that consumers behave in this manner, the CPI provides an exaggerated measure of inflation because it does not take into account this pattern of substitution.

To illustrate, suppose that the market basket consists of 10 apples and 10 oranges. The table below shows that the price of apples doubled, while the price of oranges remained the same. As expected, consumers responded by substituting oranges for apples.

Time Period	Price per apple	Quantity of apples	Price per orange	Quantity of oranges
1	\$1.00	10	\$1.00	10
2	\$2.00	5	\$1.00	15

Using the formula for a price index, and assuming that time period 1 is the base period, this example shows how a fixed-weight index, like the CPI, overstates the higher cost of living.

$$\text{Price Index} = \frac{\$30}{\$20} \times 100 = 150$$

The consumer would need to spend \$25 to purchase 5 apples and 15 oranges in the second period, while the combination of 10 apples and 10 oranges cost \$20 in period 1. A fixed-weight index uses base period quantities in each period so it would appear that the consumer needs to spend \$30 in time period 2. It is true that the consumer would need to spend \$30 in order to continue purchasing 10 apples and 10 oranges (base period quantities), but if the consumer is just as happy with 5 apples and 15 oranges, then a 50 percent increase in expenditure is not necessary. This is a concern because many workers' wages and social security benefits are tied to the CPI. If, for example, the CPI indicated a 50 percent increase in the cost of living, when in fact the increase in the cost of living was lower, then social security benefits would be increased more than is needed to keep pace with the rising cost of living and this places an additional burden on wage-earners who pay taxes to support social security.

Inflation rates are generally reported on an annual basis. The annual rate of inflation is the percentage change in the price index from one year to the next.

$$\textbf{annual inflation rate} = \frac{\mathbf{CPI}_{\text{year 2}} - \mathbf{CPI}_{\text{year 1}}}{\mathbf{CPI}_{\text{year 1}}} \times \mathbf{100}$$

The data below provide an example.

Year	CPI	Annual Inflation Rate
1	100	
2	110	10 %
3	120	9 %
4	125	4 %

According to the above data, prices rose 20 percent between year 1 and year 3 and 25 percent between year 1 and year 4, while the annual rate of inflation was 10 percent from year 1 to year 2, approximately 9 percent from year 2 to year 3, and approximately 4 percent from year 3 to year 4.

A useful technique developed to adjust for inflation is the calculation of real or constant dollar values from nominal or current dollar values using the following formula:

$$\textbf{Real Value} = \frac{\textbf{Nominal Value}}{\textbf{PI}_2/\textbf{PI}_1}$$

Any Price Index (PI) may be used in this formula, such as the CPI. The subscript "2" refers to the current period and the subscript "1" refers to a previous period. For many applications, there may be a series of nominal income values from different years that need to be converted into real income values in order to see how real income or purchasing power has changed over time. To accomplish this, the above formula can be simplified.

Given a value for nominal income in time period t (the current time period), the value for real income in time period t can be found by using the simplified version of the above formula.

$$\textbf{Real Income}_t = \frac{\textbf{Nominal Income}_t}{\textbf{CPI}_t} \times 100$$

Suppose your nominal income rose from $20,000 last year to $22,000 this year and, at the same time, the CPI rose from 160 to 176. Then, real income was $12,500 last year, and is also equal to $12,500 using the above formula. The fact that real income remained unchanged indicates that there was no change in purchasing power, even though nominal income rose. Why? Because nominal income rose 10 percent, but prices also rose 10 percent on average.

Similarly, if you earned $20,000 last year and there was 10 percent inflation, how much would you need to earn this year to have the same real income and purchasing power? Since 10 percent of $20,000 is $2,000, the answer is $22,000.

As another example, suppose you wanted to know how a nominal income of $60,000 in the current year compares to a nominal income of $50,000 in a previous year. Remember that when there is inflation, having more dollars does not guarantee greater purchasing power. If the price index rose 10 percent (from 100 to 110), you could calculate the real value of current income using the formula:

$$\text{Real Value} = \frac{\$60{,}000}{110/100} = \frac{\$60{,}000}{110} \times 100 = \$54{,}545$$

Thus, earning $60,000 in a world with 10 percent inflation is comparable to earning $54,545 in a world with no inflation. Note that nominal income rose 20 percent in this example, but real income rose only 10 percent. This is because prices or the cost of living rose 10 percent. A close approximation of the percentage change in any real value can be found by subtracting the inflation rate from the percentage change in the nominal value.

$$\text{Percentage change in real value} = \text{percentage change in nominal value} - \text{inflation rate}$$

Types of Inflation

For the economy as a whole, prices may be rising on average as a result of events that cause demand to increase in a number or markets, or as a result of events that cause supply to decrease in a number of markets. The primary cause of inflation is the money supply growing at a faster rate than total output. Increases in the money supply can lead to increases in the total (aggregate) demand for goods and services, which may put upward pressure on the price level. When an increase in aggregate (total) demand results in an increase in the price level, the result is **demand-side inflation,** which is sometimes referred to as **demand-pull inflation** because an increase in aggregate demand pulls up prices. On the supply side of the economy, unanticipated events or **supply shocks**, such as hurricanes that disrupt oil supply lines, may cause input prices to increase which puts upward pressure on the price level, resulting in **supply-side inflation.** Inflation that stems from higher costs of production pushing up prices is also referred to as **cost-push inflation**. The model of aggregate demand and aggregate supply, presented in Chapter 6, is designed to illustrate the causes and effects of a changing price level.

Consequences of Inflation

As the price level rises, the value of the dollar falls and a greater amount of money is required to purchase the same amount of output. This problem would be negligible if each individual's income rose in proportion to the increase in the price level, but such proportional changes are unlikely. Rather, inflation tends to have **redistributive effects**, causing some groups and individuals to be better off, while others are worse off. Additional consequences of inflation are related to uncertainty, increased speculation, and shortened time horizons.

NAME____ SECTION#_______________

Print Last Name, First Name

UNEMPLOYMENT

1. The unemployment rate is:
   a. the percentage of the population over age 18 that is out of work and actively seeking work.
   b. the percentage of the labor force that is considered to be unemployed.
   c. estimated by the Bureau of Economic Analysis on a weekly basis.
   d. monitored and estimated by Congress on a daily basis.

2. Which of the following is counted as unemployed by the Bureau of Labor Statistics?
   a. A full-time student without a job who is part of the civilian population
   b. A 24-year old male without a job who is currently available for work, and actively seeking work
   c. Anyone over the age of 16 who is included in both the civilian population and the institutional population and is currently not working for pay
   d. Anyone who is working less than 10 hours a week for pay and actively looking for a 20 hour per week job

3. A person is classified as employed by the Bureau of Labor Statistics (BLS) if he/she:
   a. worked 15 unpaid hours on a family-owned farm during the survey week.
   b. held a part-time job while searching for a full-time, permanent position.
   c. worked as little as 1 hour for pay during the survey week.
   d. All of the above would be classified as employed.

Use the data below to answer questions 3 and 4:

	Unemployed	Employed
Year 1	**7.5 million**	**142.5 million**
Year 2	**7.3 million**	**144.7 million**
Year 3	**7.0 million**	**144.7 million**
Year 4	**7.7 million**	**147.3 million**

4. The number of workers in the labor force in Year 2 is _______, and the unemployment rate is approximately ______ percent.
   a. 144.7 million; 5
   b. 144.7 million; 4.8
   c. 152 million; 5
   d. 152 million; 4.8

5. The unemployment rate is lowest in year:
   a. 1.
   b. 2.
   c. 3.
   d. 4.

NAME____ SECTION#________________

Print Last Name, First Name

6. Structural unemployment occurs when:
   a. the skills demanded in labor markets and the location of job openings do not match the skills and locations of people seeking work.
   b. workers accept jobs that are temporary.
   c. workers leave one job to search for another.
   d. the number of unemployed workers exceeds the number of job vacancies.

7. Which of the following best describes an individual who is frictionally unemployed?
   a. A new college graduate who is currently without a job but who has had several interviews that promise to result in job offers
   b. A skilled engineer who is unable to find an engineering position due to a downturn in the overall economy
   c. A former production line worker who has been unable to find a job in manufacturing after he/she was replaced by a robot
   d. An agricultural worker who does not have work in the winter months

8. An autoworker that has been laid off because the demand for autos has declined due to an economy-wide downturn is considered to be:
   a. seasonally unemployed.
   b. structurally unemployed.
   c. frictionally unemployed.
   d. cyclically unemployed.

9. If the economy is operating at full employment, then:
   a. the unemployment rate is zero percent.
   b. structural and frictional unemployment have been eliminated.
   c. the unemployment rate is equal to the natural rate of unemployment.
   d. cyclical unemployment is greater than the sum of structural and frictional unemployment.

10. The type of unemployment associated with recessions is:
    a. seasonal unemployment.
    b. structural unemployment.
    c. frictional unemployment.
    d. cyclical unemployment.

NAME____ SECTION#________________

Print Last Name, First Name

UNEMPLOYMENT

1. Officially, individuals who are not currently working are classified as unemployed if:
   a. they have been out of work for more than six weeks.
   b. they desire to work.
   c. they are willing and able to work and are actively seeking employment.
   d. they are willing and able to work but are not actively seeking employment.

Use the data below to answer questions 2 – 4:

	Labor Force	Total Population	Employed
Year 1	**140 million**	**300 million**	**128 million**
Year 2	**142 million**	**305 million**	**129 million**
Year 3	**144 million**	**310 million**	**130 million**

2. The number of unemployed workers in Year 2 is:
   a. 2 million.
   b. 163 million.
   c. 15 million.
   d. 13 million.

3. The unemployment rate in Year 1 is approximately:
   a. 8.6 percent.
   b. 9.4 percent.
   c. 12 percent.
   d. 4 percent.

4. The unemployment rate __________ between Year 1 and Year 2 and __________ between Year 2 and Year 3.
   a. increased; increased
   b. decreased; increased
   c. increased; decreased
   d. decreased; decreased

5. Which of the following statements is ***true***?
   a. Cyclical unemployment is associated with changes in the cycle of technology, while structural unemployment is associated with recession.
   b. When the economy is experiencing cyclical unemployment, the number of job-seekers exceeds the number of jobs available.
   c. Individuals that are cyclically unemployed must be retrained or relocated to find employment; individuals that are structurally unemployed have the skills demanded in the labor market but are still in the job search process.
   d. Frictional and structural unemployment occur when the economy is in a recession; cyclical unemployment occurs in a booming economy.

NAME____ SECTION#______________

Print Last Name, First Name

6. A skilled individual who lost his/her job due to a downturn in overall economic activity is considered to be ______________________ if he/she is unable to find another job.
   a. cyclically unemployed
   b. seasonally unemployed
   c. underemployed
   d. a discouraged worker

7. Suppose the natural rate of unemployment is 5 percent, there is 2.5 percent frictional unemployment, and the actual rate of unemployment is 8 percent. Then:
   a. structural unemployment is 2.5 percent and cyclical unemployment is 3 percent.
   b. structural unemployment is 2.5 percent and cyclical unemployment is 5.5 percent.
   c. structural unemployment is 3 percent and cyclical unemployment is 5 percent.
   d. structural unemployment is 3 percent and cyclical unemployment is 2.5 percent.

8. Macroeconomic policy is primarily aimed at eliminating:
   a. seasonal unemployment.
   b. frictional unemployment.
   c. structural unemployment.
   d. cyclical unemployment.

9. The phantom unemployed:
   a. claim they are employed when in fact they are unemployed.
   b. claim they are not in the labor force when in fact they are.
   c. are working, but are paid in cash in order to evade income taxes.
   d. claim they are actively seeking work when in fact they are not.

10. Official unemployment statistics are more likely to ***understate*** the true unemployment problem when:
   a. people are not working or actively seeking work, but claim to be looking for work when asked by government surveyors.
   b. underemployed workers are counted among the employed and there are discouraged workers.
   c. the Bureau of Labor Statistics is unable to contact some of the households randomly selected for the survey.
   d. unemployment is frictional rather than structural in nature.

NAME____ SECTION#______________
Print Last Name, First Name

UNEMPLOYMENT AND INFLATION

INSTRUCTIONS: Fill in the following ten blanks with the correct word or phrase.

Officially, someone is considered unemployed if he/she is out of work, is willing and able to work, and is (1) ____.

Workers that leave one job to search for another and job-seekers that have recently entered the labor force are considered to be (2) _____________________________ unemployed.

A person that must be retrained or relocated to be employed is considered to be (3) ______________________________ unemployed.

The type of unemployment associated with economic downturns and recessions is called (4) ______________________________ unemployment.

The rate of unemployment that occurs when the economy is at full employment is called the (5)____.

People who are willing and able to work but have given up actively seeking employment due to lack of success are called (6) ____.

The major macroeconomic goals include (7) ______________________________, (8) _____________________________________, and economic growth.

During inflationary periods, the purchasing power of the dollar (9) _____________________.

(10) ______________________________ inflation occurs when the total (aggregate) demand for goods and services in the economy increases faster than the total (aggregate) supply of all goods and services.

NAME____ SECTION#______________
Print Last Name, First Name

INFLATION

Fill in blanks 1 – 3 based on the following information:

Suppose the cost of a consumer's market basket rose from $200 in the base year to $210 in the current year.

1. The CPI in the base year is _______________.

2. The CPI in the current year is _______________.

3. The percentage change in prices between the base year and the current year is ________.

Fill in blanks 4 – 7 based on the following information:

Use the table below with mid-2018 Regional CPI data from the Bureau of Labor Statistics to calculate the real salary for each city (1982-84 = 100).

City	Price Index	Nominal Salary	Real Salary
New York	273	$57,330	4.______________
Philadelphia	251	$52,220	5.______________
Dallas	232	$49,880	6.______________

7. In which city will purchasing power be greatest? ________________________________

Complete the table below and fill blanks 8 - 10.

Year	CPI	Annual Inflation Rate
1	100	
2	106	8.__________%
3	9.__________	8.5 %
4	120	10.__________%

NAME____ SECTION#______________

Print Last Name, First Name

UNEMPLOYMENT AND INFLATION

1. In order to be classified as unemployed, with the exception of workers who have been temporarily laid off and are waiting to report back to work, a person must:
   a. have filed for unemployment compensation.
   b. not have a job.
   c. not have worked during the survey week and currently be available for work.
   d. not have worked during the survey week, be actively looking for work, and currently be available for work.

2. Structural unemployment occurs when:
   a. the actual unemployment rate exceeds the natural rate of unemployment.
   b. unemployed workers do not have the skills needed for the available jobs.
   c. the number of unemployed workers exceeds the number of job vacancies.
   d. workers leave one job to search for another job requiring similar skills.

3. In a population of 300 million people, 150 million are in the labor force and 138.75 million are employed. The unemployment rate is:
   a. 2.5%.
   b. 5%.
   c. 5.3%.
   d. 7.5%.

4. When the actual unemployment rate is equal to the natural unemployment rate:
   a. frictional unemployment exceeds structural unemployment.
   b. structural unemployment exceeds frictional unemployment.
   c. cyclical unemployment is zero.
   d. there is some cyclical unemployment.

5. All of the following are considered to be part of the labor force ***except***:
   a. persons who like to work but are not employed or actively seeking employment.
   b. persons who are laid off and are currently seeking other jobs.
   c. part-time workers who are seeking full-time employment.
   d. persons who are employed in positions for which they are overqualified.

6. The inflation rate calculated using the Consumer Price Index (CPI) measures:
   a. the percentage change in the cost of a representative market basket of consumer goods and services.
   b. the percentage change in the cost of all goods and services purchased by every consumer each year.
   c. the percentage change in the cost of living for all consumers.
   d. the average percentage change in the prices of all goods and services produced.

NAME____ SECTION#_______________

Print Last Name, First Name

Use the information in the table below to answer questions 7 – 10:

Year	Nominal Income	CPI (1982-1984 = 100)
2008	$48,000	215.303
2009	$49,000	214.537
2010	$51,000	218.056
2011	$53,000	224.939
2012	$54,000	229.594
2013	$55,000	232.597

7. This person's real income in 2011 was approximately __________. This means the purchasing power of his/her income _______________ slightly from 2010 to 2011.
   a. $23,562; decreased
   b. $23,562; increased
   c. $53,000; decreased
   d. $53,000; increased

8. The inflation rate for 2009 was _______, rounded to the tenth. The inflation rate for 2013 was ______, rounded to the tenth.
   a. –0.4%; 3%
   b. –0.4%; 1.3%
   c. 7.7%; 3%
   d. 7.7%; 1.3%

9. Based on the answer to #8, what nominal income in 2013 would keep this person's purchasing power the same as in 2012?
   a. $54,702
   b. $54,000
   c. $23,216
   d. $55,715

10. You do not have to do any calculations to know that the purchasing power of this person's income increased from 2008 to 2009 because:
    a. nominal income increased from $47,000 to $48,000.
    b. the CPI decreased from 215.303 to 214.537.
    c. nominal income increased and the CPI decreased.
    d. the percentage change in nominal income was less than the percentage change in the CPI.

NAME____ SECTION#______________
Print Last Name, First Name

INFLATION

1. Inflation is:
   a. an increase in the average level of prices of goods and services over time.
   b. not an economic problem because each individual's income rises in proportion to the increase in the price level.
   c. a one-time increase in the price of all goods and services.
   d. an increase in the purchasing power of the dollar over time.

2. The purchasing power of the dollar:
   a. is unaffected by inflation.
   b. decreases during inflationary periods.
   c. increases during inflationary periods.
   d. cannot be predicted during inflationary periods.

Use the data below to answer questions 3 – 5:

Year	**CPI**
1	**100**
2	**103**
3	**106.5**
4	**111**
5	_____

3. The base year is:
   a. year 1.
   b. year 2.
   c. year 3.
   d. year 4.

4. Between year 3 and year 4, prices rose by approximately:
   a. 4.5 percent.
   b. 4.2 percent.
   c. 4 percent.
   d. 11 percent.

5. If prices rose by 5.4 percent in year 5, then the CPI in year 5 is approximately:
   a. 100.
   b. 105.4.
   c. 116.4.
   d. 117.

6. Inflation is:
   a. regarded as an economic problem because every person's nominal income rises in proportion to the increase in the price level.
   b. regarded as an economic problem because it can have redistributive effects, lead to increased speculation, and cause greater uncertainty.
   c. regarded as an economic problem because when there is inflation, everyone is worse off.
   d. not regarded as an economic problem because every person's nominal income rises in proportion to the increase in the price level.

Use the data below to answer questions 7 – 8:

Year	**CPI**
1	**100**
2	**103**
3	**106.5**

7. John earned $50,000 in year 1. In year 2, he would need to earn at least __________ in order to maintain constant purchasing power.
   a. $46,948
   b. $52,900
   c. $53,250
   d. $51,500

8. If John's nominal salary in year 3 is $45,000, his real salary in year 1 dollars is approximately:
   a. $45,000.
   b. $42,253.
   c. $47,925.
   d. $53,250.

9. If you know that inflation will be 4 percent next year and you want to request a 6 percent increase in your ***real*** salary, then you should request that your nominal salary be increased by:
   a. 8 percent.
   b. 2 percent.
   c. 10 percent.
   d. 6 percent.

10. If an increase in the money supply causes spending to increase and this higher spending results in higher prices, the resulting inflation comes from:
    a. the supply side of the economy and is called demand-pull inflation.
    b. the supply side of the economy and is called cost-push inflation.
    c. the demand side of the economy and is called cost-push inflation.
    d. the demand side of the economy and is called demand-pull inflation.

CHAPTER 5 National Income Accounting

Just as firms need accounts in order to function and know where they stand, economists and policymakers need accounts for the national economy. Measures of total economic activity are needed to analyze the current state of the economy and formulate policy. National income accounting provides measures of the economy's output and income which, combined with information about unemployment and inflation, allow identification of economic problems and evaluation of policy alternatives. The Department of Commerce's **Bureau of Economic Analysis (BEA)** reports national income and production data in the National Income and Product Accounts (NIPA), which can be accessed at www.bea.gov.

Macroeconomic Aggregates

Macroeconomists view the economy in terms of totals, or aggregates, which are composed of the sum of individual actions. These aggregates are found in the national income accounts data, collected and published by government agencies. They are derived by adding up, or aggregating, the economic activities of individuals, firms, and government. It is impractical to add tons of wheat, yards of cloth, and number of houses together, so the data are calculated in terms of their market values, which are reflected in dollar amounts spent to purchase the output. Prices change over time, so it is necessary to adjust the data for inflation to get real GDP after a measure for nominal GDP is derived. The adjustment to get real GDP is explained later in this chapter. There are two ways to measure total output in an economy: Gross Domestic Product (GDP) and Gross National Product (GNP).

Gross Domestic Product (GDP) is the total market value of all **final** goods and services produced by domestically **located** resources (production within a particular country regardless of ownership) during a one-year period. GDP is the value of only **final** goods and services, so it is important to avoid **double-counting** intermediate goods which are inputs to the production of final goods and services. The value of final goods and services is measured by summing the value added, or the increase in market value of a product, at each successive stage of production. For example, if a firm produces paper and sells it to a publisher, the price of the book sold by the publisher includes the cost of the paper, so it would not make sense to include both the value of the paper and the value of the book in GDP.

GDP is estimated by summing all expenditures on output, including consumption spending (C), gross private domestic investment spending (I), government spending (G), and net exports, or exports minus imports (EX – IM). The **expenditure approach** derives from the fact that all output produced is purchased by consumers, business firms, the government, or foreigners.

$$\mathbf{GDP = C + I + G + (EX - IM)}$$

Consumption spending (C) is the largest component of GDP and includes household spending on durable goods like cars and furniture, nondurable goods like food and clothing, and services like health care and financial planning. The value of all consumption goods and services produced during the year is estimated by adding up how much households spent on these items to get **personal consumption expenditures (PCE)**, often abbreviated as just **C**.

Gross private domestic investment spending (I) includes business spending on capital such as machines, tools, and equipment, spending on new residential and non-residential construction, and changes in inventory. In the national income accounts, the **consumption of fixed capital,** or **depreciation,** measures the amount of capital consumed during the year. Capital (machines, tools, and equipment) is consumed when it is used up, worn out, or becomes obsolete. **Net private domestic investment spending** excludes depreciation.

Net private domestic investment = Gross private domestic investment – depreciation

The nation's capital stock is growing (and the production possibilities frontier is shifting outward) when net private domestic investment is positive, which means that gross private domestic investment exceeds depreciation, so firms are spending enough on machines, tools, and equipment to both replace depreciated capital and add to their stock of capital. If net investment is equal to zero, then there is no change in the capital stock; and if net investment is negative, the capital stock is declining. The U.S. economy has experienced positive net investment, and therefore an increasing capital stock, during most years for which data is available, except during the Great Depression of the 1930s.

Gross private domestic spending also includes changes in inventory. The reason for this is that goods that were produced during the year may not be sold until the next year. When this happens, consumption spending for the year will not correspond to all of the goods produced that year, so the government corrects for this by counting the value of goods produced and not yet sold (changes in inventory) as part of investment spending. If there were a lot of goods produced in the previous year and added to inventory, and then purchased in the current year, it is possible that inventories could be smaller at the end of the current year, so the value for changes in inventory could be negative.

Government spending (G) corresponds to government consumption expenditures and gross investment, so government purchases of goods, services, and capital (body armor for the military, the services of teachers, soldiers, police officers, etc.) are included in G, but G does not reflect transfers such as welfare or social security payments.

The final component of GDP is net exports. Net exports of goods and services (**X_{NET} = EX – IM)** is the difference between exports and imports. The value of **exports (EX)** measures output that was produced in the U.S., but purchased by foreigners. Finally, **import spending (IM)** is subtracted, since domestic spending (C, I, and G) includes spending on imported goods and services. Foreign-produced goods and services are not part of U.S. GDP. Note that adding net exports (EX – IM) achieves both adjustments. The value of net exports will be positive whenever exports exceed imports, and the country is running a **trade surplus**; net exports will be negative when imports exceed exports, and there is a **trade deficit**. The U.S. has incurred large trade deficits in each year since the mid-1980s.

The BEA reports that current-dollar GDP in 2017 was $19,485.4 billion, and is projected to be about $20.65 trillion in 2018. In terms of C + I + G + (EX – IM), in 2017 GDP was:

$13,321.4 bi + $3,368 bi + $3,374.4 bi + (–$578.4 bi) = $19,485.4 billion

Personal Consumption Expenditures (PCE = C) of $13,321.4 billion is by far the largest component of GDP. Household spending on consumer durables, nondurables, and services accounts for almost 70% of total spending on final output in the U.S. There is a $0.1 billion, or $100 million, difference between the GDP reported by the BEA and the sum of the spending reported by the BEA due to rounding and statistical discrepancy.

Gross National Product (GNP) is the total market value of all final goods and services produced by domestically **owned** resources (production by resources owned by members of a particular nation regardless of where the production takes place) during a one-year period. GNP equals GDP plus net foreign factor income.

Both GDP and GNP measure the country's total output during the year. GDP receives more media attention than GNP, but both are valid ways to define a country's production. Both can be found by summing consumption (C), gross private domestic investment (I), government purchases (G), and net exports (EX – IM). The specific products that would be classified as exports or imports differ somewhat depending on whether GDP or GNP is being constructed.

The difference between GDP and GNP is **net foreign factor income**, which is income earned by domestically-owned resources abroad minus income earned by foreign-owned resources here.

- Output produced by domestically-owned resources abroad is not counted in GDP, since GDP measures production on U.S. soil, so it must be added to GDP to arrive at GNP. For example, if a graduate of the University of North Texas goes to Italy to play professional basketball, his output (measured by the income he receives) would be considered part of Italy's GDP and part of U.S. GNP.
- Output produced by foreign-owned resources here is counted in GDP, but does not fit the definition of GNP, so it is subtracted from GDP to arrive at GNP. For example, if Toyota operates a factory in the U.S., the entire value of this output is part of U.S. GDP because production occurs on U.S. soil. If the factory employs U.S. auto workers, their contribution is also part of U.S. GNP, but the profit income paid to the owners of Toyota who live in Japan is not part of U.S. GNP.

GNP = GDP + net foreign factor income

GDP and GNP are the largest economic aggregates and are very close in amount in the United States. Estimated current dollar (nominal) U.S. GDP in the second quarter of 2018 is $20.4 trillion and estimated U.S. GNP for the same period is $20.7 trillion. Other measures of aggregate income and output are derived from GDP and GNP. Net Domestic Product (NDP) and Net National Product (NNP) reflect total output after subtracting the value of capital that was depreciated or lost during the production process, so these measures correspond to the amount of output that is still available for consumption or for adding to the nation's wealth.

NDP = GDP – consumption of fixed capital (depreciation)

NNP = GNP – consumption of fixed capital (depreciation)

Producing the nation's output generates payments to the factors of production in the form of wages, rent, interest, and profit. The total value of expenditures is equal to the value of the incomes generated in production, except that businesses do not pay out as income the amount deducted for depreciation or indirect business taxes paid to government. The **income approach** derives from the fact that production generates income for workers, real estate and natural resource owners, lenders, and business owners.

The most commonly cited income measures are derived from GNP rather than GDP, so these reflect income earned by U.S. citizens. Income measures can be estimated by adding together all the sources of income, or by starting with GNP and adjusting. National Income (NI) is the income earned by resources, but households do not actually receive all the income they earn and some households receive income which is unearned.

National Income (NI): the total <u>earnings</u> of labor and property from the production of goods and services.

NI = wages + rent + interest + corporate profits + proprietors' income + farm income

NI = NNP – indirect business taxes

Personal Income (PI): the total <u>income received</u> by persons from all sources, before personal taxes have been deducted.

PI = NI – corporate taxes – retained earnings – social security taxes + transfer payments + net interest

Disposable Income (DI): the income remaining to persons after payment of personal taxes. DI can be either spent (consumed) or saved.

DI = PI – Personal taxes = Consumption spending + Personal Saving = C + S

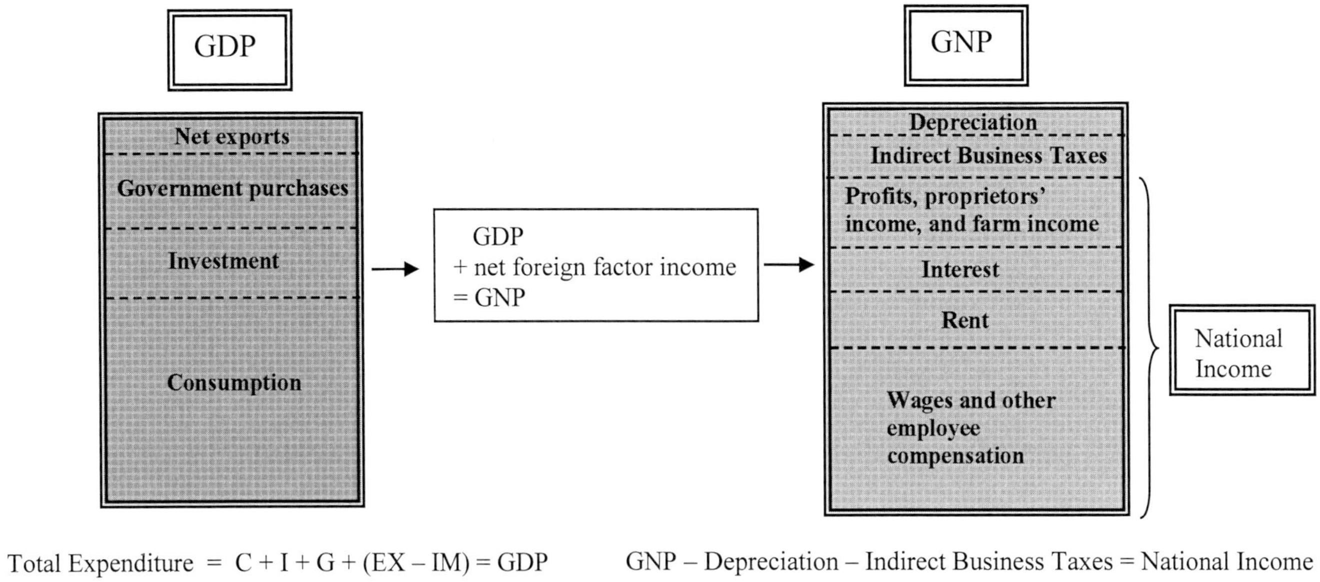

Real and Nominal GDP

GDP data are based on market prices, and prices change over time. Thus, it is useful to transform **nominal GDP**, or the money value of output measured in current prices, into **real GDP** or constant-dollar GDP, which is the value of current output using the prices of another time period. Nominal GDP is current output at current prices, while real GDP is current output at base period prices, keeping in mind that the base period is often the previous year.

Recall that the consumer price index (CPI) is constructed using a representative basket of goods and services purchased by the typical consumer. GDP includes goods and services purchased by other firms as well as by the government and by foreigners, so the CPI doesn't necessarily reflect the change in the average prices of all goods and services included in GDP. A different kind of price index, the GDP Implicit Price Deflator, is used to measure how the overall price level is changing over time. The GDP Deflator is constructed as a changing-weight, or **chain-weight**, index with product quantities determined by current production.

As a simple example, assume GDP consists of bread and toasters and the economy produced 100 loaves of bread plus 5 toasters in the base year. If each loaf of bread is worth \$1 and each toaster is worth \$20, the market value of base year output is (\$1)(100) + (\$20)(5) = \$200. In the base year, nominal GDP and real GDP are always the same number.

	Price per loaf	Quantity of bread	Price per toaster	Quantity of toasters	GDP Deflator
Base Year	\$1	100	\$20	5	100
Current Year	\$2	200	\$25	8	167

Both prices and quantities increased from the base year to the current year in this example. Current year nominal GDP is equal to (\$2)(200) + (\$25)(8) = \$600, so nominal GDP is three times larger in the current year compared to the base year. This does not mean that the economy produced three times as much output!

In this example, the GDP Deflator increased from a value of 100 in the base year to a new value of 167 in the current year. The GDP Implicit Price Deflator is estimated and published by the Bureau of Economic Analysis in NIPA Table 1.1.9, and would need to be obtained for real-world analysis. In problems such as this example, the GDP Deflator is provided for the purpose of calculating real GDP. Real GDP for a given year (t) is calculated using the formula:

$$\textbf{Real GDP}_t = \frac{\textbf{Nominal GDP}_t}{\textbf{GDP Deflator}_t} \times 100$$

In the simple example with bread and toasters, nominal GDP increased from \$200 to \$600, while the GDP Deflator increased from 100 to 167. To find out what happened to output, calculate real GDP in the current year and compare to the base year.

$$\textbf{Real GDP in current year} = \frac{\$600}{167} \times 100 = \$360$$

This calculation shows that <u>real</u> GDP increased from \$200 in the base year to \$360 in the current year. This answer can be easily confirmed with the price and quantity data since this is a simplified example with only two products. In the current year, 200 loaves of bread and 8 toasters are produced. If there had been no inflation since the base year, the price per loaf of bread would remain \$1 and the price per toaster would remain \$20, so the value of current output would be (\$1)(200) + (\$20)(8) = \$360 = real GDP.

The percentage change in real GDP from one year to the next provides a measure of how much output has changed annually (the economy's growth rate).

$$\textbf{annual growth rate} = \frac{\text{Real GDP}_{\text{year 2}} - \text{Real GDP}_{\text{year 1}}}{\text{Real GDP}_{\text{year 1}}} \times 100$$

$$\text{annual growth rate} = \frac{\$360 - \$200}{\$200} \times 100 = 80 \text{ percent}$$

The base year for the GDP Implicit Price Deflator is currently 2012: nominal GDP and real GDP are equal in the base year because the Price Index is 100 in 2012. Current-dollar, or nominal, GDP was \$19,485.4 billion in 2017 when the GDP deflator was 107.948. The deflator increased from 100 in 2012 to 107.948 in 2017, which means prices rose approximately 8% from 2012 to 2017. How much was real GDP in 2017?

$$\textbf{Real GDP in 2017} = \frac{\text{Nominal GDP in 2017}}{\text{GDP Deflator in 2017}} \times 100$$

$$\textbf{Real GDP in 2017} = \frac{\$19{,}485.4 \text{ billion}}{107.948} \times 100 = \$18{,}050.728 \text{ billion}$$

In 2012 dollars, real GDP in 2017 was \$18,050.7 billion. In most years, both nominal and real GDP increase, but nominal GDP increases at a faster rate because it reflects both the increase in real output and the increase in prices. However, real GDP declines during recessionary periods. This was the case recently when real GDP declined from \$15,626 billion in 2007 to \$15,604.7 billion in 2008 and declined even further to a low of \$15,208.8 in 2009. It increased in 2010 to \$15,598.8 billion and has been increasing since that time.

Other Issues

An increase in real GDP does not necessarily mean that people are better off. For example, suppose total real GDP increased by 5 percent but there are 20 percent more people to share that output. This concern can be addressed by calculating **per capita real GDP** (real GDP divided by population). However, per capita real GDP still does not tell us anything about how output is distributed. Most modern economies experience a gradual increase in real per capita GDP each year, but there is still poverty and inequality. In addition, no attempt is made to adjust output measurements for environmental damage. Some economic activity, such as rebuilding after a hurricane, cleaning up an oil spill, or fighting a war, can cause GDP to rise, but that doesn't mean that hurricanes, oil spills, and wars are improving people's living standards.

The GDP measure of output has several problems and omissions. Only market transactions and a few imputed values, such as the market value of owner-occupied houses, are included in GDP. Non-market activities, such as a homemaker's services, volunteer activities, and the labor component of do-it-yourself jobs, are not counted. Leisure time, unreported income, and the underground economy are not included either. These omissions can be especially significant when comparing countries, since non-market activities are more important in some countries than in others. International data are available from several sources, including the *CIA World Fact Book* at www.cia.gov and the World Bank at www.worldbank.org.

GDP and Economic Growth

One of the major macroeconomic goals for the economy is economic growth. Growth is commonly measured by the change in real output, or real GDP, over time. The graph below shows real GDP between 2005 and 2013, a period during which the economy experienced a downturn, followed by an expansion. Although the economy fluctuates in the short run, the long-run trend shows economic growth.

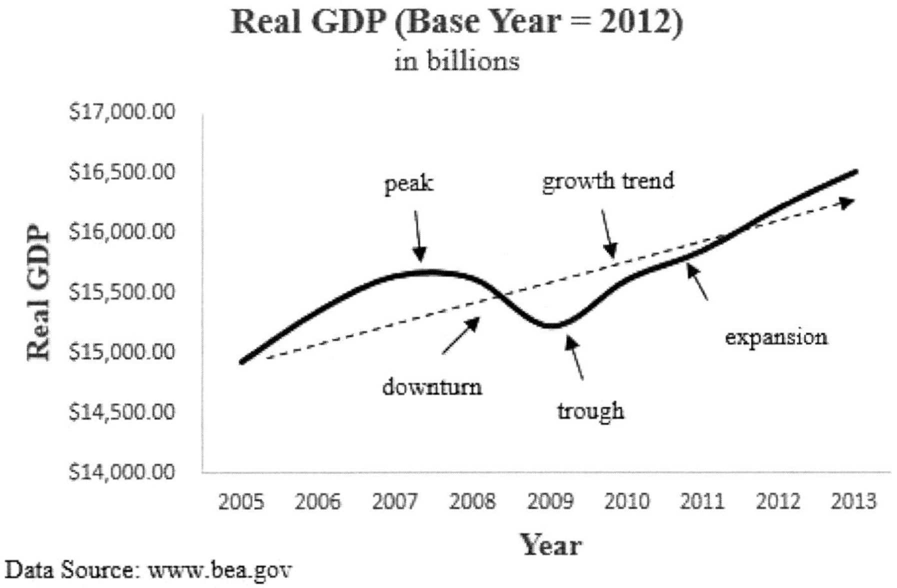

Several sources contribute to economic growth. Improvements in productivity achieved through investment in human capital, investment in physical capital, and investment in research and development cause the economy's production possibilities curve to shift outward, and the economy's ability to produce increases. Increases in technology that result from research and development often lead to improvements in production methods which also increase production possibilities. Increases in the resources available for production, such as an increase in the size of the labor force, increase the economy's production possibilities. Factors that increase the economy's production possibilities – increases in productivity, resources, and technology – contribute to economic growth.

Supply-Side economists argue that the focus of macroeconomic policy should be on promoting long-term growth, using such means as reduced taxation to stimulate work and investment and reduced regulation to stimulate business expansion. Other economists favor an approach known as Industrial Policy, which means using policies to stimulate industries that are well positioned for success in the global marketplace.

Real GDP has grown substantially over the long term, as shown in the graph below. Despite the Great Depression and other periods of recession, the overall picture is one of economic expansion.

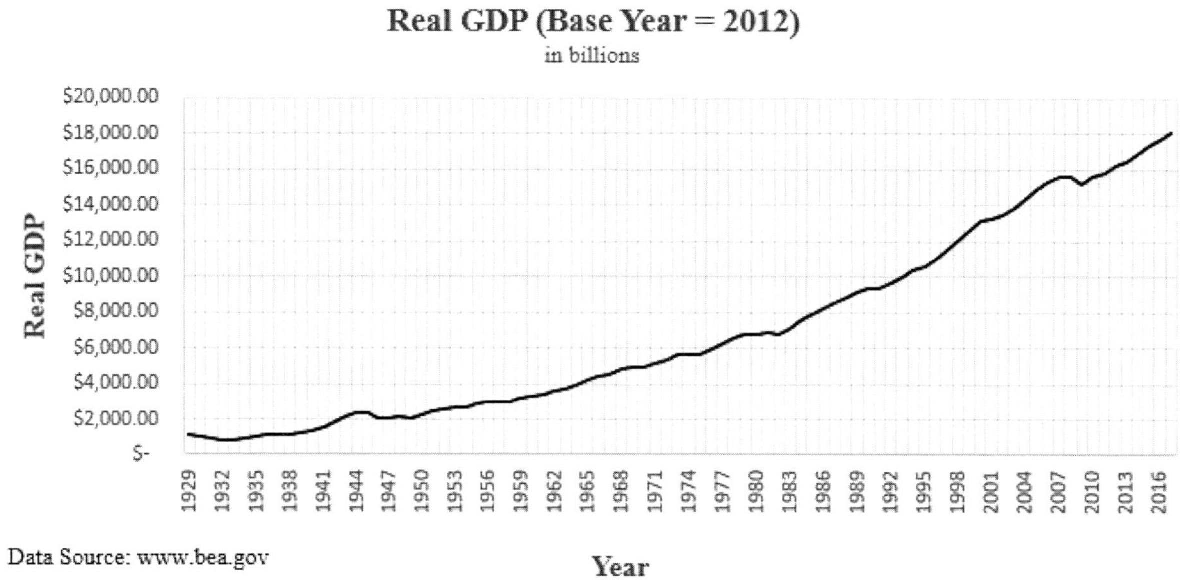

Per-capita GDP, or GDP divided by the population, is used as a measure of our material standard of living. In order to achieve improved living standards, an economy must grow faster than its population so that per-capita GDP is rising over time. A necessary condition for increasing per-capita GDP is increasing labor productivity (measured as the economy's total output divided by the number of workers or labor force).

Though growth in U.S. labor productivity has slowed in recent years, U.S. living standards continue to show improvement over time. Workers generally become more productive through education and training (investment in human capital) and through the employment of tools and machines (investment in physical capital). Technological advance, which generally requires investment in research and development (R&D), may be the key to greater economic prosperity in the future.

Real GDP for the U.S. now measures in the trillions of dollars; numbers so big it is difficult to grasp, and looking at the difference in real GDP from one year to the next might not be easy to interpret. **Economic growth** is usually expressed as the **percentage change in real GDP** from one year to the next because it is more useful for making comparisons across time periods and across countries. In the rate of change calculation below, "t" represents a given time period and "t – 1" represents the previous time period.

$$\%\text{ change in Real GDP} = \frac{\text{Real GDP}_t - \text{Real GDP}_{t-1}}{\text{Real GDP}_{t-1}} \times 100$$

If, for example, real GDP was $10 trillion in year 1 and $10.4 trillion in year 2, then real GDP increased by $400 billion from year 1 to year 2. This means that from year 1 to year 2, real GDP grew 4 percent, which is easier to comprehend than a $400 billion increase.

$$\%\Delta\text{Real GDP} = \frac{\$10.4\text{ trillion} - \$10\text{ trillion}}{\$10\text{ trillion}} \times 100 = 0.04(100) = 4\%$$

The Foreign Sector

A very important component of GDP is net exports (EX – IM). The U.S. economy is inextricably linked to the rest of the world. This can easily be seen by the prevalence of both **imports** and **exports** in our economy. The United States currently exports more than ten percent of total domestic output and imports an even higher percentage. Imports represent a **leakage** from the circular flow of income while **exports** are an injection into the flow of income. An increase in exports, all other things equal, increases the flow of income. An increase in imports, all other things equal, decreases the flow of income. In the GDP formula, imports and exports are accounted for by the net export term, (exports – imports). The balance of trade between the U.S. and our trading partners has been of concern in recent decades. When exports exceed imports, a **trade surplus** exists. When imports exceed exports, a **trade deficit** exists. The U.S. continues to experience a trade deficit, which means the U.S. consumes more than it produces.

In addition to goods and services, capital also moves between countries. A **capital inflow** represents a flow of foreign money into the United States. Capital moving from the U.S. to other countries is a **capital outflow**. Capital flows are not always in balance. A capital account surplus occurs if more capital is flowing in than flowing out. A capital account deficit occurs if more capital is flowing out than is flowing in. Our current trade deficit is related to our capital account surplus.

Most economists believe that free and open trade is beneficial to all countries. There are, however, reasons given for using **trade barriers** to restrict international trade. Two common trade barriers are quotas and tariffs. A **quota** is a legal limit on the amount of a good that may be imported. A **tariff** is a tax on imports. Both tend to raise the price of the imported good. Arguments in favor of restricting trade include protecting national defense, protecting domestic jobs, and protecting infant industry.

One of the consequences of erecting trade barriers is retaliation from other countries: if the U.S. places a barrier to imports from a country, that country is likely to respond in-kind by placing a barrier to U.S. exports into that country.

<u>The Exchange Rate</u>

Changes in the exchange rate can have an impact on net exports and GDP. The exchange rate is the domestic price of a foreign currency. An increase in the exchange rate means that foreign currency is more expensive, which makes Americans less likely to purchase foreign goods, travel abroad, or purchase foreign assets, ceteris paribus. Thus, the demand for foreign currency is downward-sloping because the quantity demanded falls when the price of foreign currency rises.

When foreign currency costs more, dollars cost less for foreigners who wish to purchase them. In response to cheaper dollars, foreigners are more likely to purchase our goods, travel here, and purchase our assets. Note that when foreigners are buying more dollars, they are also selling more foreign currency. Thus, the supply of foreign-currency is upward-sloping because the quantity supplied rises when the price of foreign currency rises.

When the value of the dollar falls, or depreciates, relative to a foreign currency, U.S. exports become relatively cheaper and foreign imports become relatively more expensive. This means that exports increase and imports decrease, leading to an increase in net exports and an increase in GDP, ceteris paribus. Depreciation of the dollar helps U.S. companies that export goods and services. However, depreciation of the dollar means that U.S. citizens traveling in foreign countries will need more dollars to buy the foreign currencies and travel abroad becomes more expensive.

Given the downward-sloping demand for foreign currency and the upward-sloping supply of foreign currency, the foreign currency market is in equilibrium at the point where supply and demand intersect. The exchange rate is determined by the forces of supply and demand, so events that cause supply or demand to shift will cause the exchange rate to change.

There are many events that can cause a change in the equilibrium exchange rate. If one country experiences more rapid inflation than the other, the exchange rate is likely to change as a result. This theory is based on the notion of purchasing power parity. This idea is easiest to understand by using a simple example, as is provided on the next page.

Assume that a cup of coffee costs $3 in the U.S. and 45 pesos in Mexico. The price of the cup of coffee is the same to a consumer only if $1 trades for 15 pesos in the foreign currency market. When the price of a product is the same internationally, there is purchasing power parity.

Suppose Mexico experiences rapid inflation so that the price of a cup of coffee increases to 60 pesos. Then, purchasing power parity is re-established only if the price of $1 increases to 20 pesos. More rapid inflation abroad therefore tends to cause the international value of the dollar to rise, so that the dollar is said to appreciate, or strengthen, in value.

This theory works moderately well to predict long-run exchange rate movements. In the real world, it takes time for the exchange rate to adjust enough to re-establish purchasing power parity because international trade flows and patterns of consumption are slow to change. In the above example, the inflation in Mexico causes coffee (and other goods) to be more expensive when purchased in Mexico and paid for with dollars (verify that the dollar cost of a Mexican cup of coffee is $4 when the peso price of coffee is 60 and $1 trades for 15 pesos). When foreign goods are more expensive, American consumers respond by purchasing a lower quantity of the foreign output and the demand for foreign currency declines. A leftward shift of the demand for foreign currency curve causes the price of foreign currency to fall, which means the foreign currency depreciates or weakens against the dollar and also means that the dollar appreciates or strengthens against the foreign currency.

Another event believed to contribute to real-world exchange rate movements is when the interest rate in one country rises compared with the interest rate in another country. For example, if Japanese interest rates rise while U.S. interest rates remain constant, then Japanese financial assets become more attractive. This will likely trigger a capital outflow and an increase in the demand for foreign currency since many in the U.S. will choose to purchase foreign currency in order to acquire foreign assets such as bonds. This will cause the value of the yen to rise, which means the yen appreciates internationally and the dollar depreciates.

EXAMPLE: Use the data below to calculate Net Exports, GDP, NDP, GNP, NNP, National Income (NI), Net Investment, Personal Income (PI), and Disposable Income (DI). Verify that DI = C + S.

Personal Consumption Expenditures (C)	\$600 billion
Gross Private Domestic Investment (I)	\$500 billion
Government Expenditures (G)	\$300 billion
Exports (EX)	\$20 billion
Imports (IM)	\$50 billion
Consumption of Fixed Capital (depreciation)	\$75 billion
Indirect Business Taxes	\$20 billion
Net Foreign Factor Income	\$10 billion
Corporate Taxes	\$55 billion
Retained Earnings	\$225 billion
Social Security Taxes	\$180 billion
Net Interest	\$5 billion
Transfer Payments	\$210 billion
Personal Taxes	\$300 billion
Personal Saving	\$140 billion

All numbers are in billions of dollars:

Net Exports = EX – IM = 20 – 50 = -30 (Trade Deficit)

GDP = C + I + G + (EX – IM) = 600 + 500 + 300 + (20 – 50) = 1,370

NDP = GDP – Depreciation = 1,370 – 75 = 1,295

GNP = GDP + net foreign factor income = 1,370 + 10 = 1,380

NNP = NDP + net foreign factor income = 1,295 + 10 = 1,305

NI = NDP – indirect business taxes + net foreign factor income = 1,295 – 20 + 10 = 1,285

Net Investment = I – Depreciation = 500 – 75 = 425

PI = NI – corporate taxes – retained earnings – social security taxes

+ transfer payments + net interest

= 1,285 – 55 – 225 – 180 + 210 + 5 = 1,040

DI = PI – Personal taxes = 1,040 – 300 = 740

DI = Personal Saving (S) + Consumption spending (C) = 140 + 600 = 740

NAME____ SECTION#______________

GDP AND NATIONAL INCOME ACCOUNTING

1. Gross Domestic Product measures the total market value of:
   a. all final goods and services produced by resources owned by a country's citizens, regardless of where the resources are located.
   b. all final goods and services produced by resources located within a country's borders, regardless of who owns the resources.
   c. all intermediate goods plus the market value of all final goods and services produced by a country's resources.
   d. all economic transactions that affect a country's citizens, regardless of where the transactions occur.

2. The expenditure approach to calculating GDP is represented by the equation:
   a. GDP = C + I + G + (EX - IM).
   b. GDP = NI + net foreign factor income.
   c. GDP = C + I + G + (EX + IM).
   d. GDP = C + I + G – IM.

3. Estimated GDP:
   a. includes the value of services performed in the home, such as cleaning and cooking, but does not count the value of such services if they are purchased in the marketplace.
   b. reflects the value added at each stage of production only once to avoid double-counting.
   c. does not include the value of domestically produced output sold abroad (exports).
   d. includes the values of all financial transactions and sales of used goods.

4. Which of the following ***would not increase*** the 2018 GDP estimate for the U.S.?
   a. The value of automobiles produced in the U.S. in 2017 and sold in the U.S. in 2018
   b. The value of beer produced in the U.S. in 2018 and purchased by customers in restaurants in Canada in 2018
   c. The value of insurance-approved dental and medical services performed in the U.S. in 2018
   d. All of the above would increase the 2018 GDP estimate for the U.S.

5. The total income earned by factors of production in a given year is equal to:
   a. gross domestic product.
   b. gross national product.
   c. national income.
   d. personal income.

NAME____ SECTION#______________

Use the data below to answer questions 6 – 10:

Consumption Expenditures (C)	**$12,100 billion**
Investment Expenditures (I)	**$2,800 billion**
Government Expenditures (G)	**$3,200 billion**
Exports (EX)	**$2,500 billion**
Imports (IM)	**$2,760 billion**
Depreciation	**$2,200 billion**

6. Gross Domestic Product (GDP) is equal to ________.
   a. $22,800 billion
   b. $25,560 billion
   c. $19,760 billion
   d. $17,840 billion

7. Net Domestic Product (NDP) is equal to __________.
   a. $14,800 billion
   b. $17,000 billion
   c. $15,640 billion
   d. $20,600 billion

8. ***Net*** investment expenditures:
   a. equal $2,800 billion
   b. equal $600 billion
   c. equal $500 billion
   d. cannot be calculated from the information given.

9. Net exports are equal to __________.
   a. $5,260 billion
   b. –$260 billion
   c. – $560 billion
   d. $2,500 billion

10. Which of the following is true for this economy?
   a Net investment is positive, which increases the potential for economic growth
   b. A trade deficit exists
   c. Net Domestic Product is less than Gross Domestic Product, which means the unemployment rate is higher than the natural rate
   d. The data indicate that all of the above are true for this economy.
   e. Only a. and b. are true for this economy.

NAME____ SECTION#______________

NATIONAL INCOME ACCOUNTING

1. The largest component of U.S. GDP is:
   a. personal consumption expenditures.
   b. gross private domestic investment.
   c. government consumption expenditures and gross investment.
   d. net exports of goods and services.

2. The expenditure approach to calculating GDP adds up spending only on ***final*** goods and services to:
   a. get an accurate measure of changes in the price level during the time period in question.
   b. account for the fact that domestic resources may work and produce in foreign countries.
   c. avoid the problem of double counting, and thus overstating the value of production in the economy.
   d. eliminate the effect of inflation on the value of output.

3. Which of the following ***would*** increase measured U.S. GDP for 2018?
   a. Computer chips produced in the U.S. in 2018 and purchased by Japanese manufacturers in 2018
   b. Purchases by American consumers in 2018 of sweatshirts made in Japan in 2018
   c. The value of U.S.-made cars produced in 2016 and sold to American consumers in 2018
   d. The value of volunteer services performed in the U.S. by Americans in 2018

4. If gross investment spending is greater than depreciation (consumption of fixed capital), then net investment is:
   a. positive and the economy's capital stock is growing.
   b. positive and the economy's capital stock is contracting.
   c. negative and the economy's capital stock is growing.
   d. negative and the economy's capital stock is contracting.

5. In the national income accounts, the term depreciation refers to:
   a. the amount by which actual GDP falls short of potential GDP.
   b. the difference between nominal GDP and real GDP.
   c. the rate at which the value of stocks and bonds fall in equity and capital markets.
   d. the value of capital that is used up, worn out, or becomes obsolete during the year.

6. If the value of imports exceeds the value of exports in a given year, then:
   a. net exports are negative and there is a trade surplus.
   b. net exports are negative and there is a trade deficit.
   c. net exports are positive and there is a trade surplus.
   d. net exports are positive and there is a trade deficit.

7. Disposable Income (DI) is:
   a. the total before-tax income received by persons from all sources.
   b. the income remaining to persons after all personal taxes have been deducted.
   c. the total earnings of labor and property from the production of goods and services.
   d. National Income (NI) minus indirect business taxes.

8. GDP divided by the population is called:
   a. net national product.
   b. net domestic product.
   c. per capita GDP.
   d. average national income.

Use the information below to answer questions 9 – 10:

All values in billions of dollars ($billions)

Personal consumption expenditures (C)	**10,417.1**
Gross private domestic investment (I)	**1,818.0**
Net exports of goods and services (EX_{NET})	**– 500.2**
Government consumption expenditures and gross investment (G)	**3,020.2**
Consumption of Fixed Capital (Depreciation)	**1,896.1**

9. Gross Domestic Product (GDP) is equal to __________.
   a. $14,119 billion
   b. $14,755.1 billion
   c. $14,505.4 billion
   d. $16,651.2 billion

10. Which of the following statements is ***true*** according to the data provided above?
   a. The value of the nation's capital stock is declining.
   b. Net Domestic Product is equal to $12,257.9.
   c. This country is experiencing a trade deficit.
   d. All of the above statements are true.
   e. Only statements a. and c. are true.

NAME____ SECTION#______________

NATIONAL INCOME ACCOUNTING PROBLEMS

Use the information below to answer questions 1 – 10 (all figures are in billions):

Personal Consumption Expenditures = $9,000
Gross Private Domestic Investment = $2,450
Government Purchases = $2,600
Transfer Payments = $720
Exports = $420
Imports = $540
Depreciation (Consumption of Fixed Capital) = $1,430
Indirect Business Taxes = $225
Net Foreign Factor Income = $25
Social Security Taxes = $590
Net Interest = $315
Retained Earnings = $610
Corporate Income Taxes = $450
Personal Taxes = $2,250

1. GDP = $__________________ billion

2. GNP = $__________________ billion

3. NDP = $__________________ billion

4. NNP = $__________________ billion

5. Net Private Domestic Investment = $__________________ billion

6. The value for net investment in #5 indicates that the nation's capital stock is

   ______________________________.

7. National Income = NI = $__________________ billion

8. Personal Income = PI = $__________________ billion

9. Disposable Income = DI = $__________________ billion

10. Personal Saving = $__________________ billion

NAME____ SECTION#________________

REAL GDP, THE GDP DEFLATOR, AND GROWTH

Use the information below to fill in blanks 1 – 10. Use the space at the bottom of the page for your calculations.

Year	Nominal GDP	Real GDP	GDP Deflator
1	$11,200 billion	$11,200 billion	1.__________
2	$12,113.92 billion	2.____________	104
3	3.____________	$11,880.96 billion	110

4. The base year is year ___________.

5. In the base year, the GDP deflator = ____________.

6. Nominal GDP ________________________ between year 1 and year 2.

7. Real GDP __________________________ between year 1 and year 2.

8. The economy grew at a rate of __________% between year 1 and year 2.

9. Nominal GDP ________________________ between year 2 and year 3.

10. The economy grew at a rate of __________% between year 2 and year 3.

NAME____ SECTION#______________

NATIONAL INCOME ACCOUNTS

Use the data below to answer questions 1 – 3:

Consumption Expenditures	**$ 9,500 billion**
Wages	**$ 7,000 billion**
Rent	**$ 250 billion**
Interest Income	**$ 200 billion**
Corporate Profits	**$ 500 billion**
Proprietors' Income	**$ 800 billion**
Farm Income	**$ 150 billion**
Personal Income	**$11,000 billion**
Personal Taxes	**$ 1,100 billion**

1. National income (NI) is equal to _________.
   a. $7,950 billion
   b. $8,750 billion
   c. $8,900 billion
   d. $10,000 billion

2. Disposable income (DI) is equal to __________.
   a. $7,000 billion
   b. $8,100 billion
   c. $9,100 billion
   d. $9,900 billion

3. Personal saving is equal to _________.
   a. $1,500 billion
   b. $900 billion
   c. $400 billion
   d. $500 billion

4. Disposable income is the income:
   a. that is taken out of your pay and disposed of by government.
   b. available to households for spending and saving.
   c. earned by the factors of production in a given time period.
   d. received by persons from all sources before payment of personal taxes.

5. In the national income accounts, investment includes:
   a. purchases by businesses of new machines, tools, and equipment.
   b. changes in business inventories.
   c. all new construction, including new residential housing.
   d. All of the above are included

6. National income (NI) is:
   a. the sum of all net income earned in the production of goods and services.
   b. the income remaining to persons after payment of personal taxes.
   c. the income earned by the factors of production.
   d. the total income received by persons from all sources before payment of personal taxes.

Use the information below to answer questions 7 and 8:

A landowner in Arkansas clears some acreage and sells the trees to a lumber mill for $10,000. The lumber mill cuts the trees into boards and sells them to a furniture manufacturer for $16,000. The furniture-making company manufactures $35,000 worth of furniture with the wood. A distributor buys the furniture and sells it to consumers for $50,000.

7. How much did this set of transactions add to GDP?
   a. $50,000 since this is the value of the furniture, the final good
   b. $35,000 + $50,000 = $85,000
   c. $16,000 + $35,000 + $50,000 = $101,000
   d. $10,000 + $16,000 + $35,000 + $50,000 = $111,000

8. What was the value added by the lumber mill?
   a. $4,000
   b. $6,000
   c. $16,000
   d. $20,000

9. Only the values added at each stage of production are included when calculating GDP:
   a. to measure real GDP rather than nominal GDP.
   b. because final market values are artificially inflated.
   c. to avoid double counting.
   d. in order to accurately measure well-being.

10. Which of the following items would be included in measured GDP?
   a. The value of non-market activities, such as a homemaker's services
   b. The value of volunteer services
   c. The value of underground (illegal) activity
   d. The value of services provided by government employees
   e. None of the above items are included in measured GDP

NAME______________________________ SECTION#__________

NOMINAL GDP, REAL GDP, AND ECONOMIC GROWTH

1. Nominal GDP measures the quantities of goods and services produced in the:
   a. current year and valued at current prices.
   b. current year and valued at constant (base) prices.
   c. base year and valued at current prices.
   d. base year and valued at future prices.

2. Real GDP measures the quantities of goods and services produced in the:
   a. current year and valued at current prices.
   b. current year and valued at constant (base) prices.
   c. base year and valued at current prices.
   d. base year and valued at future prices.

3. If nominal GDP rose from one year to the next:
   a. total spending fell.
   b. real spending also rose.
   c. prices rose (there was inflation).
   d. total spending also rose.

4. If 2005 is the base year, then real GDP in 2006 is a measure of:
   a. the market value of goods and services produced in 2005, assuming no change in the price level between 2005 and 2006.
   b. the market value of goods and services produced in 2006, assuming no change in the price level between 2005 and 2006.
   c. the current market value of goods and services produced in 2005.
   d. the current market value of goods and services produced in 2006.

5. If, in a given year, nominal GDP is $11,850 billion and the GDP deflator is 120, then real GDP is:
   a. $8,500 billion.
   b. $14,220 billion.
   c. $9,875 billion.
   d. $9,500 billion.

6. Of the following measures, the one that is the best measure for tracking economic growth over time is:
   a. the absolute change in nominal GDP.
   b. the percentage change in nominal GDP.
   c. the absolute change in real GDP.
   d. the percentage change in real GDP.

7. All of the following contribute to economic growth ***except***:
   a. increases in technology.
   b. increases in research and development.
   c. increases in labor productivity.
   d. increases in the average level of prices.

8. If growth in real GDP exceeds population growth:
   a. material living standards would likely decline.
   b. material living standards would likely increase.
   c. per-capita GDP would decrease.
   d. productivity would decrease.

9. If nominal GDP rose from $6,500 billion in the base year to $7,030.4 billion in the current year and the current year GDP Deflator is 104, then the economy's growth rate is:
   a. approximately 2.3 percent.
   b. 4 percent.
   c. 6.4 percent.
   d. approximately 10.6 percent.

10. If the current GDP deflator is 108.6 and nominal GDP is $7,400 billion, then real GDP in base-year dollars is approximately:
   a. $6,814 billion.
   b. $7,507 billion.
   c. $8,036 billion.
   d. $8,281 billion.

NAME____ SECTION#________________

THE FOREIGN SECTOR

1. The exchange rate is:
   a. the foreign price of a foreign currency.
   b. the domestic price of a foreign currency.
   c. the velocity at which foreign currency flows through the economy.
   d. the rate at which imports and exports flow through world markets.

2. A tax placed by the government on imports into a country is a:
   a. tariff.
   b. quota.
   c. voluntary export restraint.
   d. nontariff barrier.

3. A country that imports more than exports has a:
   a. budget deficit.
   b. budget surplus.
   c. trade deficit.
   d. trade surplus.

4. A country that exports more than it imports has a:
   a. budget deficit.
   b. budget surplus.
   c. trade deficit.
   d. trade surplus.

5. An increase in the value of the U.S. dollar relative to the Mexican peso should result in a(n) __________ in U.S. imports from Mexico and a(n) __________ in U.S. exports to Mexico.
   a. increase; increase
   b. increase; decrease
   c. decrease; increase
   d. decrease; decrease

6. If the U.S. dollar appreciates in value relative to other currencies, exports from the U.S. become ______________ and imports to the U.S. become ______________.
   a. more expensive; more expensive
   b. more expensive; less expensive
   c. less expensive; more expensive
   d. less expensive; less expensive

7. Suppose the exchange rate between the U.S. dollar and the British pound is initially \$2 = 1 pound. If the dollar appreciates relative to the pound, then:
   a. deflation is likely to occur in Britain.
   b. aggregate demand is likely to decrease in Britain.
   c. \$2 will exchange for more than one pound.
   d. \$2 will exchange for less than one pound.

8. A stable economy with relatively high real rates of interest:
   a. can only exist in theory, not in practice.
   b. would probably experience an inflow of capital.
   c. discourages foreign investment.
   d. is necessarily the result of a trade surplus.

9. The theory of purchasing power parity predicts that when the U.S. experiences more rapid inflation than Japan:
   a. the dollar will appreciate against the yen.
   b. the dollar will depreciate against the yen.
   c. the yen will depreciate against the dollar.
   d. there will be no change in the value of the dollar or the yen.

10. The theory of interest parity predicts that when interest rates in the U.S. increase compared to foreign interest rates, there will be a:
   a. capital inflow, causing the dollar to strengthen internationally.
   b. capital inflow, causing the dollar to weaken internationally.
   c. capital outflow, causing the dollar to strengthen internationally.
   d. capital outflow, causing the dollar to weaken internationally.

Practice Exam I

The answers to this practice exam are on page 110.

1. Which of the following represents a positive statement?
   a. Government should redistribute income from the rich to the poor to promote a more equitable society.
   b. U.S. income is not equally distributed, even after adjusting for a progressive system of taxation and transfer payments made to the poor.
   c. No one should be unemployed in a country as large as the United States.
   d. Wealthy U.S. citizens do not pay their fair share of taxes.

2. If an economist wants to isolate the relationship between price and quantity demanded, she would use the:
   a. scarcity assumption.
   b. ceteris paribus assumption.
   c. fallacy of composition.
   d. fallacy of division.

3. An example of capital, as the term is used in a principles of macroeconomics course, is:
   a. a corporate jet.
   b. a $10,000 corporate bond.
   c. 10,000 shares of a corporation's stock.
   d. the bank account balance of a corporation.

4. A primary focus of macroeconomics is:
   a. why the fundamental problem of scarcity exists.
   b. why business firms pursue maximum profit instead of maximum revenue.
   c. how firms can achieve the goal of profit maximization.
   d. how the economy can achieve the goals of full employment, price stability, and economic growth.

5. "If the federal government plans to increase spending on the space program, then it will have to decrease its spending on other government programs." This statement ***best*** represents the concept of:
   a. the fallacy of false cause.
   b. opportunity cost.
   c. limited wants and needs.
   d. demand.

6. Statements that require a value judgment and cannot be disproven based on facts:
   a. should never be made.
   b. are called positive statements.
   c. are called negative statements.
   d. are called normative statements.

7. In the design of public policy, the fallacy of composition may occur if:
   a. it is assumed that because event B follows event A, event A causes event B.
   b. it is assumed that other influences on a relationship are held constant.
   c. it is assumed that because a policy is good for one sector of the economy, it is also good for the economy as a whole.
   d. it is assumed that because a policy is good for the economy as a whole, it must also be good for each individual sector of the economy.

Use the graph below to answer the next 2 questions.

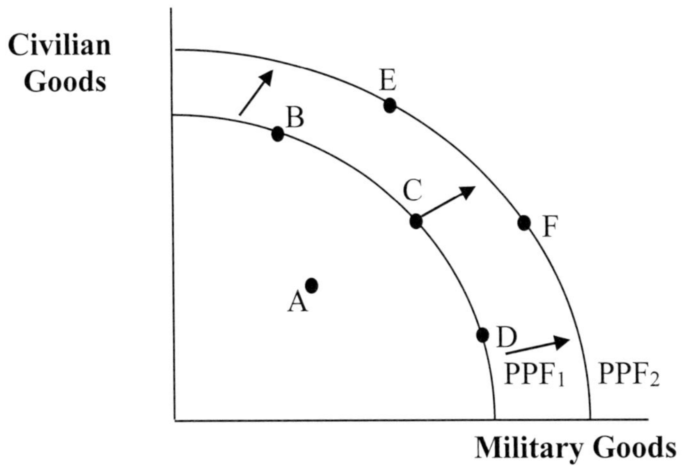

8. For this economy to move from PPF_1 to PPF_2 requires:
   a. a less efficient allocation of existing resources.
   b. economic growth brought about by, for example, technological innovation.
   c. producing at point C on PPF_1 in order to have an even mix of outputs.
   d. an increase in current consumption to reduce government military spending.

9. If this economy is on PPF_2, production is inefficient at point(s):
   a. F.
   b. A & E.
   c. A, B, C, & D.
   d. A only.

10. The simple circular flow model illustrates that:
   a. households are demanders and suppliers in product markets (output markets).
   b. businesses are demanders and suppliers in resource markets (input markets).
   c. households are suppliers in resource markets (input markets) and demanders in product markets (output markets).
   d. businesses are suppliers in product markets (output markets) and demanders in resource markets (input markets).

11. Which statement below is ***false***?
   a. Scarcity forces all societies to decide how best to use available resources.
   b. Capitalism requires private ownership of inputs and outputs.
   c. Government directs resources to their highest valued use in a market economy.
   d. Planned, or command, economies rely heavily on government direction of production and central planning.

12. Individual buyers and sellers interacting to determine what outputs will be produced helps describe a:
   a. market economy.
   b. command economy.
   c. planned economy.
   d. central economy.

Use the data in the Production Possibilities Schedule below to answer the next 3 questions.

Production Possibilities Schedule

Combination	School Buses	Refrigerators
A	0	20
B	1	18
C	2	14
D	3	8
E	4	0

13. The opportunity cost of moving from point C to point D and gaining the third school bus is:
   a. 6 refrigerators.
   b. 8 refrigerators.
   c. 14 refrigerators.
   d. 12 refrigerators.

14. The PPF that results from this production possibilities schedule will:
   a. be a straight line, indicating constant opportunity cost.
   b. be a straight line, indicating increasing opportunity cost.
   c. bow outward, indicating constant opportunity cost.
   d. bow outward, indicating increasing opportunity cost.

15. The combination of 2 school buses and 10 refrigerators:
   a. is unattainable given current resources and technology.
   b. represents an inefficient use of resources.
   c. is the optimal way of using current resources and technology.
   d. fully employs the resources and technology available.

16. According to the law of demand, an increase in the price of beef leads to, ceteris paribus:
   a. a decrease in the demand for beef.
   b. an increase in the demand for beef.
   c. a decrease in the quantity demanded of beef.
   d. an increase in the quantity demanded of beef.

Use the graph of the chocolate market below to answer the next three questions.

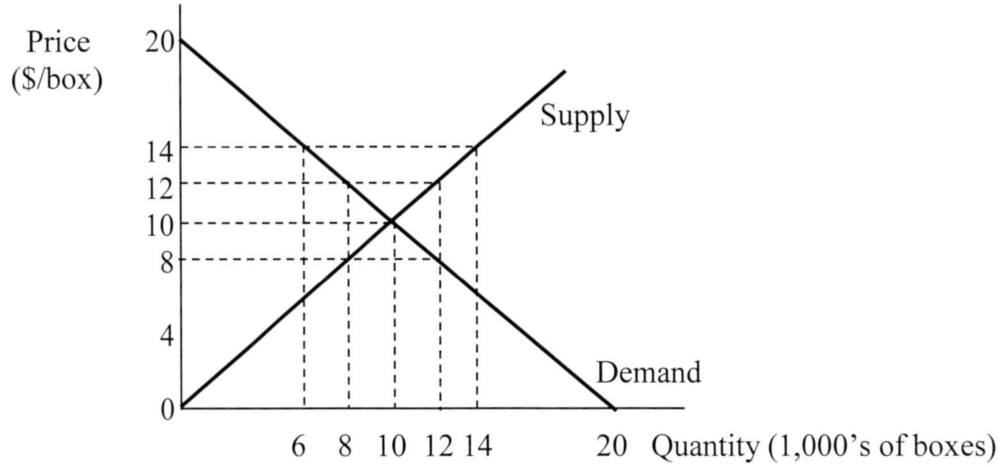

17. A price of $8 per box of chocolates results in:
   a. equilibrium in the chocolate market.
   b. a shortage of 2,000 boxes of chocolates.
   c. a shortage of 4,000 boxes of chocolates.
   d. an increase in the quantity supplied of chocolates.

18. At equilibrium, buyers of chocolates pay ______ per box and purchase ______boxes.
   a. $10; 10,000
   b. $8; 10,000
   c. $12; 8,000
   d. less than $10; between 8,000 and 12,000

19. Which of the following describes the adjustment in a market when the price in the market is above the equilibrium price for the market?
   a. A surplus exists, which causes an increase in price, a decrease in quantity demanded, and an increase in quantity supplied
   b. A shortage exists, which causes a decrease in price, a decrease in quantity demanded, and an increase in quantity supplied
   c. A shortage exists, which causes an increase in price, a decrease in quantity demanded, and an increase in quantity supplied
   d. A surplus exists, which causes a decrease in price, an increase in quantity demanded, and a decrease in quantity supplied

20. If the demand for chewing gum increases, ceteris paribus:
   a. the supply of chewing gum must also increase.
   b. the equilibrium price and quantity of chewing gum will both increase.
   c. the equilibrium price of chewing gum will increase leading the quantity supplied of chewing gum to decrease.
   d. the equilibrium price of chewing gum will decrease if chewing gum is an inferior good.

21. Which of the following events will most likely cause an increase in the supply of apple juice, ceteris paribus?
   a. An increase in the demand for apple juice
   b. An increase in the price of apple juice
   c. An increase in the price of orange juice
   d. An increase in the number of apple trees planted in orchards

22. If supply decreases at the same time that demand decreases, then:
   a. both equilibrium price and quantity will increase.
   b. equilibrium quantity will increase and equilibrium price will decrease.
   c. equilibrium quantity will decrease but the change in equilibrium price cannot be determined from the information given.
   d. equilibrium price will increase but the change in equilibrium quantity cannot be determined from the information given.

23. The law of supply indicates that:
   a. price and quantity supplied are directly (positively) related.
   b. price and supply are directly (positively) related.
   c. supply and demand are directly (positively) related.
   d. supply and demand are inversely (negatively) related.

24. Which of the following is ***not*** a macroeconomic policy goal of a market economy?
   a. Full employment
   b. Price stability
   c. Equal income distribution
   d. Economic growth

25. A recent college graduate who is looking for a job and has had several interviews that indicate a job offer is forthcoming is considered to be ______________ unemployed until a job is accepted and started.
   a. frictionally
   b. seasonally
   c. structurally
   d. cyclically

26. In a population of 300 million people, 125 million are employed and 8 million are unemployed. The labor force is _____ and the unemployment rate is _____.
   a. 125 million; 8 percent.
   b. 133 million; 6.4 percent.
   c. 300 million; 2.67 percent.
   d. 133 million; 6 percent.

27. Suppose a technological breakthrough leads domestic manufacturers to decrease the number of workers employed. These unemployed workers are considered to be:
   a. frictionally unemployed.
   b. structurally unemployed.
   c. cyclically unemployed.
   d. temporarily laid-off and therefore not unemployed.

28. To be considered unemployed, a person must:
   a. qualify for unemployment benefits.
   b. be willing and able to work.
   c. be willing and able to work and actively seeking a job.
   d. have had a job at some point in the past year.

29. When the economy is operating at the natural rate of unemployment:
   a. the unemployment rate is 0%.
   b. there is some low level of cyclical unemployment but 0% frictional unemployment.
   c. there is some low level of structural and frictional unemployment but 0% cyclical unemployment.
   d. all people who are willing and able to work have a job.

30. Cyclical unemployment is associated with:
   a. workers moving between jobs.
   b. changes in technology that change the skills demanded in the labor market.
   c. downturns in the overall economy.
   d. inflationary periods.

31. Inflation occurs when:
   a. the average price level rises.
   b. the price of a good or service rises.
   c. consumer incomes increase.
   d. some prices change faster than other prices.

Use the information in the table below to answer the next two questions.

Year	Nominal Income	CPI
2000	$40,000	172.2
2001	$42,000	177.1
2002	$43,000	179.8

32. This person's real income in 2002 was _______ which was __________ his/her real income in 2001.
   a. $23,915; greater than
   b. $24,970; greater than
   c. $23,915; less than
   d. $24,970; less than

33. The inflation rate for 2001 was approximately:
   a. 1.5%.
   b. 2.8%.
   c. 4.9%.
   d. 1.7%.

34. Gross domestic product is:
   a. the sum of payments to the factors of production in a given time period.
   b. the total market value of all final goods and services produced within a country's borders in a given time period.
   c. the sum of the values of all economic transactions that occur within an economy in a given time period.
   d. the value of all production that occurs by the factors of production owned a country's citizens.

35. Which of the following items ***would*** increase U.S. GDP for 2019?
   a. The value of cars made in the U.S. in 2018 and sold in 2019
   b. The value of shoes produced in Brazil and sold in the U.S. in 2019
   c. The value of stock market transactions that occurred in the U.S. in 2019
   d. The value of bicycles produced and sold in the U.S. in 2019

36. When economists talk about the growth rate of the economy, they measure that growth rate with the:
   a. absolute change in nominal GDP.
   b. percentage change in nominal GDP.
   c. absolute change in real GDP.
   d. percentage change in real GDP.

37. All of the following events are likely to contribute to economic growth ***except:***
   a. an increase in the technology used to produce outputs.
   b. an increase in the productivity of labor.
   c. an increase in the U.S. price level relative to foreign price levels.
   d. an increase in the amount of capital.

Use the information in the table below to answer the next three questions.

All figures are in billions of dollars

Consumption Spending.	6,576.0
Investment Spending	1,589.6
Government Purchases.	1,712.8
Net Exports	-488.6
Depreciation	1,022.3
Indirect Business Taxes	460.3
Net Foreign Factor Income	0.0

38. Gross domestic product is:
   a. $9,389.8 billion.
   b. $9,878.4 billion.
   c. $10,367 billion.
   d. $8,367.5 billion.

39. Net domestic product is:
   a. $9,389.8 billion.
   b. $9,878.4 billion.
   c. $10,367 billion.
   d. $8,367.5 billion.

40. Net investment is:
   a. $1,589.6 billion.
   b. $1,022.3 billion.
   c. $567.3 billion.
   d. impossible to calculate from the information given.

Answers to Practice Exam I

1. b	11. c	21. d	31. a
2. b	12. a	22. c	32. a
3. a	13. a	23. a	33. b
4. d	14. d	24. c	34. b
5. b	15. b	25. a	35. d
6. d	16. c	26. d	36. d
7. c	17. c	27. b	37. c
8. b	18. a	28. c	38. a
9. c	19. d	29. c	39. d
10. c	20. b	30. c	40. c

CHAPTER 6 Aggregate Demand/Aggregate Supply Analysis

The last two chapters have demonstrated how important macroeconomic variables are measured. Economic models explain how and why these variables change over time. The Aggregate Demand/Aggregate Supply model shows the determination of the economy's price level (P) and output level (Q), and also provides information about other variables. In general, changes in output or real GDP are inversely related to changes in the unemployment rate. For example, if the unemployment rate falls, assuming no change in the size of the labor force, there are more workers producing output, which results in a higher output level.

Aggregate Demand

Demand decisions are made when someone decides to purchase a good or service, or spend. All income payments generated in the economy accrue to households, and households use income to pay taxes, purchase consumer goods and services, and save. The largest component of aggregate demand is **consumer spending** (C). Consumer spending includes the purchase of food, clothes, appliances, health care services, automobiles, and all the other things that people purchase on a daily basis.

Another component of aggregate demand is **investment spending** (I), which refers to spending on capital goods (machines, tools, etc.), new construction, and changes in business inventory. When households save, funds are made available to finance investment spending, but the decision to save (e.g., deposit money in a savings account, a mutual fund, stocks, or bonds) is not the same as the decision to invest. Investment spending occurs when an entrepreneur is starting a new business or expanding an existing business.

A third component of aggregate demand is **government spending** (G). Within the public sector, all levels of government collect taxes or borrow, using the proceeds to purchase goods and services and make transfer payments. Transfer payments can be thought of as income redistributed from some households to others. For example, workers pay social security taxes, and retired individuals receive social security benefits. Government spending occurs when the public sector is purchasing goods and services, not making transfer payments.

In a **closed economy**, there are only three types of spending—consumer, investment, and government. In an **open economy**, there is also foreign trade as goods and services are imported from abroad and exported to other countries. It is useful to remember the formula provided by national income accounting for total output:

$$\mathbf{GDP = C + I + G + (EX - IM)}$$

where C denotes the consumer spending of households, I is the investment spending of business firms, G equals government spending (excluding transfer payments), EX stands for spending by foreigners on our exports, and IM represents import spending.

The combined spending of the household sector, the business sector, and the public sector equals C + I + G, but part of this spending is for the purchase of imported goods and services. By definition, imports were produced elsewhere, so it makes sense to subtract spending on imports from the total so that the remainder represents domestic spending on domestic output. Finally, add export spending so that the total, C + I + G + (EX – IM), represents the total amount of spending on goods and services produced within the country. When thinking about aggregate demand, think about the demand decisions being made not only by consumers, but also by business firms, the government, and foreigners when they want to purchase goods and services produced in the U.S. economy.

Aggregate demand (AD) is the relationship between the quantity demanded of all goods and services and the price level, holding other things that influence quantity demanded fixed. A change in the price level leads to a movement along the aggregate demand curve and a change in the quantity demanded of real GDP. For example, in the graph below, when the price level falls from P_1 to P_2, quantity demanded increases from Q_1 to Q_2 and there is a movement along curve AD from point **a** to point **b**.

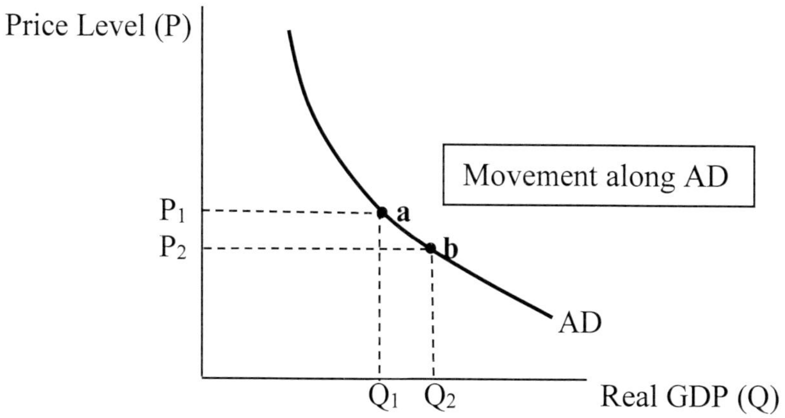

The relationship between the price level and the quantity demanded of real GDP is inverse so the AD curve is downward-sloping. AD slopes downward for three reasons:

1) the **real balance, or wealth, effect** - as the price level decreases, the purchasing power of money balances increases and people can purchase more goods and services; at a higher price level, the purchasing power of wealth declines, causing quantity demanded to decline. Real wealth increases as the price level decreases, ceteris paribus.

2) the **interest rate effect** – the interest rate is the price of money and tends to follow the price level. As the price level decreases, interest rates tend to fall, and business and household spending impacted by the interest rate increases; a higher price level leads to higher interest rates, which in turn reduces the quantity of real GDP demanded.

3) the **international trade effect** – as the domestic price level decreases, assuming no change in foreign prices, the U.S. tends to export more and import less, and spending on domestic output increases; if U.S. prices rise relative to foreign prices, the opposite occurs.

Many factors affect demand decisions and result in a shift of the aggregate demand curve. An increase in AD is shown as a rightward shift, from AD_1 to AD_2 in the graph below, for example. When AD increases, this means that some event other than a change in the price level has caused consumers, business firms, government, or foreigners to be willing and able to purchase more U.S. goods and services. The shift from point **a** to point **b'** can be explained by many different factors, but cannot be attributed to a change in the U.S. price level (P).

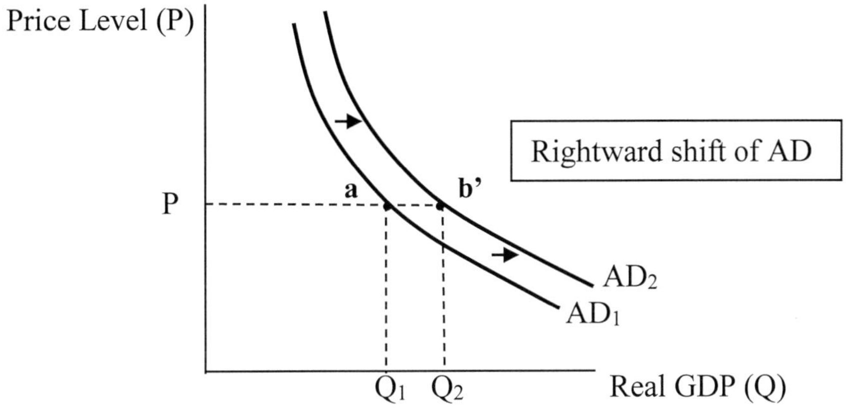

The AD curve shifts to the right whenever some event causes consumers, business firms, the government, or foreigners to demand more goods and services. These events are summarized in the chart below.

What can cause a change in C?
1. Wealth
2. Interest Rates
3. Taxes or Transfers
4. Expectations or consumer confidence

What can cause a change in I?
1. Interest Rates
2. Taxes
3. Expectations or business confidence

What can cause a change in G?
1. Fiscal Policy decisions
2. A change in the desired size of the public sector

What can cause a change in EX - IM?
1. Foreign income
2. Exchange rates

If a change in C, I, or EX – IM was caused by a change in the price level, it will be shown as a movement along the AD curve. Since a change in the price level will cause a change in real wealth, the interest rate, and net exports (the three reasons why AD is downward-sloping), it can be very difficult to avoid confusing a movement along AD and a shift. Consider a sample multiple choice question such as the one below:

Which of the following will cause aggregate demand to shift to the right?
a. an increase in the price level
b. a decrease in the price level
c. an increase in household wealth
d. a decrease in household wealth

The correct answer is "c", not 'b", because a change in the price level causes a movement along the aggregate demand curve rather than a shift of the aggregate demand curve. An increase in household wealth that occurs generally leads to more spending by consumers and an increase in aggregate demand, which is modeled as a rightward shift of the AD curve.

Economic analysis involves taking real-world events and relationships, translating them into models used to explain the events and relationships, and then using those models to make predictions about economic variables. AD is a simple model of the relationship between two macroeconomic variables: the price level and the quantity of real GDP. There are a number of events that cause aggregate demand to shift, and many of these are described below to help you become familiar with the terminology as well as the economic intuition.

- When the stock market is booming, people are wealthier, so they are likely to purchase more goods and services. Therefore, a stock market boom causes the AD curve to shift to the right. On the other hand, a stock market crash results in a leftward shift of the AD curve.

- Consumers are much more likely to purchase big-ticket items on credit when interest rates are low. Therefore, lower interest rates cause AD to shift to the right, while higher interest rates cause AD to shift to the left.

- Lower tax rates result in more take-home pay, giving households more purchasing power. Tax cuts will cause AD to shift to the right, and tax hikes will cause AD to shift to the left.

- If retired individuals receive bigger social security checks, they will have more to spend. An increase in government transfer payments will lead to a rightward shift of AD, and a decrease in government transfer payments causes a leftward shift.

- When consumers are confident about the future and feel secure in their jobs, they are more likely to make purchases, so an increase in consumer confidence will cause AD to increase. If consumers are worried about a recession or being laid off from their jobs, AD will likely decrease as they cut back on unnecessary spending.

- If people expect product prices to rise in the future, they will probably rush to buy while prices are still low. Therefore, an expectation of higher prices in the future causes AD to shift to the right, while an expectation of lower prices causes AD to fall or shift to the left.

- Business owners are more likely to borrow money to finance investment projects when interest rates are low, so a decrease in interest rates will cause AD to increase and an increase in interest rates will cause AD to decrease.

- Lower taxes on corporate profits provides corporations with greater liquidity and raises the expected rate of return on investment in new machines. Lower business taxes will cause AD to shift to the right and higher business taxes will cause AD to shift to the left.

- Business owners are more likely to engage in expansion when they are optimistic about the future. An increase in business confidence causes AD to increase. More pessimistic expectations cause AD to fall or shift to the left.

- The federal government can engage in expansionary fiscal policy by increasing government spending, leading to an increase in AD. Contractionary fiscal policy means lower government spending and causes AD to shift to the left.

- An increase in foreign income means that our trading partners have more to spend, so export demand is expected to rise, causing AD to shift to the right. A recession abroad would likely hurt U.S. exports by causing AD to shift to the left.

- A depreciation of the U.S. dollar means that foreign currency is more expensive, and therefore foreign goods and services cost more. At the same time, a weaker U.S. dollar will make U.S. goods and services cheaper for foreign consumers. A depreciation of the U.S. dollar, or an appreciation of foreign currency, causes AD to shift to the right, while a strengthening of the U.S. dollar in foreign currency markets results in a leftward shift of AD.

The ability to predict aggregate demand shifts is the first step in the analysis. The next step involves the aggregate supply function, which is necessary to identify macroeconomic equilibrium.

Aggregate Supply

Supply decisions are made within the business sector and are assumed to be motivated by the desire to maximize profits. Supply decisions are closely associated with input demand decisions as business firms decide how many workers to hire and which other inputs to use in order to produce goods and services. In microeconomics, supply functions are upward-sloping, reflecting the law of supply, but what about the aggregate supply function? Economists have introduced the element of time to explain the behavior of aggregate supply.

Aggregate supply (AS) shows the relationship between the quantity supplied of all goods and services and the price level, ceteris paribus. The aggregate supply curve is believed to be upward-sloping in the short run because many input prices are fixed for a particular time period due to contractual agreements. If the cost of production remains constant and the price level rises, then the price per unit of output sold increases while the cost of producing each unit of output stays the same. This means the profit per unit increases, creating an incentive for producers to increase output. As long as some input prices are fixed, causing costs of production to remain relatively constant, an increase in the price level causes an increase in the quantity supplied of goods and services (holding other things the same); this indicates that the **short-run aggregate supply curve (SRAS)** is upward sloping.

A change in the price level leads to a movement along the SRAS curve and a change in the quantity supplied of real GDP. For example, in the graph below, when the price level increases from P_1 to P_2, quantity supplied increases from Q_1 to Q_2, and there is a movement along curve SRAS from point **a** to point **b**.

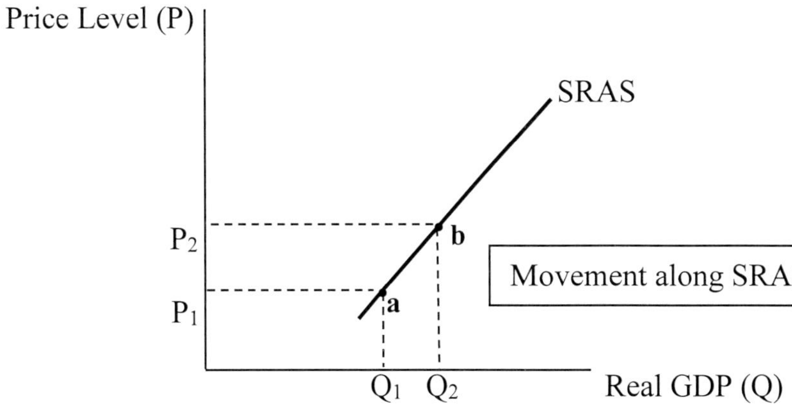

Other things that affect the supply decision can also change, and when they do, they will cause the SRAS curve to shift. For example, a shift from $SRAS_1$ to $SRAS_2$ in the graph below is a leftward shift, or a decrease in short-run aggregate supply. In this case, the shift from point **b** to point **b'** is caused by some factor other than a change in the U.S. price level.

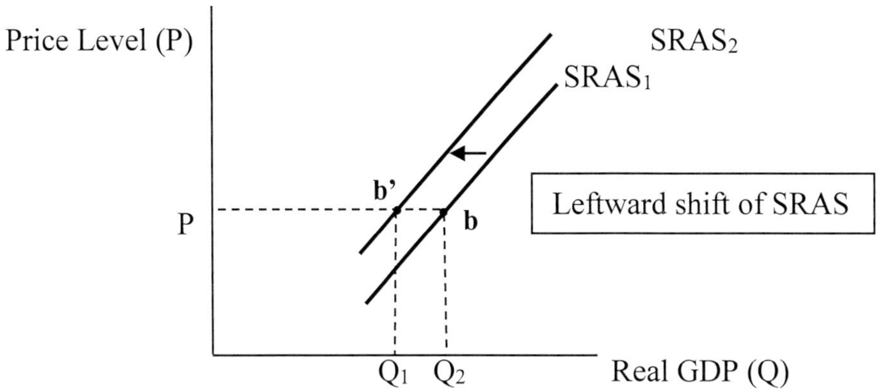

The SRAS curve is drawn assuming input prices are fixed, and when input prices change, the result is a shift in the SRAS curve. The SRAS will decrease, or shift to the left, when costs of production increase due to higher input prices, such as a higher wage rate. Energy is an important input in all industries, so a change in the price of energy has an aggregate effect. During the 1970s, for example, high energy costs were believed to cause the SRAS curve to shift leftward, and this phenomenon was called an **adverse supply shock**. Similarly, the SRAS curve increases or shifts to the right when costs of production fall due to lower input prices, such as a lower wage rate or lower energy costs. The SRAS curve also shifts to the right when the quantity or productivity of resources rises, or when technology improves. If input costs are rising, but at the same time, worker productivity is improving, the effect on the SRAS curve cannot be predicted without information about the size of the two shifts.

The **Long-Run Aggregate Supply curve (LRAS)** is vertical at the full-employment, or potential, level of real GDP (Q_N) in the long run. Potential output is the level of output the economy can produce when the economy is operating at full-employment, or the natural rate of unemployment (U_N). This potential output is often referred to as **natural real GDP (Q_N)**. Natural real GDP depends on real factors, such as technology and worker productivity, and not the price level, which is why the LRAS curve is vertical.

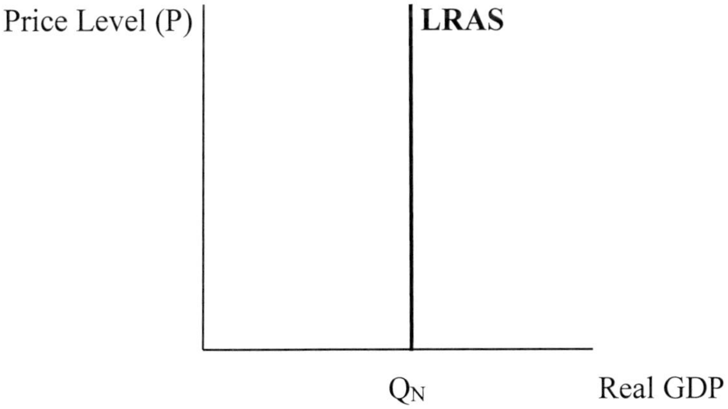

Factors that affect full-employment, or natural, real GDP (Q_N) include technology, worker productivity, and the stock of capital. When these factors lead to an increase in potential real GDP, the LRAS curve shifts to the right. The factors that shift the LRAS curve also shift the SRAS curve. However, a change in input prices does not cause the LRAS curve to shift.

Macroeconomic Equilibrium

In product markets, equilibrium occurs where the quantity demanded equals the quantity supplied, or at the point where supply and demand intersect. This happens because a surplus causes price to fall and a shortage causes price to rise. Macroeconomic equilibrium occurs when *aggregate* quantity demanded equals *aggregate* quantity supplied, or at the point where aggregate demand intersects aggregate supply.

Short-run equilibrium occurs at the point of intersection between the AD curve and the SRAS curve, while long-run equilibrium occurs at the intersection of all three curves (AD, SRAS, and LRAS). The economy may be in short-run equilibrium at an output level either above or below Q_N. If real GDP is equal to Q_N, then the economy is in long-run equilibrium.

The interaction of aggregate demand and short-run aggregate supply establishes short-run equilibrium in the economy. Graphically, short-run equilibrium occurs at the intersection of the AD and SRAS curves. In the graph below, the equilibrium price level is P_E and the equilibrium level of real output produced and purchased in this economy is Q_E.

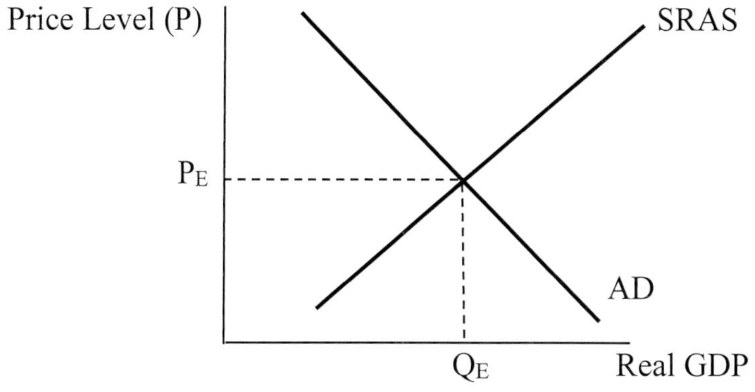

This graph does not indicate whether or not the economy is producing at full employment, nor does it reveal anything about whether the economy is experiencing inflation or recession. The picture just provides a starting point, and it is necessary to add a shift and then compare the new equilibrium point with the original equilibrium point in order to draw any conclusions about what is happening in the economy.

This model is used to predict the consequences of many different events that have caused either AD to shift or SRAS to shift. In the graphs below, different shifts are shown, leading to predictions about how the economy is affected by each single shift.

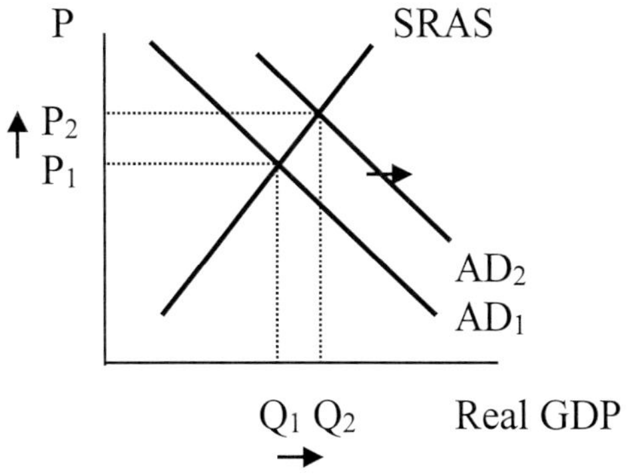

An increase in aggregate demand (rightward shift) causes equilibrium price and equilibrium quantity to increase. This kind of shift leads to inflation, but also leads to higher output. Generally, when equilibrium output rises, the economy is creating more jobs and the rate of unemployment falls.

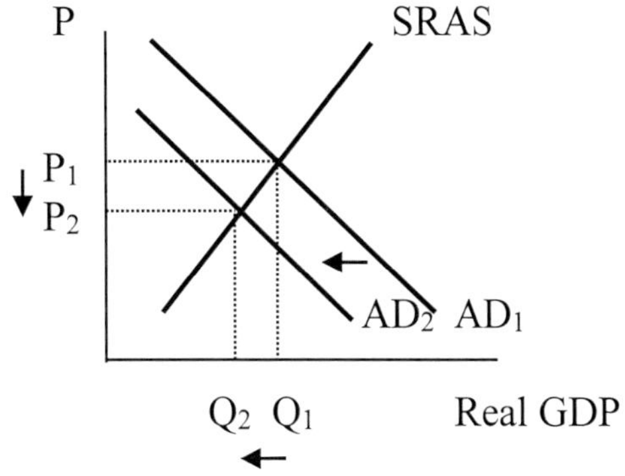

A decrease in aggregate demand (leftward shift) causes equilibrium price and equilibrium quantity to decrease. The reduction in equilibrium output is associated with fewer jobs and higher unemployment, and the lower equilibrium price level indicates deflation.

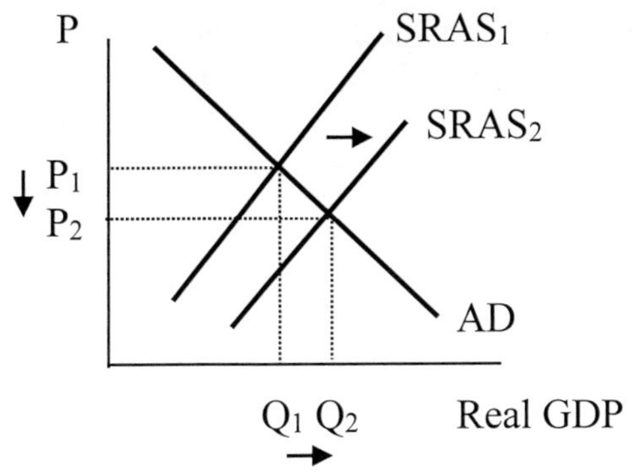

An increase in short-run aggregate supply (rightward shift) causes equilibrium price to decrease and equilibrium quantity to increase. Higher output is associated with lower unemployment. By itself, an increase in SRAS would lead to deflation, but this rarely occurs.

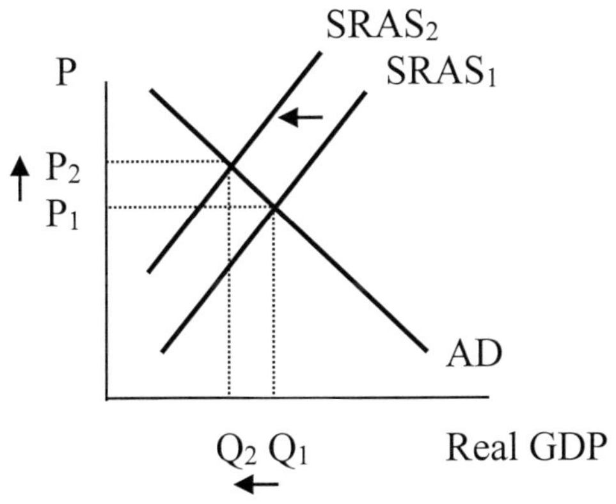

A decrease in short-run aggregate supply (leftward shift) causes equilibrium price to increase and equilibrium quantity to decrease. This combination of events, lower output and higher unemployment with higher inflation (sometimes referred to as **stagflation**), is not desirable.

Mainstream economic thinking has long held that the economy's actual real GDP (Q) will naturally gravitate toward the full-employment or natural level of real GDP (Q_N), causing the actual rate of unemployment (U) to gravitate toward the full-employment or natural rate of unemployment (U_N) in the **long run**. An economic downturn or recession only occurs in the **short run** when unemployment is higher than the natural rate.

- $U = U_N$ and $Q = Q_N$ when the economy achieves full employment
- $U > U_N$ and $Q < Q_N$ when the economy is in a recession

This natural tendency toward full-employment in the long run is called the economy's self-regulating or self-correcting mechanism and is associated with **Classical Economics**. The belief that short-term economic fluctuations will automatically stabilize led many Classical economists to favor a ***laissez-faire*** approach to macroeconomic policy, but this approach was challenged when the economy entered the Great Depression.

Keynesian Economics, one of the important macroeconomic schools of thought today, was developed to explain the way the economy behaved during the Great Depression, and what government policymakers can do to prevent the economy from again entering such a severe and prolonged downturn. Keynesian analysis focuses on the economy's short-run behavior. Many policymakers rely on Keynesian principles to manage the economy, so the modern study of macroeconomics is largely concerned with understanding the policy options (fiscal policy and monetary policy).

The long-run aggregate supply curve (LRAS) is a vertical line and indicates that equilibrium output is equal to full-employment output in the long run. **Long-run equilibrium** occurs where the AD curve intersects both SRAS and LRAS. The graph below illustrates an economy in long-run equilibrium.

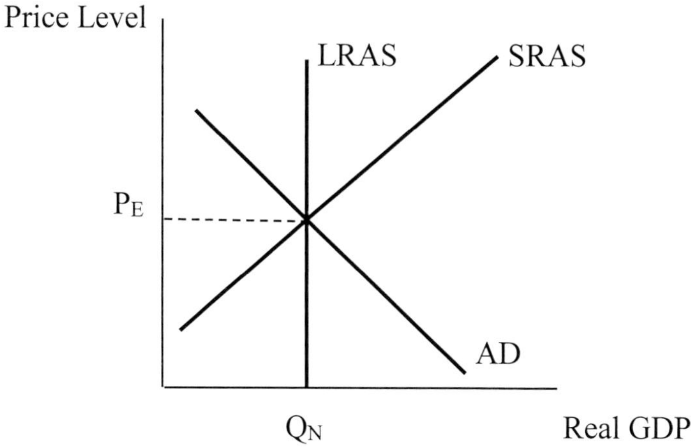

When the economy is in long-run equilibrium, real GDP is equal to full employment, or natural, real GDP (Q_N) and the unemployment rate is equal to the natural rate (U_N), so the economy is not in a recession. The important question to consider has to do with how the economy reaches long-run equilibrium, beginning from a short-run equilibrium that is either below or above full-employment output. This model is also useful for understanding how the economy grows over time, but that topic is addressed in the next chapter.

Economic growth occurs as the economy's potential, or full-employment, level of real GDP increases. The graph illustrates an increase in LRAS combined with an increase in the aggregate demand curve. If policymakers are successful in accommodating growth, then the AD curve will keep pace with the LRAS curve, allowing the economy to achieve economic growth with a stable price level.

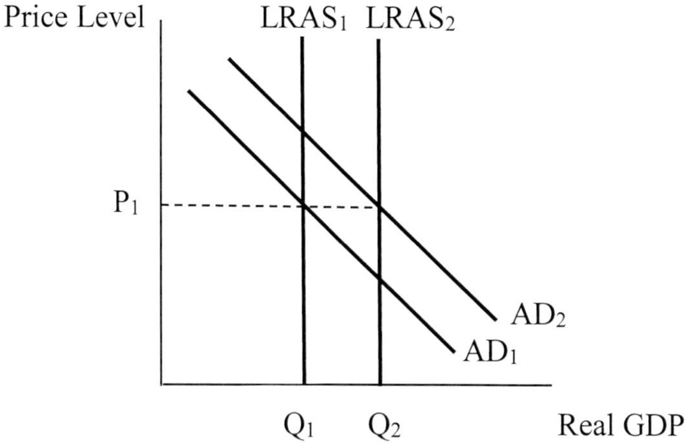

Recessionary and Inflationary Gaps

Given the large number of events that can cause aggregate demand to shift, it is not surprising to learn that aggregate demand could shift to the left, leading to a short-run equilibrium that is below full-employment output (a recessionary gap), or to the right, leading to a short-run equilibrium that is above full-employment output (an inflationary gap). Both possibilities are considered in this section, and the process by which these gaps close without government intervention is described. The central debate in Macroeconomics concerns whether it is best to take a *laissez-faire* approach and allow the economy to correct itself through shifts of the short-run aggregate supply curve, or use policy to shift the aggregate demand curve and close gaps.

Short-run equilibrium may occur at a level of real GDP that is below full-employment, or natural, real GDP (Q_N) if people are not spending enough to purchase all the output that could be produced given full employment. Because of weak spending, business inventories increase at a rate faster than anticipated, and in response to the unplanned increases in inventories, businesses cut back production and lay off workers. When this happens, there is a **recessionary gap**, as illustrated in the graph below.

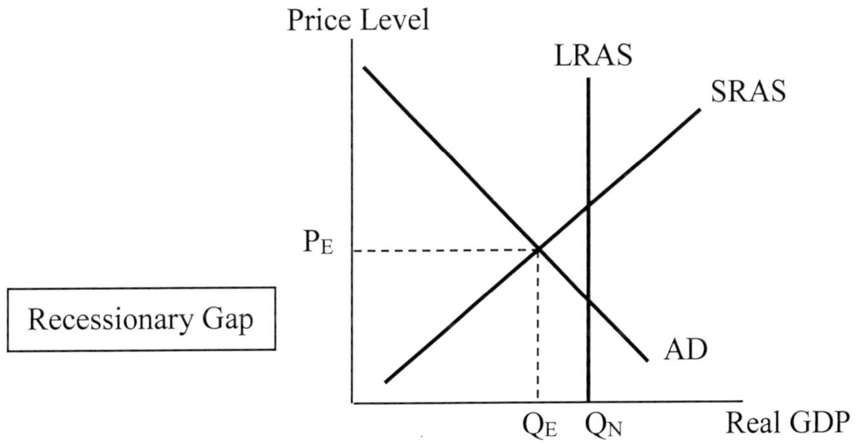

When there is a recessionary gap, equilibrium real GDP (Q_E) is below full-employment real GDP (Q_N), and the actual rate of unemployment is higher than the natural rate ($U > U_N$). These conditions (low production levels and high unemployment levels) are associated with a recession.

Because the unemployment rate is higher than the natural rate, a recessionary gap is associated with a surplus in the labor market, implying that the wage rate is above equilibrium. The wage rate may be "stuck" above equilibrium due to the minimum wage, union contracts, or other factors, but the model assumes that wages will eventually decrease, resulting in a rightward-shift of the short-run aggregate supply curve. If policymakers decide to intervene before wages fall, then the gap may be closed as a result of a rightward shift of aggregate demand. Therefore, more information is needed before predicting what will happen next.

The Bureau of Economic Analysis officially records a recession when these conditions persist for a period of time, usually 6 months. A recessionary gap is a short-run phenomenon and the economy is not expected to remain in a recession in the long run.

Eventually, labor market conditions will lead to lower wage rates, causing the SRAS curve to shift to the right. This shift will move the economy toward equilibrium at full-employment output, or Q_N. Policymakers must decide whether to wait for the economy to self-correct or to take action to close a recessionary gap. Macroeconomic policy can be used to shift the AD curve to the right, which will also move the economy toward full-employment equilibrium. These are considerations that will be examined more carefully in the next few chapters.

Short-run equilibrium may also occur at a level of real GDP that is above Q_N. If short-run equilibrium, or actual, real GDP is greater than natural real GDP, then people are spending more than businesses anticipated, and inventories are depleted at a rate faster than expected. In response to unplanned inventory decreases, businesses increase production by hiring more workers and purchasing other inputs, and an **inflationary gap** emerges, as illustrated in the graph below.

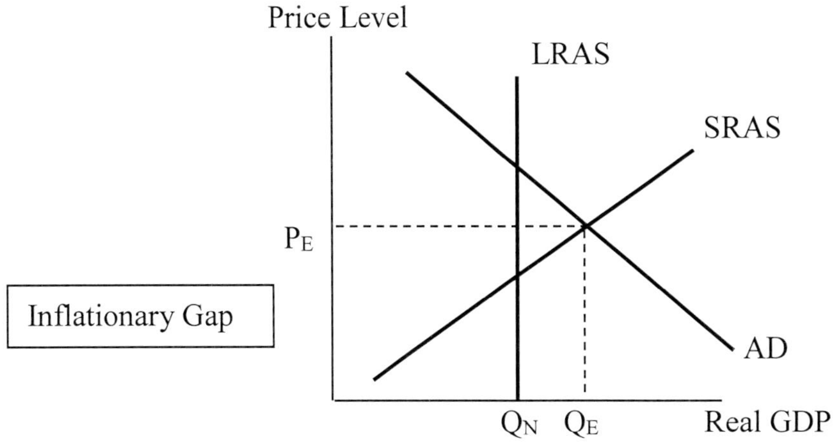

When there is an inflationary gap, equilibrium real GDP (Q_E) is above full-employment real GDP (Q_N), and the actual rate of unemployment is lower than the natural rate ($U < U_N$). Since output is high and unemployment is low, the economy is booming. Although a booming economy is desirable, these conditions put upward pressure on the equilibrium price level and lead to inflation, which is undesirable.

As with a recessionary gap, the economy's self-correcting mechanism works to eliminate an inflationary gap in the long run. However, the self-correcting process involves more inflation. If no action is taken, tight labor market conditions lead to higher wage rates, causing the SRAS curve to shift to the left. As SRAS shifts leftward, real GDP returns to Q_N, but the price level rises. Policymakers generally prefer to intervene and prevent an inflationary gap from becoming a problem by restraining aggregate demand. A detailed discussion of inflation-fighting policies and the Federal Reserve is presented later in this book.

NAME____ SECTION#______________

Print Last Name, First Name

AGGREGATE DEMAND

1. The relationship between the quantity of real GDP demanded by all sectors of the economy and the price level is given by the:
   a. long-run aggregate supply curve.
   b. short-run aggregate supply curve.
   c. aggregate demand curve.
   d. natural real GDP curve.

2. Ceteris paribus, an increase in the price level leads to:
   a. a decrease in the purchasing power of the dollar.
   b. a decrease in the quantity demanded of real GDP.
   c. a decrease in the demand for real GDP.
   d. All of the above are true
   e. Only a. and b. are true

3. All of the following help explain why the aggregate demand curve is downward sloping ***except:***
   a. the nominal balance effect.
   b. the real balance effect.
   c. the interest rate effect.
   d. the international trade effect.

4. The increase in the purchasing power of a given money income that occurs when the domestic price level falls refers to:
   a. the nominal balance effect.
   b. the real balance effect.
   c. the interest rate effect.
   d. the international trade effect.

5. The international trade effect occurs in an open economy because an increase in the U.S. price level relative to foreign price levels leads to:
   a. an increase in the quantity of U.S. goods demanded by Americans and a decrease in the quantity of U.S. goods demanded by foreigners.
   b. an increase in the quantity of U.S. goods demanded by both Americans and foreigners.
   c. a decrease in the quantity of U.S. goods demanded by foreigners and no change in the quantity of U.S. goods demanded by Americans.
   d. a decrease in the quantity of U.S. goods demanded by both Americans and foreigners.

6. Ceteris paribus, the aggregate demand curve will shift to the left as a result of:
   a. a decrease in household wealth.
   b. a decrease in the price level.
   c. a decrease in personal taxes.
   d. a decrease in interest rates.

NAME____ SECTION#________________
Print Last Name, First Name

7. Ceteris paribus, if consumers become more optimistic regarding future job prospects and income, consumer spending will ____________ and the aggregate demand curve will shift to the _____________.
   a. increase; right
   b. increase; left
   c. decrease; left
   d. decrease; right

Use the graph below to answer questions 8 – 9:

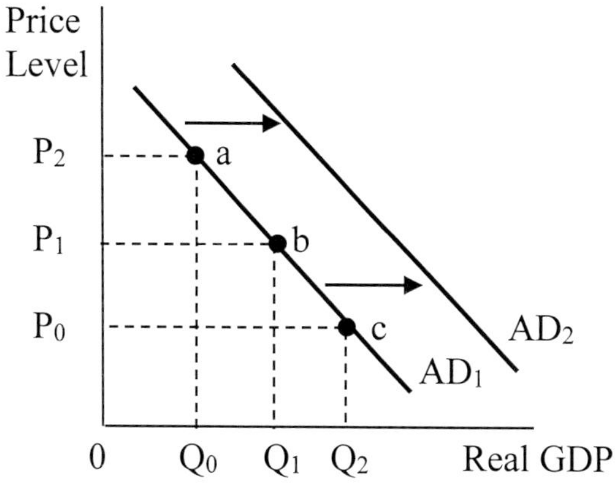

8. A movement along AD_1 from point **b** to point **c** illustrates:
   a. an increase in aggregate demand and results in a lower price level and a higher real GDP.
   b. an increase in aggregate demand and results in a higher price level and a higher real GDP.
   c. a decrease in the price level and results in an increase in the demand for real GDP from AD_1 to AD_2.
   d. a decrease in the price level and results in an increase in the quantity demanded of real GDP from Q_1 to Q_2.

9. Which of the following may cause AD_1 to shift to the right to AD_2?
   a. An increase in consumer income and wealth
   b. An increase in personal and corporate income tax rates
   c. An increase in the interest rate
   d. An increase in the natural rate of unemployment

10. The components of aggregate demand include:
   a. spending by domestic and foreign consumers on both exports and imports.
   b. spending for consumption purposes but not spending for investment purposes.
   c. spending by consumers, business firms, government, and foreigners on domestic output.
   d. private sector spending but not public sector spending.

NAME____ SECTION#______________

Print Last Name, First Name

AGGREGATE SUPPLY

1. Ceteris paribus, the short-run aggregate supply curve shows:
   a. a direct relationship between the quantity supplied of all goods and services and the price level.
   b. an inverse relationship between the quantity supplied of all goods and services and the price level.
   c. the amount of output all producers in a particular industry are willing and able to supply at different prices.
   d. the amount of output all producers are able to buy at different prices.

2. The short-run aggregate supply curve is upward sloping because:
   a. producers respond to higher prices and profits by increasing output.
   b. producers respond to higher prices and profits by restricting output.
   c. the quantity supplied of real GDP and the price level are inversely related.
   d. the supply of real GDP and the demand for GDP are directly related.

3. If the price of a major input, such as oil, increases:
   a. output prices are likely to fall, ceteris paribus.
   b. input prices are likely to fall, ceteris paribus.
   c. the SRAS curve shifts to the left, ceteris paribus.
   d. the SRAS curve shifts to the right, ceteris paribus.

4. Ceteris paribus, an increase in the price level causes:
   a. the SRAS curve to shift to the right.
   b. the SRAS curve to shift to the left.
   c. an increase in the quantity of real GDP supplied (movement along SRAS).
   d. a decrease in the quantity of real GDP supplied (movement along SRAS).

5. Which of the following events would lead to a rightward shift of the short-run aggregate supply curve?
   a. An increase in the wage rate
   b. An increase in the price of oil
   c. A beneficial supply shock
   d. A decrease in the price level

6. The long-run aggregate supply (LRAS) curve is:
   a. vertical at short-run equilibrium real GDP.
   b. vertical at natural real GDP, or potential output.
   c. horizontal at short-run equilibrium real GDP.
   d. horizontal at natural real GDP, or potential output.

NAME________________________________ SECTION#____________

Print Last Name, First Name

7. If the economy is in equilibrium at natural real GDP, an economy-wide decrease in the cost of producing outputs will, ceteris paribus:
   a. increase aggregate supply resulting in an increase in real GDP, a decrease in the unemployment rate, and a decrease in the price level.
   b. decrease aggregate supply resulting in a decrease in real GDP, an increase in the unemployment rate, and an increase in the price level.
   c. increase aggregate demand resulting in an increase in real GDP, a decrease in the unemployment rate, and an increase in the price level.
   d. decrease aggregate demand resulting in a decrease in real GDP, an increase in the unemployment rate, and a decrease in the price level.

8. Ceteris paribus, when the short-run aggregate supply curve is upward-sloping, an adverse supply shock:
   a. leads to an increase in the price level and a decrease in real GDP.
   b. has no impact on the price level but leads to an increase in real GDP.
   c. leads to an increase in both the price level and real GDP.
   d. has no impact on the price level or real GDP.

9. In the AD/AS model, economic growth is best illustrated by a:
   a. movement up along a given aggregate supply curve.
   b. movement down along a given aggregate supply curve.
   c. leftward shift of the long-run aggregate supply curve.
   d. rightward shift of the long-run aggregate supply curve.

10. Ceteris paribus, a rightward shift of the short-run aggregate supply (SRAS) curve causes:
   a. an increase in the price level, which in turn causes quantity demanded to fall.
   b. an increase in the price level, which in turn causes quantity demanded to rise.
   c. a decrease in the price level, which in turn causes quantity demanded to fall.
   d. a decrease in the price level, which in turn causes quantity demanded to rise.

NAME____ SECTION#_______________
Print Last Name, First Name

AD/AS, SHIFTS, AND EQUILIBRIUM

INSTRUCTIONS: Fill in the following ten blanks with the correct word or numerical value.

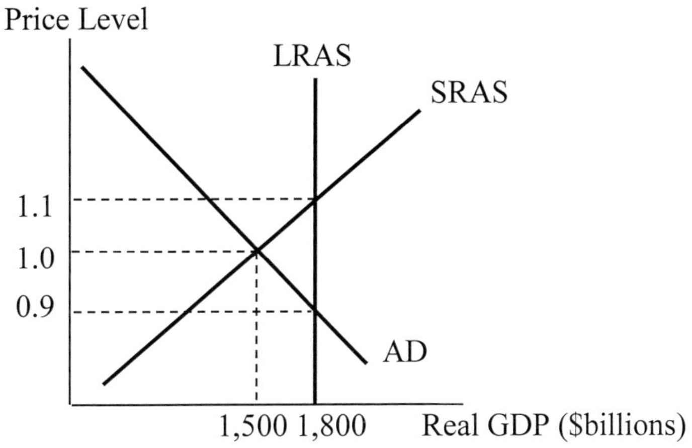

If the economy represented by the above graph is able to achieve full employment, real GDP will be equal to (1) $____________ billion. In short-run equilibrium, real GDP will be equal to (2) $____________ billion and the price level will be (3) _________. This economy's short-run equilibrium implies the existence of a/an (4) ________________________________ gap.

If the economy is initially in short-run equilibrium when economic events cause aggregate demand (AD) to increase and move to full employment, the price level will increase to (5) __________ and real GDP will increase to (6) $_____________ billion. If the economy is initially in short-run equilibrium when falling wage rates cause the short-run aggregate supply (SRAS) curve to shift to the right such that the price level decreases to 0.9, real GDP will increase to (7) $______________ billion. If real GDP is equal to $1,500 billion, the unemployment rate is (8) ___________________ than the natural rate of unemployment, so there is a (9) ____________________ in the labor market, and the wage rate is expected to (10) _______________________________, ceteris paribus.

NAME____ SECTION#______________
Print Last Name, First Name

AD/SRAS SHIFTS

INSTRUCTIONS: Draw graphs with aggregate demand (AD) and upward-sloping short-run aggregate supply (SRAS) curves to illustrate the short-run impact of each of the following on the equilibrium price level (P) and the equilibrium level of real output (GDP). In each case, indicate whether the unemployment rate (U) will rise or fall as the economy adjusts to a new short-run equilibrium.

1. Investment spending falls due to higher interest rates

2. The demand for U.S. exports increases due to increased foreign income

3. Energy prices fall due to the development of less expensive alternative fuels

4. A booming stock market causes an increase in consumer wealth

NAME____ SECTION#________________
Print Last Name, First Name

AGGREGATE DEMAND/AGGREGATE SUPPLY MODEL

Use the graph below to answer questions 1 – 2:

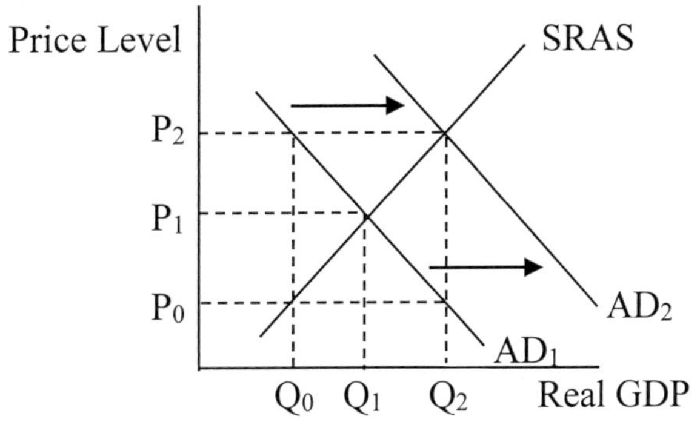

1. Suppose that the demand for all goods and services in the economy increases from AD_1 to AD_2. What is the new short-run equilibrium price level (P) and quantity of output (Q = real GDP)?
   a. P_0 and Q_0
   b. P_1 and Q_1
   c. P_1 and Q_2
   d. P_2 and Q_2

2. Which of the following events would most likely cause the increase in aggregate demand shown above, i.e. the shift from AD_1 to AD_2?
   a. A decrease in the price level
   b. A decrease in household wealth
   c. A decrease in consumer confidence
   d. A decrease in interest rates

3. Assuming the short-run aggregate supply curve is upward sloping, an adverse (negative) supply shock while aggregate demand remains unchanged, results in a __________ price level, ____________ output (real GDP) and ___________ unemployment.
   a. higher; lower; higher
   b. lower; lower; higher
   c. lower; higher; lower
   d. higher; higher; lower

4. The economy's natural rate of unemployment is:
   a. the unemployment rate associated with the full-employment level of output.
   b. greater than zero because there is some structural and frictional unemployment even when the economy is at full-employment real GDP.
   c. equal to the actual rate of unemployment in the long run, according to many mainstream economists.
   d. All of the above are true

NAME____ SECTION#______________

Print Last Name, First Name

5. An increase in investment spending causes the aggregate ________ curve to shift to the ________ in the short run, ceteris paribus.
   a. demand; right
   b. demand; left
   c. supply; right
   d. supply; left

Use the graph below to answer question 6:

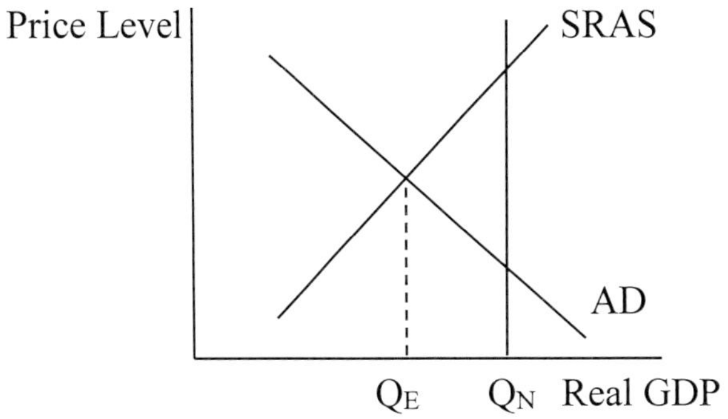

6. The diagram above shows an economy experiencing:
   a. an inflationary gap.
   b. a recessionary gap.
   c. short-run equilibrium at full-employment.
   d. long-run equilibrium.

7. If the short-run equilibrium level of real GDP is greater than full-employment real GDP, then the economy is in a(n) __________ gap with unemployment _________ the natural rate of unemployment.
   a. inflationary; above
   b. inflationary; below
   c. recessionary; above
   d. recessionary; below

8. A breakthrough in technology used in production that shifts SRAS to the right results in:
   a. a lower price level at a higher level of real GDP.
   b. a lower price level at a lower level of real GDP.
   c. a higher price level at a lower level of real GDP.
   d. a higher price level at a higher level of real GDP.

9. If the economy is initially in equilibrium at the full-employment level of real GDP and a growing economy boosts consumer and investor confidence, ceteris paribus, the aggregate demand curve will shift to the ________ causing the price level to ________.
   a. left; rise
   b. right; fall
   c. left; fall
   d. right; rise

10. When the actual level of output produced is less than the full-employment level of output:
   a. the actual unemployment rate exceeds the natural unemployment rate.
   b. the actual unemployment rate is less than the natural unemployment rate.
   c. the actual unemployment rate is equal to the natural unemployment rate.
   d. the economy is in long-run equilibrium.

NAME____ SECTION#____________

Print Last Name, First Name

AGGREGATE SUPPLY/AGGREGATE DEMAND MODEL

Use the graph below to answer questions 1 – 2:

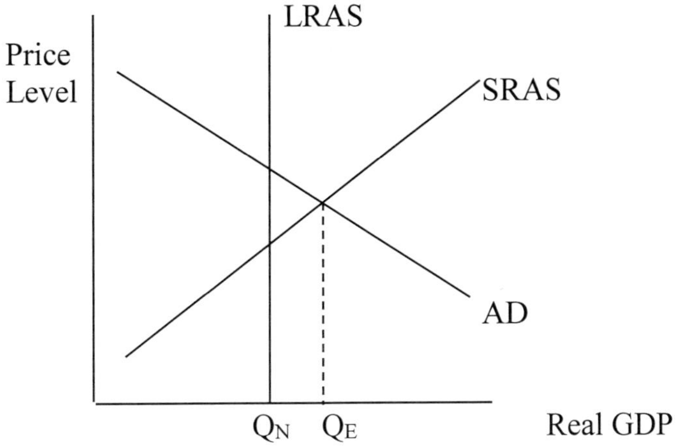

1. This graph depicts an economy:
   a. in a recessionary gap, so unemployment is below the natural rate.
   b. in an inflationary gap, so unemployment is above of the natural rate.
   c. in a recessionary gap, so unemployment is above of the natural rate.
   d. in an inflationary gap, so unemployment is below the natural rate.

2. Which of the following could cause the economy depicted above to move to equilibrium at full-employment output?
   a. A rightward shift of the SRAS curve
   b. A leftward shift of the SRAS curve
   c. A rightward shift of AD curve
   d. All of the above will move this economy to equilibrium at full employment.

3. In the long run, when prices are perfectly flexible:
   a. aggregate supply is vertical and a market economy is self-correcting.
   b. a market economy cannot self-correct.
   c. government will be required to set prices to maintain equilibrium.
   d. changes in aggregate demand cause equilibrium real GDP to change.

4. An increase in consumer confidence when the SRAS curve is upward sloping:
   a. leads to an increase in the price level but has no impact on real GDP.
   b. has no impact on the price level but leads to an increase in real GDP.
   c. leads to an increase in both the price level and real GDP.
   d. has no impact on the price level or real GDP.

NAME____ SECTION#______________

Print Last Name, First Name

5. In the long run, if continued increases in aggregate demand are not matched by similar increases in aggregate supply, then, ceteris paribus:
   a. the full-employment level of real GDP will increase.
   b. a recessionary gap will emerge.
   c. the price level will increase.
   d. the inflation rate will be greater than the unemployment rate.

6. The vertical long-run aggregate supply curve implies that:
   a. changes in aggregate demand will have no effect on the price level.
   b. the short-run aggregate supply curve is also vertical.
   c. natural or full-employment real GDP does not depend on the price level in the long run.
   d. natural or full-employment real GDP is the same as equilibrium real GDP in the short run.

7. A rightward shift of the long-run aggregate supply curve illustrates:
   a. economic growth.
   b. a recessionary gap.
   c. an inflationary gap.
   d. a decrease in natural real GDP.

8. When the economy is in a recessionary gap:
   a. there is a surplus of labor.
   b. there is a shortage of labor.
   c. it is producing a real GDP level that is greater than natural real GDP.
   d. the unemployment rate is less than the natural unemployment rate.

9. If the actual unemployment rate is less than the natural unemployment rate:
   a. a recessionary gap exists and wages are likely to rise.
   b. an inflationary gap exists and wages are likely to rise.
   c. a recessionary gap exists and wages are likely to fall.
   d. an inflationary gap exists and wages are likely to fall.

10. An economy in long-run equilibrium is producing:
    a. a level of real GDP that is greater than its natural real GDP.
    b. where both the price level and real output are maximized.
    c. a level of real GDP equal to its natural real GDP.
    d. in the vertical range of aggregate demand.

CHAPTER 7 Classical Economics and a Self-Regulating Economy

Early macroeconomic thought, which formally began with the publication of *An Inquiry Into the Nature and Causes of the Wealth of Nations* by Adam Smith in 1776, is now referred to as the **Classical** model. In *The Wealth of Nations,* Smith explains the nature of markets and how markets, if left alone, will automatically move resources to their highest valued uses without the need for any government direction. While Adam Smith addressed many important issues in his influential book, the focus here will be on his treatment of markets and the workings of a market-based economy. The Classical model was refined during the 19th century by many economists, such as David Ricardo, Jean Baptiste Say, Thomas Malthus, and John Stuart Mill.

The basic assumption of the Classical model is that all prices in the economy – output prices, wages and other input prices, and interest rates – are perfectly flexible. Another assumption is that people have a motive for exchange. In the case of households, the motive for demand is satisfaction and in the case of businesses, the motive for supply is profit. If output prices are flexible, then shortages in output markets will clear as prices rise and surpluses will be eliminated as prices fall. Continual surpluses are not likely to occur in a particular market because suppliers, if allowed to pursue their own self-interest (profit), will not continue to devote resources to outputs that people do not want and are most likely to move resources to areas in the economy where demand is higher, and hence profits are greater. The "invisible hand" of the market will cause resources to flow naturally to their highest valued uses.

In the Classical model, the labor market is also based on the idea that markets, if left alone, will automatically move toward equilibrium. The wage rate, which is the price of labor, is assumed to be perfectly flexible. Unemployment occurs, but it will not persist for long periods because unemployment represents surplus labor. If there is a surplus of labor, the unemployed labor will bid wages down and wages will fall and the market will move toward equilibrium. If there is a shortage of labor, business firms will offer higher wages to hire workers away from other firms and wages will rise and move toward equilibrium.

The Classical credit market (loanable funds market) assumes that households save, but only if paid to do so. Interest is viewed as the reward for abstaining from current consumption; households are willing to give up current consumption only if they believe that doing so will make them better off in the future. Households are better off when paid interest on savings. Household saving represents the supply of loanable funds. Businesses are considered to be the primary borrowers, or demanders, of household savings. Interest then, is the price of money and what businesses pay households to borrow funds to finance investment spending. Once again, the market is assumed to adjust and move toward equilibrium. If the interest rate is above equilibrium, there is a surplus of loanable funds, and the interest rate will fall. If the interest rate is below equilibrium, there is a shortage of loanable funds and the interest rate will rise. Flexible interest rates, then, adjust to equate household saving and business investment spending.

One of the central tenets of the classical model is **Say's Law**, which holds that supply creates its own demand. Income not spent by households (saved) is funneled through financial markets and borrowed by business firms to finance investment. As a result, it is very unlikely that aggregate spending will be too low to support aggregate output. The model effectively ruled out negative demand shocks as a source of economic fluctuation but went on to say that, even if demand is weak, firms will respond by lowering product prices to sell everything they have produced and unemployed workers will offer to work for a lower wage. Under these conditions, not only will markets move toward equilibrium, they move toward equilibrium at a full-employment level of output. Classical theorists did not believe that a situation in which firms began lowering production levels and laying off workers for long periods was likely to occur, so it was unnecessary to plan for a government solution to an economy-wide glut (surplus), or recession. The upcoming pages use basic aggregate supply and aggregate demand graphs to show the adjustment that occurs in the overall economy when the economy is not at a full-employment equilibrium in the short run.

Given the assumptions of flexible prices, wages, and interest rates, and Say's Law being true, the model concludes that government action is unnecessary because markets automatically clear and move toward full-employment equilibrium. The Classical theorists advocated a ***laissez-faire*** policy, which roughly translates as "allow them to do" or leave them alone. In other words, government should leave households and businesses alone to pursue their own self-interest and outcomes are likely to be more efficient than if government interfered in markets.

While the general conclusion of the model is that there is no need for government to intervene in markets, most Classical economists still see a role for government in a market economy. The federal government maintains responsibility for national security, the nation's infrastructure, international relations, and other broad areas, but leaves the pursuit of full employment and economic growth to free market forces. Within this policy framework, government must avoid policies that might interfere with the workings of a market economy, such as price controls or excessive taxation. The Classical School of Thought can be regarded as a precursor to many modern schools of thought, such as Supply-Side Theory.

Today, economists do not simply assume that prices and wages are always perfectly flexible, so modern analysis must account for what might happen in the short run. Many agree that the Classical model provides a good description of how the economy operates in the long run, but it is also necessary to understand how the economy can move from a short-run equilibrium, in which there may be either a recessionary gap or an inflationary gap, to a long-run equilibrium, where the economy is at full employment.

<u>The Self-Regulating Economy: Adjusting to Gaps</u>

The Classical writers did not make use of aggregate demand and aggregate supply graphs to explain how the economy works. However, this simple model is a useful tool for illustrating how a market economy with perfectly flexible prices automatically adjusts to close recessionary and inflationary gaps.

Suppose the economy is initially in long-run equilibrium, when a negative demand shock occurs, causing AD to fall, or shift to the left. The explanation for the negative demand shock might be any number of things, such as reduced wealth due to a stock market crash or lower consumer confidence, but the consequence of a negative demand shock is straightforward: business firms will experience weakened sales. How do firms react to weakened sales? Two possibilities occur to most people – firms may react by lowering product prices or by lowering production and, with it, employment. The most reasonable prediction is that there will be a combination of lower product prices and lower production levels, especially since in the short run, firms may not be able to lower wages and other input costs, creating a reluctance to accept lower product prices.

The negative demand shock is illustrated by a leftward shift of the aggregate demand curve. As AD shifts to the left, the economy adjusts to a new short-run equilibrium in which the price level is lower and the equilibrium level of real GDP, Q_E, has fallen below the full-employment level of real GDP, Q_N, with unemployment now above the natural rate ($U > U_N$). In other words, the AD shift has created a Recessionary Gap and actual equilibrium real GDP is less than natural (full-employment) real GDP ($Q_E < Q_N$), as illustrated in the graph below.

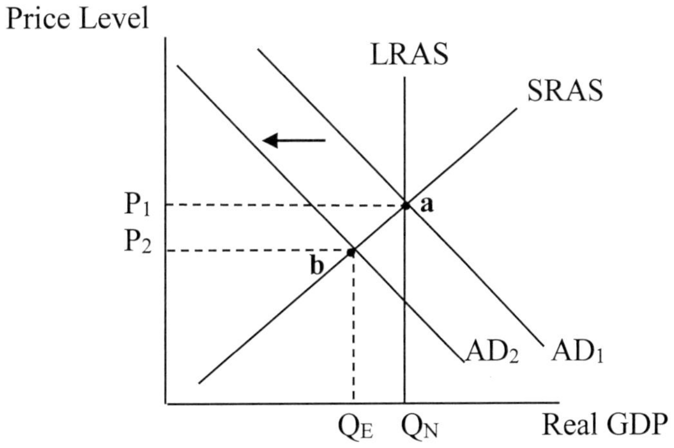

The adjustment from point **a** to point **b** indicates that the economy is entering a downturn, with downward pressure on prices, reduced output, and higher unemployment. If this downturn is considered serious enough, it will be designated a recession.

According to Classical economics, though, the economy will not remain at point **b** for a long period of time. The self-regulating mechanism will play an important role. If the economy is currently operating at point **b**, then the rate of unemployment is above the natural rate. Over time, when these workers are unable to find jobs, they will lower their wage expectations and become more willing to accept reduced wage rates. Workers who retain their jobs during this time will also become more willing to accept pay cuts in order to avoid unemployment. As long as the economy is experiencing a recessionary gap, there is a surplus of workers and there will be downward pressure on wages.

Although it may not happen immediately, eventually wages will begin to fall to clear labor market surpluses. As wages and other input prices fall, the cost of producing output falls, and lower costs of production cause SRAS to increase. Once input prices fall, the SRAS curve shifts to the right, moving the economy back toward full-employment equilibrium, as illustrated in the graph on the next page.

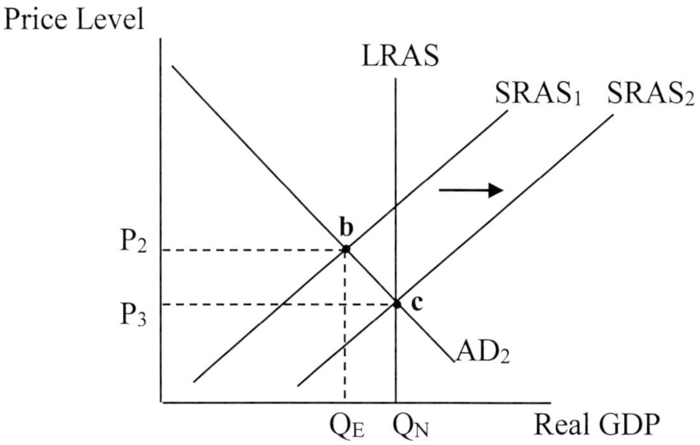

Lower input prices lead to a rightward shift of SRAS, from $SRAS_1$ to $SRAS_2$, causing the economy's short-run equilibrium to move from point **b** to point **c**. The forces causing this adjustment continue until the economy is back in long-run equilibrium at Q_N where the unemployment rate is again equal to the natural rate ($U = U_N$). Notice that the price level has fallen and is at P_3 when the adjustment is complete. The lower wages paid to labor can now purchase full-employment output (Q_N) because output prices have also fallen. In a self-regulating economy, recessionary gaps are automatically eliminated by increases in short-run aggregate supply.

This model does not reflect a real-world tendency for inflation that comes from cost-of-living increases in wages over time. In practice, what the model shows as decreasing prices and wages may simply be a decrease in the rate of growth in wages and prices that occurs over time. The price level may actually fall if the recession is severe enough, as happened in the 1930s when the price level fell approximately 25 percent between 1929 and 1933. Less severe recessions are usually characterized by lower rates of inflation and lower rates of increase in nominal wages, but it is now extremely rare for the price level to fall, indicating deflation.

Next, suppose the economy is initially in long-run equilibrium, when a positive demand shock occurs, causing AD to increase or shift to the right. The explanation for the positive demand shock might be any number of things, such as an increase in wealth from a stock market boom or higher consumer confidence, but the consequence of a positive demand shock is straightforward: business firms will experience stronger sales. How do firms react to stronger sales? The two possibilities that occur to most people is for firms to react by raising product prices or by raising production and, with it, employment. The most reasonable prediction is that there will be a combination of higher product prices and higher production levels, especially since in the short run, firms may not have to pay higher input costs, creating a desire to increase output while profit margins are high.

The increase in aggregate demand results in a short-run equilibrium for which the level of output is greater than the natural level, resulting in an inflationary gap. The increase in aggregate demand is illustrated by a rightward shift of the aggregate demand curve and the impact of the increase can be analyzed using the aggregate demand and aggregate supply model.

As AD shifts to the right, the economy adjusts to a new short-run equilibrium in which the price level is higher and the equilibrium level of real GDP (Q_E) is above the full-employment level of real GDP (Q_N), with unemployment now below the natural rate ($U < U_N$). In other words, the AD shift has created an Inflationary Gap ($Q_E > Q_N$), as illustrated in the graph below.

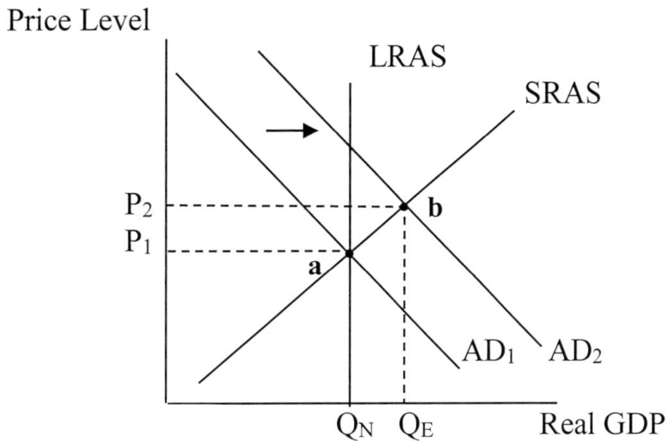

The adjustment from point **a** to point **b** indicates that the economy is entering an upturn, with upward pressure on prices, increased output, and lower unemployment. News reports about the state of the economy will probably reflect growing concern about the rate of inflation.

According to Classical economics, though, the economy will not remain at point **b** because the self-regulating mechanism will play an important role. If the economy is currently operating at point **b**, the rate of unemployment is below the natural rate. There is a shortage of workers and firms that desire to hire more labor in order to increase output will begin to bid for available workers by offering higher wages.

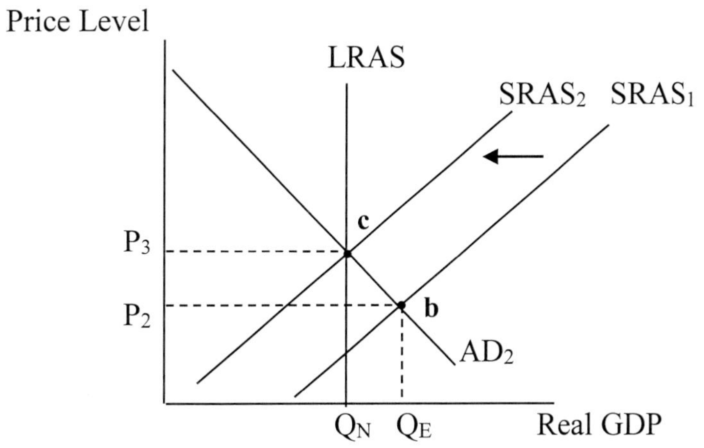

Higher wages and other input prices lead to increased costs of production and $SRAS_1$ shifts left to $SRAS_2$, causing the economy's short-run equilibrium to move from point **b** to point **c**. The forces causing this adjustment continue until the economy is back in long-run equilibrium at Q_N, where the unemployment rate is again equal to the natural rate ($U = U_N$). The inflationary gap is closed by a decrease in short-run aggregate supply.

Classical economists argued that government action is not necessary to close a recessionary gap due to the self-regulating mechanism, but the existence of an inflationary gap is a little different. The self-regulating mechanism will eliminate the gap over time, but the process involves a period of cost-push inflation following the initial period of demand-pull inflation. In this case, policymakers may choose to intervene in an effort to prevent excessive inflation. The approach to using active policy to close an inflationary gap, or even to prevent an inflationary gap from emerging, will be considered in the chapter on monetary policy.

The discussion of Classical Economics presented here represents a modern interpretation that relies very heavily on the AD/AS model. Classical Economics actually predates supply and demand analysis so the explanation presented in this book would not be found in original sources, such as Adam Smith's *Wealth of Nations* (1776) or John Stuart Mill's *Principles of Political Economy* (1848). Modern tools of analysis allow for a more technical explanation of events, but the original analysis of the Classical economists led them to similar conclusions. Today, many economists believe that the economy's long-run behavior is more important than temporary, short-run deviations from full employment, and these economists focus more on policies designed to promote long-term growth. There are also many economists today who believe that what happens in the short run is just as important as, if not more important than, what happens in the long run. Keynesian economists argue that government can manage the economy's short-run behavior to promote full employment and price stability. The basic Keynesian model is presented in the next chapter.

F.A. Hayek is an economist associated with the Austrian School of Thought. He was awarded the Nobel Prize in Economics in 1974 and was strongly opposed to the Keynesian approach. He argued that each economic bust (downturn) was caused by an earlier government-generated boom. Economic booms, according to Austrian thinkers like Hayek, are created when banks expand credit, causing the money supply to increase and shifting aggregate demand rightward. The expansionary monetary policy creates artificially low interest rates, leading to overinvestment. This can often manifest as a bubble in the stock market or the construction industry. Because of the economic boom, employment is strong and wages are up, leading to increased consumption. As domestic incomes and product prices rise, a country will increase its imports and reduce exports, leading to a growing trade deficit.

Austrians believe that every economic boom carries the seeds of its own destruction. Eventually, a crisis of confidence or excessive debt causes spenders to become nervous, and the booming economy quickly begins to unwind. When government steps in to take action designed to prevent the downturn, they are only postponing the inevitable and making it potentially worse. When the economy is in the midst of a severe downturn, it is easy to argue that government policy has the potential to bring the economy back up again. Austrian economists advocate a hands-off approach for government in order to avoid the boom and bust cycle entirely.

NAME____ SECTION #_____________
Print Last Name, First Name

THE CLASSICAL MODEL

1. The basic Classical model and the notion that a market economy is self-regulating began with:
   a. the debate between David Ricardo and Thomas Malthus.
   b. the refining of Say's Law in the late 1700s.
   c. the writing of John Stuart Mill's *On Liberty*.
   d. the publication of Adam Smith's *The Wealth of Nations*.

2. The Classical model is based on the assumption that:
   a. prices, wages, and interest rates are flexible.
   b. an increase in demand creates an equal increase in supply.
   c. a market economy, if left alone, is not likely to reach a full-employment equilibrium.
   d. a general overproduction, or "glut", of goods and services occurs when there is voluntary unemployment.

Use the graph below to answer questions 3 and 4:

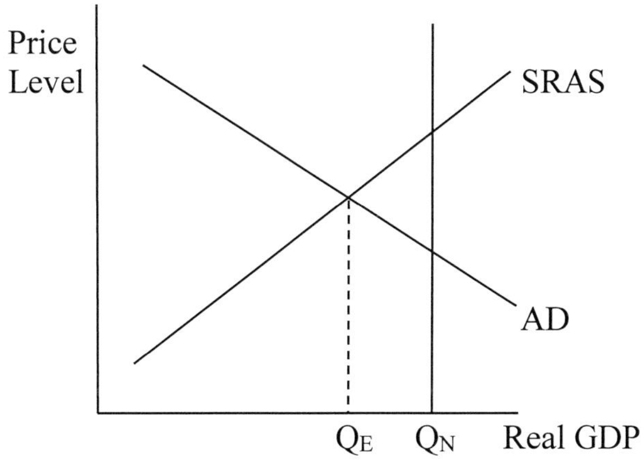

3. The economy depicted in the above graph is experiencing a(n) ________ gap. The current rate of unemployment is ________ than the natural rate of unemployment.
   a. recessionary; higher
   b. recessionary; lower
   c. inflationary; higher
   d. inflationary; lower

4. The Classical approach argues that the above gap:
   a. will automatically close because wages and other input prices will rise and SRAS will shift to the left.
   b. will automatically close because wages and other input prices will fall and SRAS will shift to the right.
   c. can only be closed if government intervenes forcing it to close.
   d. cannot occur in a market economy.

NAME____ SECTION #____________

Print Last Name, First Name

5. Which of the following is ***not*** an assumption of the Classical model?
   a. Wages are flexible
   b. Demand creates its own supply
   c. Output prices decrease when surpluses occur
   d. Say's Law is true

6. According to Say's Law:
   a. involuntary unemployment is likely to occur and persist in a market economy.
   b. demand and supply are only related in the long run.
   c. supply creates its own demand.
   d. prices and wages are not flexible downward.

7. In the Classical model, if the amount of saving exceeds the amount of investment, then:
   a. interest rates will rise to move the credit market to equilibrium.
   b. interest rates will fall to move the credit market to equilibrium.
   c. households will increase their saving to take advantage of higher interest rates.
   d. businesses will increase their borrowing to take advantage of higher interest rates.

8. When the wage rate is ***below*** the equilibrium wage rate, the Classical model argues that:
   a. downward pressure on wages will eliminate the surplus in the labor market.
   b. downward pressure on wages will eliminate the shortage in the labor market.
   c. upward pressure on wages will eliminate the surplus in the labor market.
   d. upward pressure on wages will eliminate the shortage in the labor market.

9. The Classical model leads to the conclusion that:
   a. government intervention is necessary for a market economy to achieve a full-employment equilibrium.
   b. there is no automatic mechanism that ensures that a market economy is self-regulating.
   c. government should take a *laissez-faire* approach with respect to the macroeconomy.
   d. there is no role for government in a market economy.

10. A market economy is self-regulating only if:
   a. prices in all markets can rise to eliminate shortages and fall to eliminate surpluses.
   b. Say's Law is not true.
   c. government takes an active role in managing the macroeconomy.
   d. all of the above occur simultaneously.

NAME____ SECTION #____________

Print Last Name, First Name

THE SELF-REGULATING ECONOMY

1. For an economy to be self-regulating:
   a. policymakers must be able to control the position of the aggregate demand curve.
   b. wages and other input prices must be flexible.
   c. the short-run aggregate supply curve must be vertical.
   d. equilibrium real GDP must always be equal to full-employment real GDP.

2. Economists who believe that the economy is self-regulating generally advocate:
   a. active government intervention in the economy.
   b. using monetary policy as a tool for fine-tuning the economy.
   c. a laissez-faire approach to macroeconomic policy.
   d. using fiscal policy as a tool for fine-tuning the economy.

Use the graph below to answer question 3:

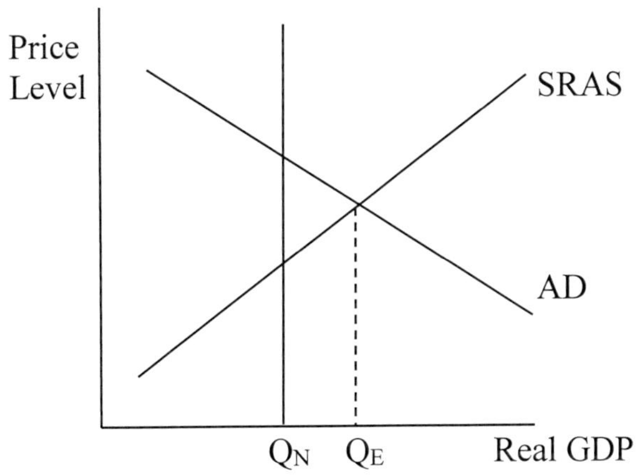

3. The economy depicted in the above graph is experiencing a(n) ________ gap. The current rate of unemployment is ________ than the natural rate of unemployment.
   a. inflationary; higher
   b. recessionary; higher
   c. inflationary; lower
   d. recessionary; lower

4. When the economy's rate of unemployment is ***higher*** than the natural rate, this creates:
   a. downward pressure on wages to eliminate the surplus in the labor market.
   b. downward pressure on wages to eliminate the shortage in the labor market.
   c. upward pressure on wages to eliminate the surplus in the labor market.
   d. upward pressure on wages to eliminate the shortage in the labor market.

5. If actual (equilibrium) real GDP is less than the full-employment, or natural, level of real GDP, then wages and other input prices are expected to:
   a. fall and SRAS to shift to the left until long-run equilibrium is achieved.
   b. fall and SRAS to shift to the right until long-run equilibrium is achieved.
   c. rise and SRAS to shift to the left until long-run equilibrium is achieved.
   d. rise and SRAS to shift to the right until long-run equilibrium is achieved.

NAME____ SECTION #______________
Print Last Name, First Name

6. In a self-regulating economy, inflationary gaps are automatically eliminated in the long run by:
   a. decreases in wage rates that cause short-run aggregate supply to shift rightward.
   b. decreases in wage rates that cause short-run aggregate supply to shift leftward.
   c. increases in wage rates that cause short-run aggregate supply to shift rightward.
   d. increases in wage rates that cause short-run aggregate supply to shift leftward.

7. Assume the economy is initially in equilibrium at the full-employment level of real GDP. If businesses and consumers become pessimistic regarding future economic conditions, ceteris paribus, the aggregate demand curve will shift to the ________, causing the level of output to ________.
   a. left; fall
   b. right; fall
   c. left; rise
   d. right; rise

8. Economists that advocate a macroeconomic policy of *laissez-faire*:
   a. believe the economy is self-regulating only if the government intervenes to move the economy to equilibrium at natural real GDP.
   b. believe the economy is self-regulating and will automatically move to equilibrium at natural real GDP in the long run.
   c. also advocate central planning and government control of resources.
   d. also advocate active government intervention in the economy.

9. Which of the following summarizes the process for closing a recessionary gap if the economy is self-regulating?
   a. Labor shortages put upward pressure on wages, which leads to higher costs of production and a decrease in short-run aggregate supply
   b. Labor shortages put downward pressure on wages, which leads to increases in employment and spending and an increase in aggregate demand
   c. Unemployed resources put upward pressure on the price level, which leads to higher wages, increases in spending and an increase in aggregate demand
   d. Unemployed resources put downward pressure on resource prices, which leads to lower costs of production and an increase in short-run aggregate supply

10. Which of the following summarizes the process for closing an inflationary gap if the economy is self-regulating?
   a. Labor shortages put upward pressure on wages, which leads to higher costs of production and a decrease in short-run aggregate supply
   b. Labor shortages put downward pressure on wages, which leads to increases in employment and spending and an increase in aggregate demand
   c. Unemployed resources put upward pressure on the price level, which leads to higher wages, increases in spending and an increase in aggregate demand
   d. Unemployed resources put downward pressure on resource prices, which leads to lower costs of production and an increase in short-run aggregate supply

NAME____ SECTION #____________
Print Last Name, First Name

THE CLASSICAL MODEL

INSTRUCTIONS: Fill in the following blanks with the correct word or phrase.

An Inquiry Into the Nature and Causes of the Wealth of Nations was written by (1) ____________________________. The basic assumption of the Classical model is that all prices in the economy are perfectly (2) ______________________. One of the central tenets of the Classical model is (3) ________________________, which holds that supply creates its own demand. The Classical theorists advocated a (4) _______________________________ policy, allowing households and businesses to pursue their own self interest. Most modern economists agree that the Classical model provides a good description of how the economy operates in the (5) ________________________, but it is also necessary to understand how the economy adjusts from a short-run equilibrium to a long-run equilibrium, where the economy is at (6) ____.

According to the Classical model, if the economy is initially in long-run equilibrium, and a negative event causes the aggregate demand curve to shift to the left, business firms will experience (7) ____________________ sales, leading some to (8) ______________________ production and employment. Although the decrease in aggregate demand causes the economy to adjust to a new short-run equilibrium for which output is below full employment, this is a temporary situation. In the long run, assuming no action is taken by policymakers, wages will (9) __________________ and the SRAS curve will shift to the (10) __________________ until full employment is restored.

NAME____ SECTION #______________
Print Last Name, First Name

RECESSIONARY AND INFLATIONARY GAPS IN A SELF-REGULATING ECONOMY

1. Add an aggregate demand (AD) curve and a short-run aggregate supply (SRAS) curve to the graph below to illustrate an economy experiencing a **recessionary gap,** and fill in the blanks with either *above* or *below*. Label all curves, the equilibrium price level (P_E), and equilibrium real GDP (Q_E).

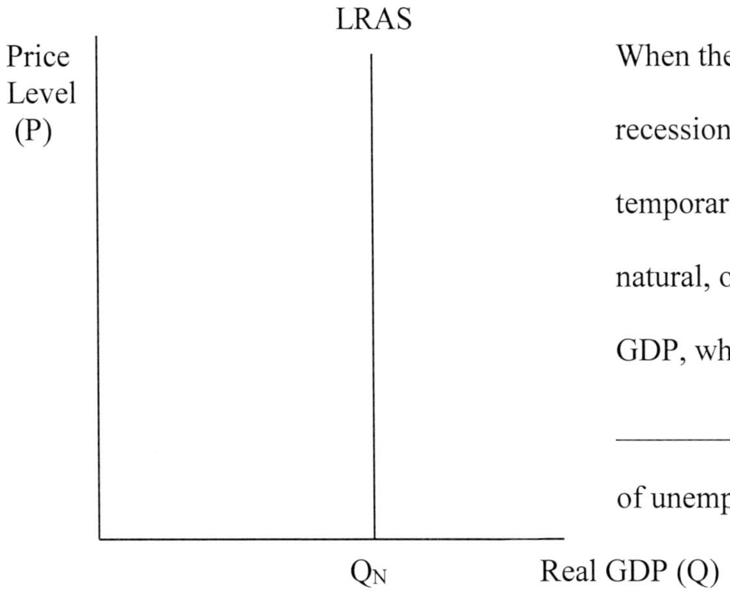

When the economy experiences a recessionary gap, real GDP is temporarily __________________ natural, or full-employment, real GDP, while the rate of unemployment is __________________ the natural rate of unemployment.

2. Add an aggregate demand (AD) curve and a short-run aggregate supply (SRAS) curve to the graph below to illustrate an economy experiencing an **inflationary gap,** and fill in the blanks with either *above* or *below*. Label all curves, the equilibrium price level (P_E), and equilibrium real GDP (Q_E).

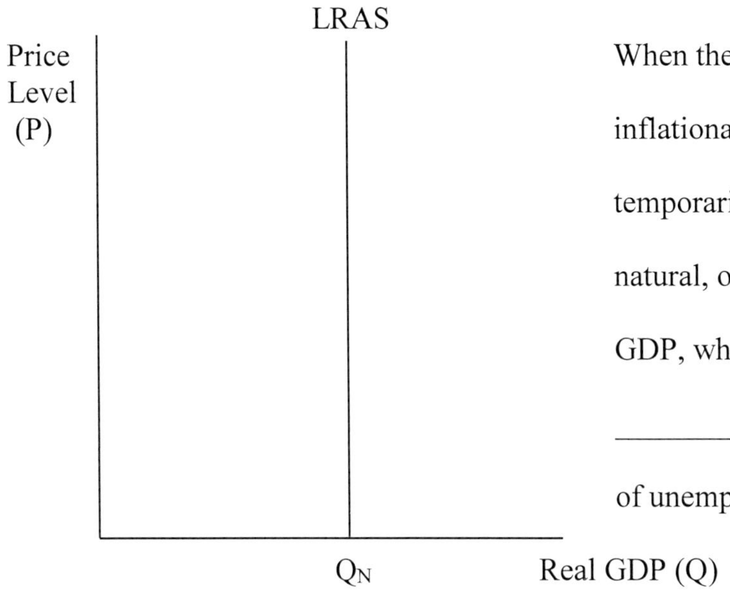

When the economy experiences an inflationary gap, real GDP is temporarily ____________________ natural, or full-employment, real GDP, while the rate of unemployment is __________________ the natural rate of unemployment.

CHAPTER 8 Keynesian Economics

The general belief that the economy is self-regulating, calling for a laissez-faire approach to macroeconomic policy, was challenged infrequently until the Great Depression in the 1930s. In his book, *The General Theory of Employment, Interest, and Money* (1936), John Maynard Keynes disagreed with the classical belief that a market economy automatically moves itself to a full-employment equilibrium. Keynes believed that the economy could settle at equilibrium below full employment because aggregate spending may not be sufficient to purchase all that is produced at full employment. He offered a new view that, without proper management by policymakers, the economy may follow a path of instability with frequent and severe economic downturns. The new view that government can and should play an active role in managing the macroeconomy is presented by the **Keynesian** model.

Observing the growing ranks of the unemployed and the reluctance of employers to hire them even at lower wages during the early 1930s, Keynes disagreed with the two cornerstones of the Classical Model: Say's Law and flexible prices. Keynes developed the important distinction between the long run and the short run and set out to build a model of short-run equilibrium. According to this model, equilibrium output and income are determined by aggregate spending in the short run, so the focus of the Keynesian model is on the components of aggregate spending and aggregate demand: consumption spending (C), investment spending (I), government spending (G), and foreign spending (EX – IM). The Keynesian model looks at what motivates each sector of the economy to spend or not spend, and the impact on those decisions on aggregate demand and the economy as a whole. In contrast to the Classical model, which focuses on the long run and automatic changes in aggregate supply, the Keynesian model is a short-run model with the focus on aggregate demand.

Keynes found that even though consumption is the largest component of aggregate spending, investment is the most volatile and therefore the source of many fluctuations in aggregate spending. He regarded government spending and taxing (fiscal policy) as a potential tool for stabilizing overall spending and recognized that the role of foreign spending grows with globalization. Because the Keynesian model rests on the assumption that prices are not always flexible, it is not a very good way to approach the study of an inflationary economy. This model is appropriate for the study of an economy experiencing an overall downturn resulting from weak demand which, according to Keynesians, is an accurate description of the Great Depression.

The legacy from the Depression era, combined with the new way of thinking embodied by the Keynesian model, is an attitude toward government policy that is in sharp contrast to the *laissez-faire* philosophy of the Classicals. In modern times, the popularity of a President often depends on the state of the economy. When the economy is doing well, people often credit the current administration; when it is doing poorly, they tend to blame the current administration. Congressional candidates are expected to demonstrate an advanced understanding of economic policy issues, and the chair of the Board of Governors of the Federal Reserve System is considered by many to be the most powerful person in the country from an economic standpoint. There is a general attitude that government can and should improve the economy's performance, and the debate is sharply focused on how best to accomplish this.

Recall that if the economy is initially in long-run equilibrium and a negative demand shock occurs, AD falls, creating a recessionary gap. The emphasis in the previous chapter was on how the economy will eventually return to full-employment equilibrium on its own due to changes in short-run aggregate supply, but this chapter considers whether government policy can be used to restore full employment more quickly.

A rightward shift of the AD curve is another way to reach full employment, and government can cause AD to increase using either fiscal stimulation (via increased government spending or tax cuts) or monetary expansion, which involves implementing policy to lower interest rates. The specifics of government policy options are addressed in other chapters because there are a lot of details involved in understanding fiscal policy and monetary policy. This chapter focuses on the basic elements of Keynesian analysis and sets the stage for policy analysis.

The economy depicted in the graph below is experiencing a recessionary gap. Equilibrium output is below the full-employment level of real GDP, and the unemployment rate is above the natural rate. This unemployment is the result of inadequate demand for goods and services throughout the economy: people do not plan to spend enough to purchase all of the output that could be produced at full employment. At this point in time, there are two options for addressing the recessionary gap: 1) waiting for the economy's self-regulating mechanism to eliminate this recessionary gap (remember, eventually lower wages will cause SRAS to shift to the right) or 2) government using its policy tools to shift AD to the right until equilibrium output is back to full employment.

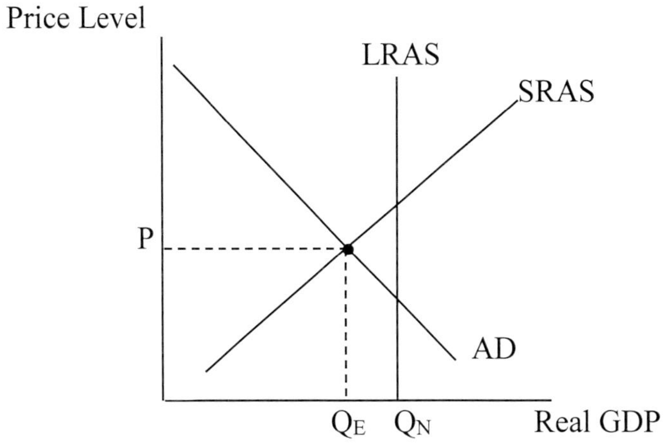

In order to implement policy to increase aggregate demand, government policy makers must know what motivates each sector of the economy to increase spending. The Keynesian approach to closing a recessionary gap will entail estimating the response of households, businesses, and foreigners to potential changes in government spending and/or taxing and using that knowledge to help cause an increase in aggregate demand.

The graph below shows the impact of an increase in aggregate demand. If policymakers can successfully cause AD to increase, AD_1 shifts out to the right to AD_2 and the economy will move from equilibrium at point **a** to equilibrium at point **b**. This adjustment is accompanied by a higher price level as P_1 increases to P_2. Higher production and output occurs and equilibrium output increases from Q_E to Q_N. Increasing output requires more employment and the unemployment rate falls. Once at point **b**, output is equal to full-employment real GDP and the unemployment rate is equal to the natural rate ($U = U_N$).

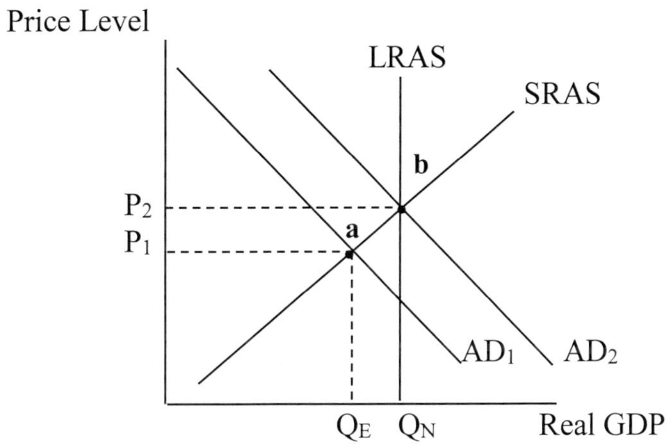

Historical evidence shows that as the economy moves from a recession to full employment, the price level increases, as from P_1 to P_2 in the above graph. The presentation of the Keynesian model provided in the next section simplifies the analysis by assuming that the price level remains fixed when AD shifts. Although this is not realistic, it is a temporary assumption that can be relaxed later. Assuming a fixed price level, the short-run aggregate supply curve is drawn as a horizontal line. If the price level is fixed, increases in AD lead to increases in output and employment without putting upward pressure on the price level, as shown below.

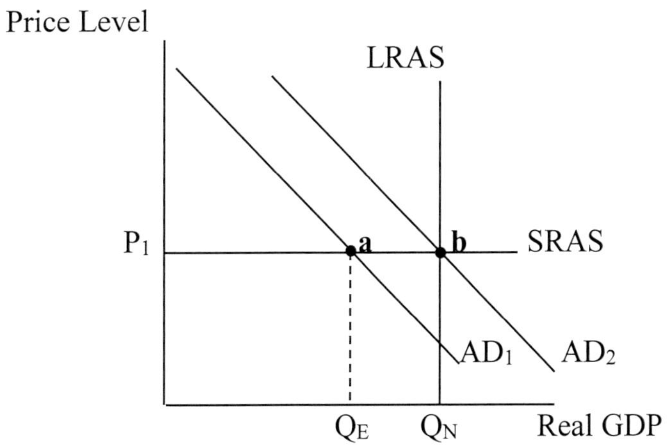

The development of the basic Keynesian model in the following pages assumes it is a fixed-price model. This means increases in spending, income and output that occur when AD increases represent increases in real spending, real income, and real output.

The Keynesian Model

John Maynard Keynes focused on the economy's behavior in the short run, unlike the Classical theorists who had argued that long-run equilibrium naturally occurs at the economy's full employment level of output and employment. According to Keynes, short-term fluctuations of real GDP, which is also called real output, occur primarily because of shifts in the aggregate demand curve that generate different levels of production and employment. Assuming that the short-run aggregate supply curve is horizontal, or equivalently, that the price level is fixed, simplifies the mathematics involved with estimating the new equilibrium output caused by a given AD shift, which in turn allows us to measure the size of the multipliers. While Keynes did not argue that the price level could not change, he did argue that prices and wages are not perfectly flexible and tend to be "sticky", especially downward.

Keynes observed that consumption spending is the largest component of aggregate demand and hypothesized that consumption is primarily a function of disposable, or after-tax, income. In other words, how much people spend depends primarily on the level of their current disposable income. Changes in current disposable income will lead to changes in current consumption spending. Before exploring the determination of equilibrium income and output in this model, the nature of the Keynesian consumption function must be understood.

The Consumption Function

The following data represent consumption spending behavior in a hypothetical economy:

Disposable Income (Y_D)	Consumption (C)	Saving (S)	$MPC = \Delta C/\Delta Y_d$	$MPS = \Delta S/\Delta Y_D$ $MPS = 1 - MPC$
$ 0	$ 500	-$500	0.75	0.25
1,000	1,250	-250	0.75	0.25
2,000	2,000	-0-	0.75	0.25
3,000	2,750	+250	0.75	0.25
4,000	3,500	+500	0.75	0.25

Consumption spending, C, depends on **disposable income**, Y_D. As disposable income increases, consumption increases, but by a smaller amount.

Consumption has two components: autonomous consumption and induced consumption. **Autonomous consumption**, C_0, is equal to consumption spending when disposable income is zero and is independent of disposable income, depending instead on household wealth, interest rates, and other economic variables. In the above example, autonomous consumption is $500. **Induced consumption**, $MPC(Y_D)$, is the additional consumption spending that occurs as disposable income increases.

The **marginal propensity to consume**, MPC, is the ratio of the change in consumption to the change in disposable income. The **MPC** gives the portion of any increase in disposable income that will be spent. In the above example, the MPC is 0.75.

Saving, S, is the difference between disposable income and consumption, or $S = Y_D - C$. The **marginal propensity to save**, MPS, is the ratio of the change in saving to the change in disposable income. The MPS gives the portion of any increase in disposable income that will be saved. In this example, the MPS is 0.25. Since disposable income must be either spent or saved, MPC + MPS = 1.

Break-even disposable income is the level of disposable income where consumption spending is just equal to disposable income. If $C = Y_D$, then S must be zero. In this example, break-even disposable income is $2,000.

The relationship between consumption and disposable income can also be expressed algebraically. The relationship is direct: an increase in disposable income leads to an increase in consumption. This means the slope of the consumption function, which is the marginal propensity to consume, is positive. The relationship is also linear: for a given unit increase in disposable income, the corresponding increase in consumption is constant.

Algebraically, the relationship between consumption and disposable income can be written using the general equation of a line (Y = mX + b). After replacing the notation, we can write the equation: $C = C_0 + MPC(Y_D)$ where C_0 is **autonomous consumption** and **MPC** is the **marginal propensity to consume**.

STEP 1: Calculate the MPC: using the data on the previous page as an example, when disposable income is $2,000, consumption is $2,000 and when disposable income is $1,000, consumption is $1,250. The change in consumption ($2,000 - $1,250) divided by the change in disposable income ($2,000 - $1,000) is equal to the MPC, $750/$1,000 = 0.75.

$$MPC = \Delta C/\Delta Y_D = \$750/\$1{,}000 = 0.75$$

STEP 2: Calculate C_0: use the equation $C = C_0 + MPC(Y_D)$ and plug in the MPC calculated in step 1 along with the coordinates of one of the points provided in the table. For example, you can write $\$3500 = C_0 + 0.75(\$4000)$ and solve for $C_0 = \$500$.

$$C_0 = \$3{,}500 - 0.75(\$4000) = \$3{,}500 - \$3{,}000 = \$500$$

STEP 3: Write the Consumption equation by plugging in the values for autonomous consumption and the MPC:

$$C = \$500 + 0.75(Y_D).$$

STEP 4: Solve for break-even disposable income by setting $Y_D = C = \$500 + 0.75(Y_D)$, which implies that $Y_D - 0.75(Y_D) = \$500$ or $0.25(Y_D) = \$500$ or $Y_D = \$500/0.25 = \$2{,}000$.

The relationship between consumption and disposable income can also be illustrated graphically. Given the equation $C = \$500 + 0.75(Y_D)$, note that this function will intersect the vertical axis at \$500 and will be linear and positively sloped. It is often convenient to use the break-even disposable income value to sketch the graph.

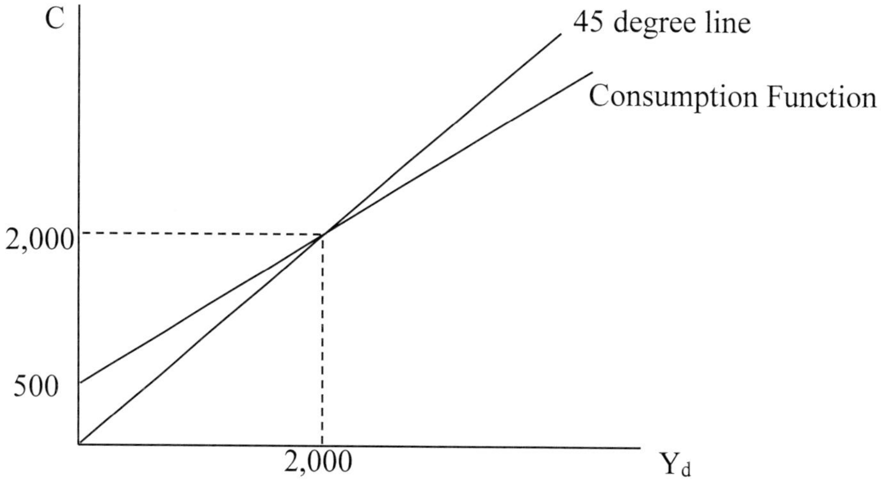

By inserting a 45 degree line, the areas of dissaving and saving can be identified. Notice that $S < 0$ (negative) at every level of disposable income between 0 and \$2,000, and $S > 0$ (positive) at every level of disposable income above \$2,000. Break-even disposable income is illustrated in the graph by the point where the consumption function intersects the 45 degree line.

Adding Investment to the Keynesian Model: Equilibrium in a Private, Closed Economy

Recall from the section on national income accounting that there are several differences between GDP and national income: depreciation, indirect business taxes, and net foreign factor income. For simplicity, the model starts by assuming no government and that these differences do not exist, so that GDP, or output, is equal to income (Y). To find equilibrium in a simple 2-sector model, ignore the public sector and the foreign sector. If there is no government, there are no taxes, so income and disposable income are identical. Remember that the price level is assumed to be fixed so that changes in income represent changes in real income.

To further simplify the model, the amount of investment spending is assumed to be autonomous. In other words, it does not depend on the amount of current income and will be the same at every level of income for a given two-sector model. Investment is assumed to be determined by other factors, such as business expectations of future sales and profits, and the quantity of investment spending depends on the expected rates of return on investment projects compared to the interest rate. Ceteris paribus, if the expected rate of return on an investment project exceeds the interest rate, or cost of funds, the project is considered profitable and will be undertaken. A greater number of projects will be considered profitable at lower interest rates than at higher interest rates, ceteris paribus, so the quantity of investment spending is inversely related to the interest rate. An increase in the interest rate leads to a decrease in the amount of investment spending and a decrease in the interest rate leads to an increase in the amount of investment spending.

The condition for equilibrium in the Keynesian model is that Total Expenditure (TE) equals Total Production (TP). If TE < TP, then businesses will experience unintended inventory accumulation and will reduce total production. If TE > TP, then businesses will experience unintended inventory depletion and will increase total production. As businesses react in this manner, the economy moves toward the equilibrium condition: TE = TP. In the 2-sector model, there are only two types of spending: consumption and investment, so TE = C + I. Total production, or total output, is assumed to equal income (Y), so the equilibrium condition may be written as: C + I = Y. At this point, a specific consumption equation and a specific value for investment spending can be used to discover where the economy's equilibrium level of output and income will occur.

Let C = \$500 + 0.75(Y) and I = \$1,500. Write the equilibrium condition:

$$C + I = Y \quad \text{or} \quad \$500 + 0.75(Y) + \$1{,}500 = Y$$

and solve this expression for Y: \$2,000 = Y – 0.75(Y) = 0.25(Y), so Y = \$2,000/0.25 = \$8,000.

The table below shows the values for consumption, investment, saving, and total expenditure associated with different income and output levels. Analyzing disequilibrium values along with the equilibrium value is helpful in understanding the concept of equilibrium.

Income and Output	**Consumption**	**Investment**	**Saving**	**C + I**
\$6,000	\$5,000	\$1,500	\$1,000	\$6,500
\$8,000	**\$6,500**	**\$1,500**	**\$1,500**	**\$8,000**
\$10,000	\$8,000	\$1,500	\$2,000	\$9,500

If businesses produce \$6,000 worth of output, households will receive \$6,000 in income, of which they will spend C = \$500 + 0.75(\$6,000) = \$5,000. Total expenditure will therefore be equal to C + I = \$5,000 + \$1,500 = \$6,500, indicating that TE > TP and inventories will be depleted. With income of \$6,000, households want to save \$1,000 but businesses want to borrow \$1,500 for investment, so there is an imbalance between desired S and desired I and between TE and TP.

If businesses produce \$10,000 worth of output, households will receive \$10,000 in income, of which they will spend C = \$500 + 0.75(\$10,000) = \$8,000. Total expenditure will therefore be equal to C + I = \$8,000 + \$1,500 = \$9,500, indicating that TE < TP and inventories will pile up unsold. With income of \$10,000, households want to save \$2,000 but businesses want to borrow \$1,500 for investment, so there is an imbalance between desired S and desired I and between TE and TP.

If businesses produce \$8,000 worth of output, households will receive \$8,000 in income, of which they will spend C = \$500 + 0.75(\$8,000) = \$6,500. Total expenditure will therefore be equal to C + I = \$6,500 + \$1,500 = \$8,000, indicating that TE = TP and the economy is in equilibrium. It is also true in equilibrium that the amount of money households choose not to spend (S = \$1,500) is exactly equal to the amount of money that businesses want to borrow and use for investment spending.

Keynes was able to describe how the spending decisions of households and businesses can determine the production decisions of businesses and can sometimes result in a level of output that is below full employment. For example, if the resources and technology of this economy are such that it is possible to produce $10,000 worth of output, the Keynesian model predicts a recessionary gap because spending plans only support $8,000 worth of output.

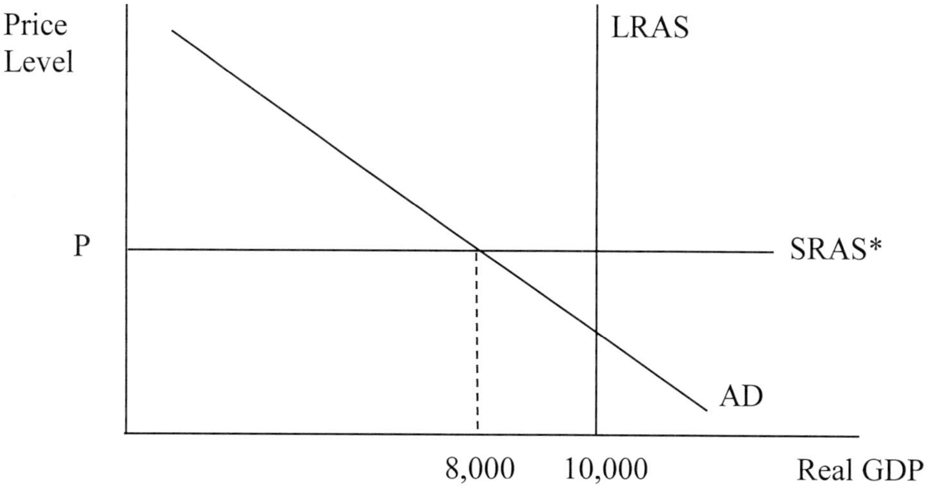

The simple Keynesian model assumes that the price level is fixed, which implies that the short-run aggregate supply curve is horizontal (depicted as SRAS* in the graph). This simplifying assumption is relaxed in the next chapter, where the short-run aggregate supply curve is assumed to be upward-sloping in the section on the real-world multiplier.

<u>The Autonomous Spending Multiplier</u>

The main significance of using the Keynesian model to calculate equilibrium output and income can be seen when the process is repeated using a different value of investment spending. Keynes observed that investment spending is the most volatile component of AD, so it is natural to wonder what happens in the economy when this value changes.

In the above example, the economy's short-run equilibrium level of output and income occurred at income equal to $8,000 because businesses were assumed to spend $1,500 for investment, which exactly offset the $1,500 of household saving. Next, repeat the calculation for equilibrium income assuming a different amount for investment spending.

If C = $500 + 0.75(Y), as before, but I = $1,250, the economy's short-run equilibrium level of output and income is now equal to $7,000 (you should verify this for yourself to learn the technique). Observe that investment spending fell from $1,500 to $1,250, a change of –$250, yet equilibrium output fell from $8,000 to $7,000, a change of –$1,000. These numbers reveal what Keynes called the multiplier effect.

Given the assumptions of this model, it can be shown that the ratio of $\Delta Y/\Delta I$, referred to as the autonomous spending multiplier, will always be equal to the reciprocal of the marginal propensity to save, or 1/MPS.

$$\text{Autonomous Spending Multiplier} = \Delta Y/\Delta I = 1/MPS$$

Once given the consumption equation for a simple model, the autonomous spending multiplier can be found by using the slope term in the equation, or the MPC. The MPC plus the MPS is always equal to one (MPC + MPS = 1) for a given consumption model, so 1 – MPC gives the MPS. The value of the autonomous spending multiplier = 1/MPS for any model. This multiplier can be used to predict how much equilibrium income and output will change (ΔY) as a result of any change in autonomous investment spending.

Example:

Given: C = \$200 + 0.9(Y) and I = \$800

Equilibrium income is \$10,000 and is found by using the equation C + I = Y. Substitute the equation for the consumption function and the value for investment into this equation to get:

$$\$200 + 0.9(Y) + \$800 = Y$$

Rewrite the equation in terms of Y by adding like terms and subtracting 0.9Y from both sides of the equation to get:

$$0.1Y = \$1{,}000 \text{ and solving for Y to get } Y = \$1{,}000/0.1 = \$10{,}000.$$

Now suppose investment spending increases from \$800 to \$1,000, so that ΔI = \$200. Since the MPC in the consumption equation is 0.9, we know that the MPS is 0.1, indicating that the autonomous spending multiplier is equal to 1/0.1 = 10. This multiplier can be used to predict the effect of the \$200 increase in investment spending on equilibrium income.

$$\Delta Y/\Delta I = 1/MPS = 10, \text{ so } \Delta Y/\$200 = 10 \text{ and } \Delta Y = (\$200)(10) = \$2{,}000$$

If income increases by \$2,000, this changes the equilibrium value from its initial amount of \$10,000 to a new amount of \$12,000. Given C = \$200 + 0.9(Y) and I = \$1,000, it can be verified that equilibrium income is equal to \$12,000.

$$\$200 + 0.9(Y) + \$1{,}000 = Y \text{ becomes } Y = \$1{,}200/0.1 = \$12{,}000$$

The next step is to add government spending and taxes to the model to find equilibrium in a three-sector model. The three sectors are the household sector, the business sector, and the government, or public, sector. With government added to the model, fiscal policy options are available and the multiplier effect also works when government spending or taxes change. The next chapter presents the extended model and fiscal policy.

The Keynesian Consumption Function: An Example

The table below is a consumption schedule for a hypothetical economy. This information can be used to develop the algebraic form of the consumption function and to answer questions, such as those presented below and on the following page. In reality, income and output are measured in trillions of dollars but the preceding and following examples use smaller numbers for illustration purposes.

Given:

Disposable Income (Y_D)	Consumption Spending (C)
$ 0	$ 500
$1,000	$1,400
$2,000	$2,300
$3,000	$3,200
$4,000	$4,100
$5,000	$5,000
$6,000	$5,900

1. What is the value of autonomous consumption? Autonomous consumption (C_0) is the value of consumption (C) when disposable income (Y_D) is equal to zero. In this example $C = \$500$ when $Y_D = \$0$, so $C_0 = \$500$.

2. What is the value of the marginal propensity to consume? The marginal propensity to consume is the change in consumption spending that occurs due to a change in income so $MPC = \Delta C/\Delta Y_D$. When income is zero, consumption spending is $500 and when income is $1,000, consumption spending is $1,400. The $1,000 increase in disposable income results in a $900 increase in consumption spending so the $MPC = \$900/\$1{,}000 = 0.9$.

3. What is the value of the marginal propensity to save? The marginal propensity to save is the change in saving that occurs due to a change in income so $MPS = \Delta S/\Delta Y_D$. If spending increases by $900 when income increases by $1,000, then saving must increase by $100, and the $MPS = \$100/\$1{,}000 = 0.1$. The identity $MPC + MPS = 1$ can also be used to find the MPS. If the MPC is 0.9, then the $MPS = 1 - 0.9 = 0.1$.

4. What is the algebraic form of the above consumption function? The general form of the relationship between consumption and disposable income is $C = C_0 + MPC(Y_D)$. The values for the MPC and C_0, found in numbers 1 and 2, can be substituted into this general equation to get the specific equation of $C = \$500 + 0.9(Y_D)$.

5. What is the value of break-even disposable income? Break-even disposable income is the level of income where consumption spending is exactly equal to disposable income and saving is equal to zero. It can be seen from the table that income and spending are equal at income equal to $5,000. Break-even disposable income can be found by setting the consumption equation equal to income and solving for income. $Y_D = \$500 + 0.9(Y_D)$ is rewritten as $0.1(Y_D) = \$500$ so $Y_D = \$500/0.1 = \$5{,}000$.

Follow the format on this page to work through the exercise on the next page.

NAME______________________________ SECTION #__________

THE BASIC KEYNESIAN MODEL

Use the information in the table below to fill in blanks 1 – 10.

Disposable Income Y_D	Consumption Spending C
$ 0	$100
$100	$180
$200	$260
$300	$340
$400	$420
$500	$500
$600	$580
$700	$660

1. Autonomous consumption is equal to $__________.

2. The marginal propensity to consume is equal to __________.

3. A $100 increase in disposable income (Y_D) leads to a(n) $__________ increase in consumption spending (C).

4. The marginal propensity to save is equal to __________.

5. A $100 increase in Y_D leads to a $__________ increase in saving.

6. At disposable income equal to $300, saving is equal to $__________.

7. Break-even disposable income is at disposable income equal to $__________.

8. The algebraic form of this consumption function is ____________________.

9. At disposable income equal to $1,000, consumption spending is equal to $__________.

10. At disposable income equal to $1,000, saving is equal to $__________.

NAME____ SECTION #______________

THE CONSUMPTION FUNCTION

Use the consumption function below to fill in blanks 1 – 5.

$$C = \$750 + 0.9(Y_D)$$

where C is consumption spending and Y_D is disposable income.

1. Autonomous consumption (C_0) = $_____________

2. Marginal propensity to consume (MPC) = _____________

3. Marginal propensity to save (MPS) = _____________

4. Break-even disposable income (Y_d) = $_____________

5. Consumption spending at disposable income of $20,000 (C) = $_______________

Use the table below to fill in blanks 6 – 10.

Disposable Income	Consumption Spending
$ 0	$1,000
1,000	1,750
2,000	2,500

6. Based on the data, autonomous consumption = $______________

7. Based on the data, the MPC = __________ and the MPS = __________

8. The equation for this consumption function is __________________________________

9. The break-even level of disposable income is $_____________

10. At disposable income of $10,000, saving is $______________

NAME____ SECTION #_____________

KEYNESIAN ECONOMICS

1. The event that brought Keynesian economics to the forefront was the:
   a. Civil War.
   b. supply shock resulting from OPEC.
   c. Great Depression.
   d. collapse of communism.

2. In *The General Theory of Employment, Interest, and Money,* Keynes disagreed with the Classical notion that:
   a. a market economy is self-regulating and always automatically moves to macroeconomic equilibrium at the full-employment level of real GDP.
   b. a market economy is self-regulating and can never achieve macroeconomic equilibrium at the full-employment level of real GDP in the long run.
   c. a decrease in aggregate demand causes the rate of unemployment to rise.
   d. an increase in aggregate demand causes the rate of unemployment to fall.

3. Keynes argued that:
   a. Say's Law is true.
   b. prices and wages are perfectly flexible.
   c. a government policy of "hands-off" is the best approach.
   d. prices and wages are not perfectly flexible in the short run.

4. Keynes believed that an economy may achieve equilibrium at a level of real GDP below the full-employment level:
   a. because of insufficient aggregate demand.
   b. when prices and wages are perfectly flexible.
   c. only if supply creates its own demand.
   d. if the long-run aggregate supply curve is vertical.

5. In the simple Keynesian model, consumption spending depends on _____________ and saving depends on _____________.
   a. the interest rate; disposable income
   b. the interest rate; the interest rate
   c. disposable income; the interest rate
   d. disposable income; disposable income

6. In the basic Keynesian model, ceteris paribus, an increase in disposable income leads to:
   a. an increase in consumption spending and a decrease in saving.
   b. a decrease in consumption spending and an increase in saving.
   c. an increase in both consumption spending and saving.
   d. a decrease in both consumption spending and saving.

7. According to Keynes, equilibrium income and output are determined by:
   a. available resources and technology in the short run.
   b. aggregate demand in the short run.
   c. the position of the long-run aggregate supply curve.
   d. the natural rate of unemployment.

8. In the short run, macroeconomic equilibrium occurs:
   a. only if the actual rate of unemployment is equal to the natural rate of unemployment.
   b. when aggregate expenditure equals total production in the economy.
   c. when government adheres to a balanced budget.
   d. only if the rate of inflation is zero.

9. In the Keynesian view, a decrease in aggregate demand will most likely cause:
   a. output and unemployment to rise.
   b. output and unemployment to fall.
   c. output to fall and unemployment to rise.
   d. output to rise and unemployment to fall.

10. If the short-run aggregate supply curve (SRAS) is horizontal, then an increase in aggregate demand leads to:
   a. an increase in real output, an increase in the price level, and a decrease in unemployment.
   b. an increase in real output, a decrease in the price level, and a decrease in unemployment.
   c. an increase in real output, no change in the price level, and a decrease in unemployment.
   d. a decrease in real output, no change in the price level, and an increase in unemployment.

NAME____ SECTION #______________

THE KEYNESIAN CONSUMPTION FUNCTION

Use the information in the table below to answer questions 1 – 5:

Disposable Income	Consumption
$ 5,000	$6,000
$ 7,500	$8,000
$10,000	$10,000
$12,500	$12,000

1. The marginal propensity to consume (MPC) is equal to:
   a. 0.2.
   b. 0.25.
   c. 0.75.
   d. 0.8.

2. The marginal propensity to save (MPS) is equal to:
   a. 0.2.
   b. 0.25.
   c. 0.75.
   d. 0.8.

3. Break-even disposable income is equal to:
   a. $6,000.
   b. $8,000.
   c. $10,000.
   d. $12,000.

4. At disposable income equal to $12,500, saving is equal to:
   a. $0.
   b. $500.
   d. $1,000.
   d. – $500.

5. Autonomous consumption is equal to:
   a. $0.
   b. $2,000.
   c. $5,000.
   d. $10,000.

6. The part of consumption spending that is independent of disposable income is called:
   a. the marginal propensity to consume.
   b. the marginal propensity to save.
   c. disposable consumption.
   d. autonomous consumption.

Use the information in the table below to answer questions 7 – 10:

Disposable Income (Y_D)	Consumption (C)
$ 0	$ 100
200	280
400	460
600	640
800	820
1,000	1,000

7. The marginal propensity to consume (MPC) is _____, and the marginal propensity to save (MPS) is _____.
   a. 0.65; 0.35
   b. 0.75; 0.25
   c. 0.8; 0.2
   d. 0.9; 0.1

8. Saving is equal to zero when disposable income is equal to:
   a. $0.
   b. $150.
   c. $600.
   d. $1,000.

9. The algebraic form of this consumption function is:
   a. $C = \$150 + 0.75(Y_d)$.
   b. $C = \$100 + 0.9(Y_d)$.
   c. $C = \$200 + 0.75(Y_d)$.
   d. $C = \$200 + 0.9(Y_d)$.

10. At disposable income equal to $2,000, consumption spending:
   a. is equal to $2,000.
   b. is equal to $1,800.
   c. is equal to $1,900.
   d. cannot be determined.

NAME____ SECTION #____________

THE KEYNESIAN MODEL

INSTRUCTIONS: Fill in the following blanks with the appropriate word or phrase.

In his book *The General Theory of Employment, Interest, and Money* (1936), (1)______________________________ disagreed with the Classical notion that a market economy automatically moves itself to a (2)____________________________ equilibrium. In particular, he disagreed with the Classicals on two important points: first, Keynes argued that prices, wages and interest rates were (3)____________________________, especially downward; and second, that Say's Law was not true in the short run. Keynes argued that, in the short run, supply does not create demand, but rather it is (4)____________________________ that determines equilibrium income, output, and employment. According to Keynes, recessions are a result of insufficient (5)____.

The Classical model focused on the **long run** and **aggregate supply** while the Keynesian approach to explaining macroeconomic changes focused on the (6)_______________________ and (7)____.

Keynes found (8)_________________________________ to be the largest component of aggregate demand, but felt that (9)__________________________________ was the most volatile component of aggregate demand. He tried to make the case that fluctuations in aggregate spending could result in instability, and Keynes argued that government could use (10)____________________________________ to help stabilize the macroeconomy.

NAME____ SECTION #__________

THE KEYNESIAN MODEL: PRIVATE CLOSED ECONOMY

Use the following model of a private, closed economy to complete the table and then fill in blanks 1 – 5, assuming there are no taxes, so $Y = Y_D$.

$$C = \$400 + 0.8(Y) \qquad I = \$800$$

(C = consumption spending, Y = income and output, and I = investment spending)

Income and Output	Consumption	Investment	Saving	C + I
$5,000	________	________	____	____
$6,000	________	________	____	____
$7,000	________	________	____	____

In this model, the MPC = (1)________ and the MPS = (2)________. Equilibrium income and output is equal to (3) $________________. If investment spending increases to $1,000, equilibrium income and output will increase to (4) $______________, implying that the value of the autonomous spending multiplier is equal to (5)____________.

Use the following model for a private, closed economy to fill in blanks 6 – 10, assuming there are no taxes, so $Y = Y_D$.

$$C = \$300 + 0.75(Y) \qquad I = \$700$$

(C = consumption spending, Y = income and output, and I = investment spending)

The simple Keynesian model predicts this economy will achieve equilibrium when income and output are equal to (6) $________________. The value of the autonomous spending multiplier is equal to (7) _______. If the full-employment output level is $4,200, then there is a(n) (8) ______________________ gap. In the simple Keynesian model with a fixed price level, the economy will achieve equilibrium at full employment following a(n) (9) ______________________ in investment spending of (10) $____________.

NAME____ SECTION #____________

THE KEYNESIAN MODEL

1. In the Keynesian model, the primary determinant of consumer spending is:
   a. disposable income.
   b. tax incentives for saving.
   c. the interest rate.
   d. a person's age.

2. Keynesian theory asserts that a free market economy with no government intervention:
   a. can never achieve equilibrium at full employment in the short run.
   b. will always achieve equilibrium at full employment in the short run.
   c. will not experience economic fluctuations in the short run.
   d. may experience economic fluctuations in the short run.

3. The essence of the Keynesian theory of unemployment is that:
   a. the unemployment rate is always equal to the natural rate due to structural and frictional types of unemployment.
   b. short-run unemployment problems are self-correcting in a market economy.
   c. government must provide public sector jobs to the unemployed.
   d. unemployment results from inadequate demand for goods and services throughout the economy.

4. If households have a tendency to save $5 of every $100 increase in income, then:
   a. the household saving rate is negative.
   b. household spending must increase by $105 when income increases by $100.
   c. the economy is in a recession.
   d. the marginal propensity to consume is 0.95 and the simple spending multiplier is 20.

5. If disposable income is $1,000 billion and consumption spending is $1,200 billion, then personal saving ___________.
   a. is -$200 billion
   b. is $200 billion
   c. is $1,800 billion
   d. cannot be determined from the information given

6. If the MPC = 0.8, the MPS = _____ and the autonomous spending multiplier = _____.
   a. 0.1; 10
   b. 0.1; 5
   c. 0.2; 10
   d. 0.2; 5

7. In the simple Keynesian model with an MPC equal to 0.80, a $50 billion increase in investment spending leads to a maximum:
   a. $50 billion increase in equilibrium income.
   b. $80 billion increase in equilibrium income.
   c. $250 billion increase in equilibrium income.
   d. $400 billion increase in equilibrium income.
   e. $500 billion increase in equilibrium income.

8. When a $2,000 increase in income causes a $1,800 increase in consumption spending:
   a. the marginal propensity to consume (MPC) is 0.9.
   b. the marginal propensity to save (MPS) is 0.20.
   c. the increase in saving is $200.
   d. All of the above are true
   e. Only a. and c. are true

9. In the simple, two-sector model, if C = $120 billion + .75(Y) and I = $30 billion, then break-even disposable income (Y_D = Y) is equal to:
   a. $120 billion.
   b. $250 billion.
   c. $480 billion.
   d. $600 billion.

10. In the simple, two-sector model, if C = $120 billion + .75(Y) and I = $30 billion, then equilibrium income (Y) is equal to:
   a. $150 billion.
   b. $480 billion.
   c. $600 billion.
   d. $1,000 billion.

NAME____ SECTION #____________

KEYNESIAN ECONOMICS

1. The marginal propensity to consume (MPC) is defined as the:
   a. fraction of disposable income that is spent by households.
   b. change in consumer spending divided by the change in disposable income.
   c. difference between disposable income and consumer spending.
   d. fraction of disposable income that is saved by households.

2. Ceteris paribus, a $100 increase in investment spending will generally:
   a. increase equilibrium income by more than $100.
   b. increase equilibrium income by less than $100.
   c. increase equilibrium income by exactly $100.
   d. have no effect on equilibrium income.

3. All of the following equations are correct ***except***:
   a. MPC + MPS = 1.
   b. 1 – MPC = MPS.
   c. MPC = C/Y_d.
   d. MPS = $\Delta S/\Delta Y_d$.

4. When the marginal propensity to consume (MPC) is 0.80, the autonomous spending multiplier is ________.
   a. 2
   b. 3
   c. 4
   d. 5

5. If the marginal propensity to consume is 0.925, then a $100 increase in disposable income leads to a:
   a. $7.50 decrease in consumption spending.
   b. $92.50 increase in consumption spending.
   c. $7.50 decrease in personal saving.
   d. $92.50 increase in personal saving.

6. If equilibrium income falls by $1,000 when investment spending falls by $250, the autonomous spending multiplier is equal to:
   a. ¼.
   b. ½.
   c. 2.
   d. 4.

7. An $8 billion decrease in investment spending when the MPC is 0.75 may potentially lead to:
   a. an increase in equilibrium income of up to $40 billion.
   b. a decrease in equilibrium income of up to $40 billion.
   c. an increase in equilibrium income of up to $32 billion.
   d. a decrease in equilibrium income of up to $32 billion.

8. Given a marginal propensity to save equal to 0.25, the simple Keynesian model leads to the conclusion that the autonomous spending multiplier is equal to ________, meaning that a $100 increase in autonomous investment spending could potentially lead to a(n) ________ increase in equilibrium income.
   a. 4; $400
   b. 4; $100
   c. 5; $500
   d. 8; $800

9. When the economy is operating where total production is less than total expenditures, all of the following are true ***except***:
   a. the economy is in a state of disequilibrium.
   b. the level of output produced is greater than what people plan to buy.
   c. businesses will increase production to increase inventories.
   d. businesses experience an unplanned decrease in inventories.

10. In the Keynesian model, when aggregate expenditure is less than aggregate output, firms are most likely to react by:
   a. increasing production and employing more workers.
   b. raising product prices and maintaining output at full employment.
   c. reducing production and laying off some workers.
   d. reducing product prices and maintaining output at full employment.

CHAPTER 9 Fiscal Policy

The three main macroeconomic goals for most economies are full employment, price stability, and economic growth. According to Keynesian theory, government, in particular Congress, can use its taxing and spending powers, or **fiscal policy**, to pursue these goals, especially the goal of full employment. The use of fiscal policy entails changes in the government's budget, which is comprised of two parts: government expenditures (G) and net taxes (T). Net taxes are equal to total tax revenue minus transfer payments made by the government (social security payments are an example of a government transfer payment).

A **budget deficit** exists when government expenditures exceed net taxes (G > T), a **budget surplus** exists when net taxes exceed government expenditures (G < T), and a **balanced budget** exists when government expenditures equal net taxes (G = T).

If the economy is experiencing a **recessionary gap**, Keynes recommended that government attempt to increase aggregate demand using **expansionary fiscal policy**: increasing government spending, decreasing taxes, or some combination of the two. Theoretically, expansionary fiscal policy will shift aggregate demand to the right to close the recessionary gap.

If an **inflationary gap** exists, government could use **contractionary fiscal policy** to decrease aggregate demand. Contractionary fiscal policy involves decreasing government spending, increasing taxes, or some combination of the two. While it is feasible in theory, in practice contractionary fiscal measures are difficult to implement for political reasons, so current U.S. policy relies more on monetary policy than fiscal policy to deal with inflation.

Fiscal policy can be directed toward private expenditures (C + I) or toward public expenditures (G). For example, a tax cut on both personal and corporate income increases the income available for the private sector to spend. Government may also increase its activity in the economy by increasing spending in areas such as infrastructure and the military. Whether policy is aimed at changing private spending or public spending will affect the relative size of the public and private sectors, as well as the mix of output in each sector.

The President and Congress make basic fiscal policy decisions during the budgetary process. To a large extent, however, current revenues and expenditures are the result of prior decisions. Only a fraction of any year's budget represents discretionary spending resulting from current decisions. A large share of government outlays are determined by previously passed laws, and the outlays occur without requiring any new legislative action on the part of Congress. Automatic changes in the government's budget are often referred to as **built-in, or automatic, stabilizers** because they change automatically as economic conditions change and they counteract the business cycle. During recessionary periods, unemployment benefits increase as more people lose their jobs and are eligible to receive them. This acts as an automatic, expansionary fiscal policy and reduces the size of the potential recessionary gap. During expansionary periods, incomes are higher and the progressive income tax structure causes tax revenues to rise. This acts as an automatic, contractionary fiscal policy and reduces the size of the potential inflationary gap.

Keynesian policy analysis focuses primarily on **discretionary fiscal policy**, or changes in government spending and taxation designed to achieve specific macroeconomic goals. These changes do not occur automatically as economic conditions change and require new action on the part of government.

Adding Government: Equilibrium in the Simplified Keynesian Model

The model is simplified by assuming that investment spending and government spending are **autonomous,** meaning their values do not depend on the level of current income. It is also assumed that taxes are lump-sum, in other words a given amount paid at one time, and the SRAS curve is horizontal. The consumption function used is the one derived in the previous chapter. If government spending is equal to tax revenues (G = T) in the model, then the government has a balanced budget. If G > T, government has a budget deficit equal to the difference between government spending and tax revenues. If G < T, government has a budget surplus equal to the difference between tax revenues and government spending. Suppose that the following information describes the economy:

$$C = \$400 + 0.75(Y - T) \quad I = \$250 \quad G = \$200 \quad T = \$200$$

Plug in T = \$200 to derive the tax-adjusted consumption function, C = \$400 + 0.75(Y – \$200) which reduces to C = \$250 + 0.75(Y).

Equilibrium is at the income where total expenditure is equal to total output and income. Total expenditure now includes consumption spending, investment spending, and government spending. Set C + I + G = Y, plug in the given values for C, I, and G, and solve for equilibrium output and income (Y):

$$\$250 + 0.75(Y) + \$250 + \$200 = Y\text{, so } \$700 = 0.25(Y)\text{, and } Y = \$700/0.25 = \$2{,}800.$$

The addition of government spending (G) and taxes (T) does not dramatically alter the mathematical steps involved in calculating equilibrium income, and these steps were presented in chapter 8.

The Government Spending Multiplier

Next, suppose that government spending is increased from G = \$200 to G = \$300, indicating that ΔG = \$100. The government spending multiplier is the same as the autonomous spending multiplier calculated in the previous chapter (1/MPS), and this multiplier can be used to predict the change in equilibrium output and income that results from a change in government spending as the additional spending works its way through the economy. In this model, the MPC is 0.75, so the MPS = 1 – MPC = 1 – 0.75 = 0.25, and the autonomous spending multiplier is 1/MPS = 1/0.25 = 4. The \$100 increase in government spending in this example becomes an increase in income for some individuals who then increase their spending by 0.75(\$100) = \$75, and so on.

The change in equilibrium income that occurs as a result of an increase in government spending is found by using the formula:

$$\Delta Y = (1/MPS)(\Delta G).$$

The new equilibrium income is the old equilibrium income plus the change in income that results from the change in government spending. The additional government spending will be multiplied four times and the new equilibrium income will be 4($100) = $400 higher, or $2,800 + $400 = $3,200.

The economy's new equilibrium level of income and output can also be calculated with the same procedure used to find equilibrium in the example on the previous page and using the new value for government spending (G = $300) to get:

$$\$250 + 0.75(Y) + \$250 + \$300 = Y, \text{ so } \$800 = 0.25(Y), \text{ and } Y = \$800/0.25 = \$3{,}200.$$

Thus, when $\Delta G = \$100$, $\Delta Y = \$400$, so $\Delta Y/\Delta G = \$400/\$100 = 4$, which is the value predicted for the autonomous spending multiplier.

The multiplier effect suggests that any change in aggregate autonomous expenditure will change income and real GDP by some multiple of the initial change in spending. Calculating the change in real GDP due to a change in spending is simplified by using the autonomous spending multiplier which is written as:

Autonomous Spending Multiplier = $1/(1\text{-}MPC) = 1/MPS = \Delta Y/\Delta I = \Delta Y/\Delta G$

This formula can be used to perform fiscal policy analysis when a change in government spending is being considered. Alternatively, it can be used to predict the impact of a change in taxes on the economy's equilibrium level of income and output.

The Tax Multiplier

Knowing the value of and understanding the spending multiplier helps to find and understand the **tax multiplier**. The tax multiplier can be used to calculate changes in real GDP that result from tax changes. Keynes argued that disposable income (Y_D) determines both consumption (C) and saving (S). Any change in Y_D will change both C and S and can be written as:

$$\Delta Y_D = \Delta C + \Delta S.$$

Suppose that the MPC is 0.75. In the simple Keynesian model, if taxes decrease by $100, Y_D will increase by $100. How much will this affect consumption and saving? Since the MPC is assumed to be 0.75, the $100 increase in Y_D causes an increase in consumption of (0.75)($100) = $75 and an increase in saving of $100 - $75 = $25.

Consumption is a component of aggregate spending, and the change in consumption (ΔC) will create a multiplier effect on real GDP. The change in real GDP (ΔY), due to the increase in consumption spending, is found by multiplying the change in consumption spending by the autonomous spending multiplier or:

$$\Delta Y = (1/MPS)(\Delta C) = (1/0.25)(\$75) = (4)(\$75) = \$300$$

Thus, a decrease in taxes causes an increase in spending and real GDP indirectly through its affect on consumption. The effect of this change in taxes (ΔT) is summarized below.

$$\mathbf{\Delta Y = (spending\ multiplier)(\Delta C) = (1/MPS)(-MPC(\Delta T)) = (-MPC/MPS)(\Delta T)}$$

Dividing both sides by ΔT yields $\Delta Y/\Delta T = -MPC/MPS$ = the tax multiplier. To illustrate, the tax multiplier can be used to calculate the effect of a \$100 decrease in taxes on income and output:

$$\Delta Y = \Delta T(\text{tax multiplier}) = \Delta T(-MPC/MPS) = -\$100(-0.75/0.25) = -\$100(-3) = \$300$$

The tax multiplier can also be found by subtracting the autonomous spending multiplier from 1.

Tax Multiplier = -MPC/MPS or Tax Multiplier = 1 – autonomous spending multiplier

For example, if the MPC is 0.75, the autonomous spending multiplier is 1/0.25 = 4 and the tax multiplier is 1 – 4 = -3 = -0.75/0.25. This implies that a change in government spending has a slightly larger effect on the economy than a change in taxes of the same magnitude. This is illustrated in the following examples.

<u>Examples of Fiscal Policy Analysis</u>

Assume the economy can be described by the following set of equations:

$$C = \$400 + 0.8(Y - T) \quad I = \$1{,}500 \quad G = \$500 \quad T = \$500$$

Then, equilibrium income and output is:

$$\$400 + 0.8(Y - \$500) + \$1{,}500 + \$500 = Y$$

$$0.2Y = \$2{,}000 \text{ therefore } Y = \$2{,}000/0.2 = \$10{,}000.$$

Suppose the full-employment level of real GDP is equal to \$11,000 for this economy. If the economy is only producing \$10,000 worth of output, there is a recessionary gap. Equilibrium in this economy is \$1,000 below full employment (natural) real GDP. Classical economists might argue that the economy will adjust to a new equilibrium at \$11,000 on its own, but Keynesian economists would urge government policymakers to make this happen using discretionary fiscal policy (note that this model is too simplified to allow for automatic fiscal policy).

The autonomous spending and tax multipliers can be used to identify some policy options, assuming the goal is to increase equilibrium income by \$1,000 (the size of the GDP gap). Recall that the autonomous spending multiplier is equal to 1/MPS. The MPC given in the consumption equation on the previous page is 0.8, so the MPS for this model is 0.2, and the spending multiplier is 1/0.2 = 5. If the spending multiplier is 5, then $\Delta Y/\Delta G = 5$. Set the $\Delta Y =$ \$1,000 to solve for the change in government spending necessary to increase equilibrium income by \$1,000:

$$\Delta G = \$1{,}000/5 = \$200.$$

Solve for equilibrium using the mathematical model to verify that if G = \$700, and everything else is the same, the new equilibrium income and output level will indeed be \$11,000.

$$\$400 + 0.8(Y - \$500) + \$1{,}500 + \$700 = Y \text{ and}$$

$$Y = \$2{,}200/0.2 = \$11{,}000$$

The tax multiplier in this case is –MPC/MPS = -0.8/0.2 = -4 and can be used to help formulate a tax policy designed to close this recessionary gap. Since $\Delta Y/\Delta T = -4$ and the desired change in equilibrium income is $\Delta Y = \$1{,}000$, the change in taxes necessary to close this recessionary gap is calculated as:

$$\Delta T = \$1{,}000/(-4) = -\$250.$$

Again, the mathematical model can be used to verify that if T = \$250, and everything else is the same, equilibrium income will increase by \$1,000:

$$\Delta Y = (-\ MPC/MPS)(\Delta T) = -4(-\$250) = \$1{,}000$$

The new equilibrium income and output level will be \$10,000 + \$1,000, which is \$11,000.

So far, two options for increasing equilibrium income by \$1,000 when the MPC is 0.8 have been identified: government can increase spending from \$500 to \$700, resulting in a budget deficit equal to \$200 since taxes are still \$500. Alternatively, government can keep its spending at \$500 and lower taxes from \$500 to \$250, resulting in a budget deficit equal to \$250. Keynes, noting that the tax policy leads to a larger budget deficit and concerned that consumers would not be reliable spenders given the state of the economy, recommended that government raise spending to give the economy the biggest possible boost. The largest boost came as a result of wartime spending (government spending rose from about \$10 billion in the early 1930s to about \$103 billion during World War II).

A third option is to change both government spending and taxing. If government must balance its budget, then any increase in government spending must be financed by an equal increase in taxes. It may seem that there would be no effect on the economy of the increase in government spending. However, as shown above, the impact on equilibrium income of an increase in government spending is greater than the impact of a decrease in taxes, implying that government spending financed by taxes will still have a stimulatory effect on the economy.

Suppose government spending increases by $1,000 when the MPC is 0.8 and that the increase in government spending must be offset by an equal increase in taxes. The impact of the increase in government spending is:

$$\Delta Y = (1/MPS)(\Delta G) = (1/0.2)(\$1{,}000) = (5)(\$1{,}000) = \$5{,}000.$$

The impact of the offsetting increase in taxes is:

$$\Delta Y = (-MPC/MPS)(\Delta T) = (-0.8/0.2)(\$1{,}000) = (-4)(\$1{,}000) = -\$4{,}000.$$

The $1,000 increase in government spending leads to a $5,000 *increase* in equilibrium income while the $1,000 increase in taxes leads to a $4,000 *decrease* in equilibrium income. The result is a net increase in equilibrium income of $1,000. The increase in equilibrium income is equal to the increase in government spending, implying that the change in government spending is multiplied one time to become new income. In this model, **the balanced budget multiplier is always equal to one**, regardless of the values of the MPC and MPS. If there is a GDP gap equal to $1,000, then it would take an increase in government spending equal to $1,000 financed by an increase in taxes equal to $1,000 to increase equilibrium income from $10,000 to $11,000. Although this would not lead to a budget deficit, Keynes did not advocate this option, probably because it would lead to such a tremendous increase in the size of the public sector relative to the rest of the economy.

The Real-World Multiplier

The results in this section reflect many simplifying assumptions, including fixed prices. In terms of the aggregate demand/aggregate supply model, the predictions of the basic Keynesian model can be related to shifts of the AD curve.

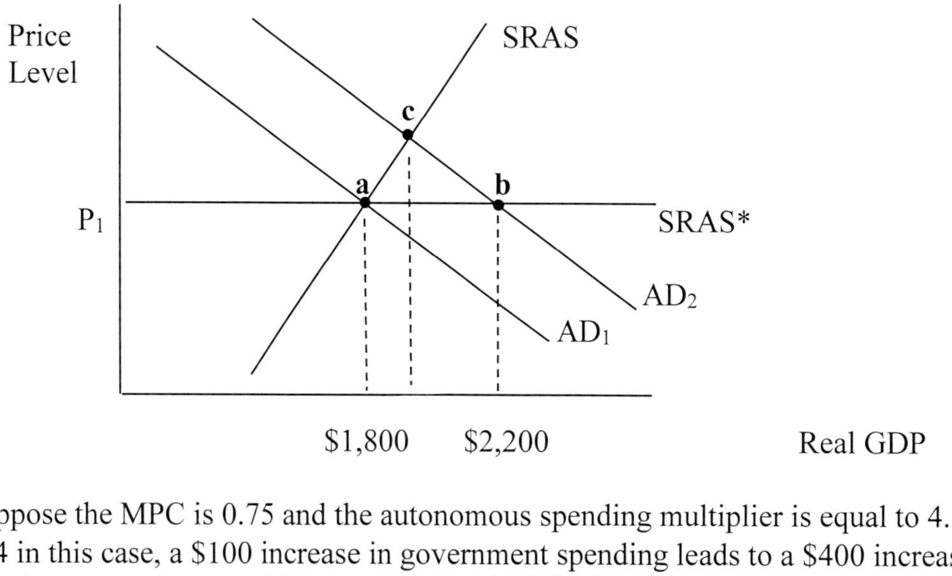

Suppose the MPC is 0.75 and the autonomous spending multiplier is equal to 4. Since $\Delta Y/\Delta G = 4$ in this case, a $100 increase in government spending leads to a $400 increase in equilibrium income and output. This implies that the initial increase in spending causes AD to shift to the right, but then the multiplier effect causes AD to continue shifting to the right from point a to point b, until the change in real GDP is, in this example, equal to $400.

In practice, the economy will actually experience such a large increase in real GDP only if prices are fixed (or the short-run aggregate supply curve is horizontal, as SRAS*). It is more realistic to assume that the SRAS curve is upward-sloping, so the new equilibrium resulting from the rightward shift in aggregate demand might actually be at point c, the point where AD_2 intersects SRAS in the graph above. This point corresponds to a level of real GDP that is greater than $1,800, but below $2,200. The assumption of fixed prices is useful because it simplifies the model and allows for easier mathematics to be used to illustrate the basic impacts of different policy options. However, the $100 increase in spending does not realistically correspond to higher production levels only; it is not likely the price level will be fixed and there will likely be a combination of higher production and higher prices when aggregate demand increases.

The upward-sloping SRAS curve is one of the reasons the real-world spending multiplier is smaller than the value predicted in the simplified Keynesian model, where the multiplier is simply 1/MPS. Another reason for the real-world spending multiplier to be less than 1/MPS is **crowding out**. Crowding out occurs when increased public sector activity reduces, or crowds out, private sector activity. Expansionary fiscal policy often involves a government budget deficit. As government increases borrowing to finance this deficit, interest rates in the economy are likely to increase, ceteris paribus. Higher interest rates can lead to decreases in private sector borrowing and spending for investment, which can negate part or all of the expansionary effect of fiscal policy and prevent the AD curve from shifting as far as predicted by the simplified model. The greater the degree of crowding out, the less effective fiscal policy will be for stimulating the economy.

Supply-Side Economics

A Keynesian, demand-side approach dominated policy decisions into the 1970s. However, a period of stagflation – relatively high rates of unemployment accompanied by significant inflation – and the failure of demand-side policies to stabilize the economy led to the development of supply-side economics. Central to the supply-side model is Say's Law, which states that "supply creates its own demand"; it is the act of selling, or supplying, that creates income and demand. The focus of policy according to the supply-side model should be on finding ways to increase the incentives for households and businesses to work, save, and invest in order to increase aggregate supply.

Supply-side policies, as the name implies, are designed to stimulate output, or aggregate supply. One such policy is a decrease in **marginal tax rates**, which is the rate applied to additional personal and business income. Taxes have a significant influence on the decisions by households to work and save and businesses to invest. Some economists argue that if marginal tax rates are too high, people will have a disincentive to work, save, and invest. Lower tax rates, according to this school of thought and some policymakers, provide incentives for businesses to increase production and investment, and for households to work and save more. Firms will invest in new plant and equipment, including new technology, and workers will work harder and longer hours if they get to keep a greater share of the income generated from production. The result is an increase in employment, productivity and output, leading to an increase in aggregate supply without putting upward pressure on prices, as might occur when demand-side policies are used to stimulate output.

The diagram on the left below shows the increase in output and the downward pressure on the price level that occurs when SRAS increases; the diagram on the right shows the increase in output accompanied by upward pressure on the price level that occurs when policy is designed to increase aggregate demand. Stimulating the supply-side of the economy does not involve trading a higher price level for a lower rate of unemployment.

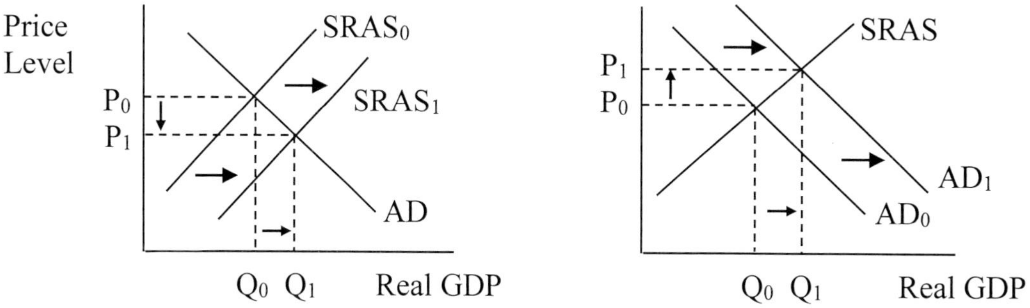

One argument against lowering tax rates, however, is the proposition that tax revenues will also fall. Economist Arthur Laffer argued this is not necessarily the case. He illustrated the possibility that tax revenues may actually fall beyond some relatively high tax rate as people and firms would legally engage in tax avoidance (by not working and not producing as much), and engage in illegal tax evasion (by not declaring income and cheating on their tax returns). The curve below shows that tax revenue increases as the tax rate increases, hits a maximum, T*, and then begins to decrease beyond some relatively high tax rate, such as t*, and is called the **Laffer Curve**.

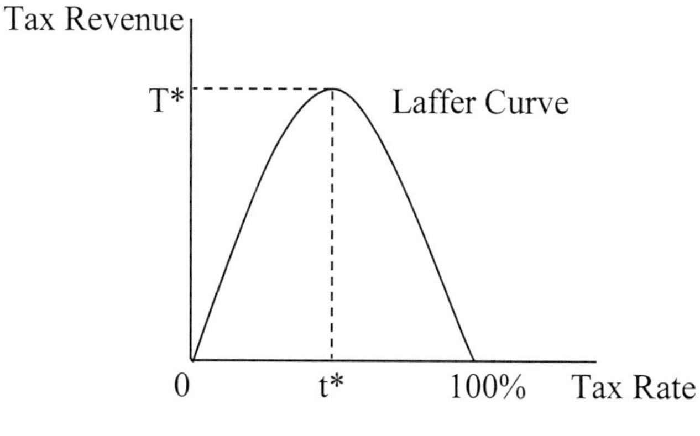

The election of Ronald Reagan in 1980 gave Congress the opportunity to pass a massive tax cut plan with the notion that the country could "produce its way" out of the inflationary environment. One significant result of the so-called supply-side tax cuts of the 1980s, coupled with large government spending increases of the time period, was rising budget deficits that led to substantial increases in the national debt. The increases in growth and employment did not materialize as dramatically as promised.

<u>The U.S. Income Tax</u>

The mathematical model presented in this chapter makes the simplifying assumption that taxes are lump-sum and do not depend on the level of income, but the largest component of federal tax revenues in the U.S. is the income tax, which is not a lump-sum tax and depends on the level of income. The model is expanded to allow for income taxes in more advanced courses, but the following presentation provides an overview of the U.S. income tax structure. The **average** income tax rate is calculated by dividing income tax payments by income:

$$\text{Average Tax Rate} = \frac{\text{income tax payments}}{\text{taxable income}}$$

There are several approaches to taxing income. A **proportional** income tax is one with a constant average tax rate. For example, if every person paid exactly 19 percent of income in taxes, the income tax would be proportional. The U.S. income tax is **progressive**, meaning that the average tax rate increases as income increases. Families with relative low incomes pay a small percentage of their income in taxes, while families with higher incomes pay a higher average tax rate. A tax is **regressive** if the average tax rate falls as income rises.

The **marginal** tax rate measures the additional income tax paid on additional income, or the change in income tax payments divided by the change in income. The symbol Δ (delta) means "change in," so:

$$\text{Marginal Tax Rate} = \frac{\Delta\text{income tax payments}}{\Delta\text{taxable income}}$$

If the marginal tax rate is greater than the average tax rate, then the average tax rate increases with income, and the income tax is progressive. The table below provides hypothetical data to illustrate the relationship between marginal tax rates and average tax rates.

Taxable Income	Marginal Tax Rate
0 - $20,000	10 percent
$20,001 - $40,000	15 percent
$40,001 - $80,000	25 percent

Suppose a family's taxable income is $30,000. According to the hypothetical tax table above, this family pays 10 percent of the first $20,000, or $2,000, plus 15 percent of the next $10,000, or an additional $1,500, so this family's income tax liability is $3,500. Its average tax rate is $3,500/$30,000 = .0.1167, or 11.67%.

The National Debt

As of November 2018, the accumulated debt of the U.S. has passed the $21.5 trillion mark. This debt originates in the budget deficits of the U.S. government and is the total stock outstanding government securities (bonds). While the size of the national debt may seem frightening to the average citizen, the bonds issued by the Treasury to finance government debt are also assets to institutions and individuals, both at home and abroad. In a sense, the decision by government to borrow money to cover its current expenditure is simply a decision to postpone taxation. At some later date, the government will impose taxes on its citizens to raise the money needed to repay borrowed funds (with interest), and a lot of this money will go back to the same people who paid the taxes. If government is paying for infrastructure or capital that will be around for a long time, then it might be prudent to defer taxation to spread the burden out, much the same as a household might use a mortgage to spread payments on a home.

U.S. government bonds that are held by U.S. citizens, private institutions, and government agencies represent internally held debt. Close to half of outstanding U.S. government debt is held by U.S. government agencies. However, a growing percentage of U.S. debt is externally held, which means the bonds are held by foreign individuals or institutions. By November 2018, more than 40 percent of U.S. government debt was held by foreign entities. Several decades ago, many people regarded the national debt as irrelevant because "we owe it to ourselves." Over this time, however, the proportion of the debt that is externally held has increased significantly, so we don't simply owe it to ourselves anymore. When the time comes for government to pay off its debt, U.S. citizens may feel the tax burden, but U.S. bondholders will not receive all of these funds—a large portion will go to foreign bondholders. In this way, some argue that the national debt is a burden on, and of concern to, future generations, since they are the ones who will ultimately have to manage this tax burden.

The issue of crowding out also raises another concern about the long-term consequences of deficit financing. If government budget deficits raise interest rates and lower investment spending, the rate at which the economy's capital stock is growing may slow down. Lower investment generally means less capital accumulation (fewer factories built, fewer machines and tools acquired, and so on). The size of our capital stock in part determines our rate of economic growth, so some argue that deficit financing is impairing economic growth.

The concerns about the size of the national debt led many to consider a balanced budget amendment to the U.S. constitution. There was not enough support in Congress for the matter to go before voters, but it is an issue that could come up again. Many state governments are constrained by balanced budget rules, but the federal government has no such constraint, other than what Congress imposes on itself (e.g. Gramm-Rudman-Hollings Act). Recall that automatic fiscal policy works to counteract economic fluctuations to a certain degree. This implies that if the federal government were required to maintain a balanced budget each year, policymakers would have to lower spending levels or raise taxes to counteract the automatic fiscal policy that would occur during a recession. Clearly, such an idea has little appeal to a Keynesian thinker, so it is not surprising that a balanced budget amendment has not been approved. Even if Congress passes a balanced budget, downturns in economic activity can trigger automatic increases in government spending and decreases in tax revenue, resulting in a **cyclical deficit**. If Congress approves a budget for which spending is greater than projected tax revenue, then there is already a **structural deficit**.

There is no consensus among economists and policy-makers as to the true burden of the debt but all agree that the size of the national debt is daunting and growing every day. The U.S. Department of the Treasury, Bureau of the Public Debt, tracks and updates the national debt daily. To view statistics on the national debt and related topics, visit their website at www.publicdebt.treas.gov and click "See the U.S. Public Debt to the Penny."

NAME____ SECTION #____________

Print Last Name, First Name

FISCAL POLICY

1. Fiscal policy is ***best*** defined as:
   a. uncontrolled government spending.
   b. altering the mix of government spending and taxing in order to balance the budget every fiscal year.
   c. changes in government spending and taxing for the purpose of achieving certain macroeconomic goals.
   d. minimizing government expenditures over the fiscal year.

2. Increases in government spending and lower taxes represent _________________, while decreases in government spending and higher taxes represent ________________.
   a. contractionary fiscal policy; expansionary fiscal policy
   b. contractionary monetary policy; expansionary monetary policy
   c. expansionary fiscal policy; contractionary fiscal policy
   d. expansionary monetary policy; contractionary monetary policy

3. Changes in government spending and taxing that counteract the business cycle and occur as a result of changing economic conditions are:
   a. discretionary stabilizers.
   b. automatic (built-in) stabilizers.
   c. discretionary budget balancers.
   d. automatic (built-in) budget balancers.

4. The increase in personal income tax payments that occurs when an economic expansion causes incomes to rise is an example of:
   a. discretionary, expansionary fiscal policy.
   b. discretionary, contractionary fiscal policy.
   c. automatic, expansionary fiscal policy.
   d. automatic, contractionary fiscal policy.

5. Suppose Congress believes that the economy is entering a recession and approves a budget that includes increased overall government spending with no corresponding increase in taxes in order to stimulate aggregate demand. This is an example of:
   a. discretionary, expansionary fiscal policy.
   b. discretionary, contractionary fiscal policy.
   c. automatic, expansionary fiscal policy.
   d. automatic, contractionary fiscal policy.

6. Suppose the economy is initially at full-employment equilibrium. Which of the following events could ***cause*** a recessionary gap, ceteris paribus?
   a. Investment increases as a result of optimistic business expectations
   b. Households save less at every level of disposable income
   c. Consumers spend less due to declining consumer confidence in the economy
   d. Congress decreases personal income tax rates

NAME____ SECTION #____________
Print Last Name, First Name

7. Which of the following is an example of automatic, expansionary fiscal policy?
   a. Lower unemployment compensation payments designed to reduce the cost of labor to businesses
   b. Higher unemployment compensation payments that occur when the economy is in a recession
   c. Higher taxes caused by increased incomes during an economic upturn
   d. Lower taxes caused by tax reform designed to lower tax rates on low-income families

8. In an economy that has automatic (built-in) stabilizers:
   a. the severity of recessions is intensified.
   b. budget deficits tend to fall during recessionary periods.
   c. income tax revenues tend to rise and transfer payments tend to fall during recessionary periods.
   d. the severity of recessions tends to be reduced.

9. Supply-side economics emphasizes:
   a. low marginal tax rates.
   b. increasing incentives to work, save, and invest.
   c. long-run effects on aggregate supply rather than short-run effects on aggregate demand.
   d. all of the above.

10. The Laffer curve suggests that:
   a. increasing marginal tax rates may actually reduce tax revenues.
   b. there is an inverse relationship between unemployment and inflation.
   c. increases in tax rates lead to increases in consumption expenditures.
   d. increases in income, output, and employment are directly related to increases in the tax rate.

NAME____ SECTION #____________
Print Last Name, First Name

THE KEYNESIAN MODEL WITH GOVERNMENT

INSTRUCTIONS: Fill in the following blanks with the correct word or phrase, according the simple Keynesian model.

The use of government spending and taxing by Congress in order to influence conditions in the macroeconomy is called (1)______________________________. When government expenditures exceed net taxes, a budget (2)____________________ exists. When government expenditures are less than net taxes, a budget (3)____________________exists. A (4)____________________ budget exists when government expenditures equal net taxes. (5)____ entails increasing government spending and/or decreasing taxes in order to increase aggregate demand. Changes in government spending and taxing that occur automatically as economic conditions change and counteract the business cycle is (6)____.

Keynes recommended the use of expansionary fiscal policy when the economy experiences a (7)______________________________ gap. He demonstrated that if government provides a stimulus, by increasing its spending or decreasing taxes, then a multiplier effect would occur which would increase aggregate demand and help move the economy toward full employment. In the simple Keynesian model, 1/MPS is the (8)________________________ multiplier, -MPC/MPS is the (9)____________ multiplier, and the balanced budget multiplier is equal to (10)_____________.

NAME____ SECTION #______________

Print Last Name, First Name

THE KEYNESIAN MODEL WITH GOVERNMENT

Use the following model of a closed economy to complete the table and then fill in blanks 1 – 10. Assume taxes are lump sum and do not change as the level of income changes. For simplicity, the model is not presented in $billions.

$$C = \$400 + 0.8(Y_D) \qquad I = \$800 \qquad G = \$500 \qquad T = \$500$$

(C = consumption spending, Y = income and output, Y_D = disposable income, $Y_d = Y - T$, I = investment spending, G = government spending and T = net taxes)

Income and Output	**Consumption**	**Investment**	**Government**	**C + I + G**
$6,000	__________	__________	__________	________
$6,500	__________	__________	__________	________
$7,000	__________	__________	__________	________

1. In this model, the MPC = __________

2. In this model, the MPS = __________

3. The equation for the tax-adjusted consumption function is ________________________

4. At income equal to $6,500, personal saving is equal to $____________________ billion

5. Equilibrium income and output is equal to $____________________ billion

6. The value of the government spending multiplier is __________

7. The value of the tax multiplier is _________

8. If government spending increases by $60 billion so government spending is $560 billion, equilibrium income and output will increase to $____________________ billion.

9. If there is lump-sum tax cut of $125 billion so taxes are $375 billion, equilibrium income and output will increase to $____________________ billion.

10. If government must balance its budget, a $125 billion lump-sum tax cut would have to be offset by a $_______________ billion decrease in government spending, resulting in a decrease in equilibrium income and output to $6,375 billion.

NAME____ SECTION #____________

Print Last Name, First Name

KEYNESIAN FISCAL POLICY

Use the graph below to answer question 1:

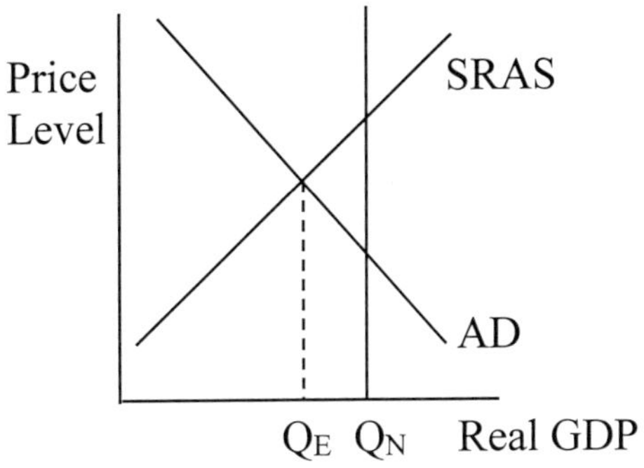

1. From a Keynesian perspective, the appropriate fiscal policy to deal with this:
   a. recessionary gap is to increase government spending and/or reduce taxes.
   b. recessionary gap is to decrease government spending and/or raise taxes.
   c. inflationary gap is to increase government spending and/or reduce taxes.
   d. inflationary gap is to decrease government spending and/or raise taxes.

2. In the simple Keynesian model with government spending (G) and lump-sum taxes (T), the tax multiplier is equal to ___________.
   a. -MPC/MPS
   b. -MPS/MPC
   c. 1/MPC
   d. 1/MPS

3. In the simple Keynesian model, when the MPC is 0.8, the autonomous spending multiplier is _________ and the tax multiplier is _________.
   a. 5; 4
   b. 5; 5
   c. 4; -4
   d. 5; -4

4. Assume the government cuts taxes by $125 billion. If the MPC = 0.8, what is the maximum potential impact on real GDP according to the simple Keynesian model?
   a. Real GDP increases by $500 billion
   b. Real GDP increases by $625 billion
   c. Real GDP decreases by $500 billion
   d. Real GDP decreases by $625 billion

NAME____ SECTION #____________

Print Last Name, First Name

5. If equilibrium real GDP falls short of full-employment (natural) real GDP by $60 million when the MPC = 0.75, which of the following would eliminate the recessionary gap that exists according to the Keynesian model?
   a. Increase G by $15 million
   b. Decrease T by $20 million
   c. Increase both G and T by $60 million
   d. Any of the above would eliminate the recessionary gap.

6. Keynesian economics suggests that the most effective way to eliminate a recessionary gap is for government to:
   a. increase its spending in order to increase aggregate demand.
   b. decrease its spending in order to balance the budget.
   c. increase taxes in order to increase tax revenues.
   d. decrease taxes and decrease government spending by the same amount.

7. If equilibrium income is $8,000 billion, full-employment income (natural real GDP) is $8,500 billion, and the MPS is 0.10, the simple Keynesian model predicts that a(n):
   a. $500 billion increase in government spending will close the recessionary gap.
   b. $10 billion increase in government spending will close the recessionary gap.
   c. $50 billion increase in government spending will close the recessionary gap.
   d. change in government spending cannot help close the recessionary gap.

Use the following information to answer questions 8 – 10:

C = \$600 billion + 0.9(Y_D)   I = \$850 billion   G = \$500 billion   T = \$500 billion

8. Equilibrium is at income (real GDP) equal to _______.
   a. $11,000 billion
   b. $14,500 billion
   c. $15,000 billion
   d. $19,500 billion

9. In this instance, the MPS is _____, the government spending multiplier is _____, and the tax multiplier is _____.
   a. 0.9; 10; -9
   b. 0.9; -9; 10
   c. 0.1; -9; 10
   d. 0.1; 10; -9

10. If government spending increases from $500 billion to $550 billion, then equilibrium income (real GDP) will:
   a. increase by $500 billion to $15,500 billion.
   b. increase by $500 billion to $15,000 billion.
   c. only increase if taxes also increase from $500 billion to $550 billion.
   d. only increase if taxes decrease by the same amount.

NAME____ SECTION #______________
Print Last Name, First Name

KEYNESIAN FISCAL POLICY

Use the following model of a closed economy to fill in blanks 1 – 10. Assume taxes are lump sum (one time payment) and do not change as the level of income changes. For simplicity, the model is not presented in $billions.

C = $250 + 0.75[Y-T], I = $500, G = $200 and T = $200

(where C = consumption spending, Y = income and output, T = taxes, I = investment spending, and G = government spending)

The simple Keynesian model predicts that this economy will achieve equilibrium when income and output are equal to (1) $________________. At equilibrium, disposable income is equal to (2) $________________, consumption spending is equal to (3) $________________, and personal saving is equal to (4) $________________. If this economy's full employment output level is $3,500, then equilibrium output is (5) ______________________________ potential output, or natural real GDP, and there is a(n) (6) _________________________________ gap. In the simple Keynesian model with fixed prices and no crowding out, the economy will move to equilibrium at full employment (natural real GDP) following a(n) (7) ____________________________ in government spending equal to (8) $_____________ (assuming no change in taxes), OR following a(n) (9) ____________________________ in taxes equal to (10) $_____________ (assuming no change in government spending).

Use the data above to verify that $\Delta Y/\Delta G = 1/MPS$ and that $\Delta Y/\Delta T = -MPC/MPS$.

NAME____ SECTION #______________

Print Last Name, First Name

INCOME TAXES

Use the following information taken from the 2018 U.S. Tax Rate Schedule for a Single Individual to fill in blanks 1 – 10.

For Taxable Income:	The Tax Due is:
$0 - $9,525	10% of Taxable Income
$9,526 – $38,700	$952.50 + 12% of the amount over $9,525
$38,701 – $82,500	$4,453.50 + 22% of the amount over $38,700
$82,501 – $157,500	$14,089.50 + 24% of the amount over $82,500
$157,501 – $200,000	$32,089.50 + 32% of the amount over $157,500
$200,001 – $500,000	$45,689.50 + 35% of the amount over $200,000
$500,001 +	$150,689.50 + 37% of the amount over $500,001

1. The marginal tax rate applied to taxable income of $12,000 is ____________.

2. The marginal tax rate applied to taxable income of $50,000 is ____________.

3. The percentage of income paid to tax increases in increments from 10% to 37% which means the U.S. Personal Income Tax is a ____________________________ tax.

4. How much of the $50,000 income will be subject to the marginal tax rate given in number 2 above? ______________________

5. How much is the total tax bill for taxable income of $50,000? ____________________

6. What is the average tax rate for taxable income of $50,000? ____________________

7. What is the marginal tax rate for taxable income of $90,000? ____________________

8. How much is the total tax bill for taxable income of $90,000? ____________________

9. What is the average tax rate for taxable income of $90,000? ____________________

10. What is the average tax rate for taxable income of $500,000? ____________________

NAME____ SECTION #______________
Print Last Name, First Name

THE PUBLIC SECTOR: TAXES AND THE NATIONAL DEBT

1. When tax receipts are greater than government expenditures during a single year, the result is:
   a. a budget surplus.
   b. a budget deficit.
   c. the structural debt.
   d. the cyclical debt.

2. When tax receipts are less than government expenditures during a single year, the result is:
   a. a budget surplus.
   b. a budget deficit.
   c. the national debt.
   d. the cyclical debt.

3. The total stock of outstanding government securities (bonds) is the:
   a. national debt.
   b. cyclical debt.
   c. budget surplus.
   d. budget deficit.

Use the data below to answer questions 4 – 6:

Income	Tax Liability
$20,000	$ 1,600
$30,000	$ 3,000
$40,000	$ 6,000
$50,000	$10,000

4. When income is $50,000, the average tax rate is:
   a. 5%.
   b. 10%.
   c. 15%.
   d. 20%.

5. As income increases, tax liability as a percentage of income:
   a. falls.
   b. remains the same.
   c. rises.
   d. initially falls, then rises.

6. The data reflect a ____________________ income tax.
   a. proportional
   b. regressive
   c. negative
   d. progressive

NAME____ SECTION #_____________

Print Last Name, First Name

7. A ____________________ tax is one for which the average tax rate decreases as income increases.
   a. progressive
   b. regressive
   c. proportional
   d. flat

8. The largest source of revenue for the federal government in the U.S. is the:
   a. sale of military equipment to foreign countries.
   b. payroll tax.
   c. personal income tax.
   d. U.S. Postal Service.

9. A balanced budget amendment to the U.S. Constitution would require that:
   a. all state governments balance their budgets.
   b. federal government spending be financed by tax revenue.
   c. tax rates must balance with interest rates in a given year.
   d. Congress use only fiscal policy to close an inflationary gap.

10. If income increases by $10,000 and the tax bill for the $10,000 increase is $3,000, then:
   a. the marginal tax rate must be equal to the average tax rate.
   b. the marginal tax rate must be greater than the average tax rate.
   c. the average tax rate is 30%.
   d. the marginal tax rate is 30%.

NAME____ SECTION #______________

Print Last Name, First Name

FISCAL POLICY AND GOVERNMENT DEBT

Use the information below to answer questions 1 – 5:

$C = \$420$ billion $+ 0.8(Y_D)$ $I = \$400$ billion $G = \$425$ billion $T = \$400$ billion

1. In equilibrium, output and income will equal _______ billion and disposable income will equal _______ billion according to the Keynesian model.
   a. $4,100; $3,700
   b. $4,100; $4,500
   c. $4,625; $4,225
   d. $4,625; $5,025

2. If full-employment real GDP in this economy is $4,750 billion, then:
   a. a recessionary gap exists.
   b. an inflationary gap exists.
   c. the economy is at full-employment equilibrium.
   d. this economy can never achieve full employment.

3. If full-employment real GDP in this economy is $4,750 billion, what is the increase in government spending that would be necessary to achieve equilibrium at full employment given the simplifying assumptions of the Keynesian model?
   a. $25 billion
   b. $31.25 billion
   c. $100 billion
   d. $125 billion

4. If full-employment real GDP in this economy is $4,750 billion, what is the decrease in taxes that would be necessary to achieve equilibrium at full employment given the simplifying assumptions of the Keynesian model?
   a. $25 billion
   b. $31.25 billion
   c. $100 billion
   d. $125 billion

5. If full-employment real GDP in this economy is $4,750 billion and the government either increases government spending or reduces taxes to achieve equilibrium at full employment, then:
   a. the initial budget deficit of $25 billion will be eliminated.
   b. there will be no effect on the government's budget.
   c. the budget deficit will be reduced, but not eliminated.
   d. the budget deficit will become larger.

6. Reductions in private consumption spending and/or investment spending that occur as a result of increased government taxing, spending, and borrowing is referred to as:
   a. automatic fiscal policy.
   b. discretionary fiscal policy.
   c. crowding out.
   d. crowding in.

7. As of November 2018, the accumulated national debt in the U.S.:
   a. had passed the $21.5 trillion mark.
   b. had been paid off due to budgetary surpluses.
   c. was all internally held.
   d. was all externally held.

8. Interest on the national debt:
   a. is negligible since the national debt is so small.
   b. creates income for bondholders, but liabilities for taxpayers.
   c. is paid only to domestic citizens since the debt is all internally held.
   d. is paid only to foreign citizens since the debt is all externally held.

9. If government spending financed by borrowing causes crowding out, then:
   a. the economy will likely grow at a slower rate due to less capital accumulation.
   b. the economy will likely grow at a faster rate due to more capital accumulation.
   c. fiscal policy is a more powerful tool for managing the economy than it would be in the absence of crowding out.
   d. there is no burden from the national debt that is shifted to future generations.

10. If a constitutional amendment was passed requiring a balanced budget for the federal government, then:
   a. automatic fiscal policy would be much more powerful than it is now.
   b. discretionary fiscal policy would be much more powerful than it is now.
   c. there would be no effect on the economy's performance according to the Keynesian model.
   d. if the government starts with a balanced budget, any increase in government spending would have to be financed by an equal increase in taxes.

Practice Exam II

The answers to this practice exam are on page 196.

1. The aggregate demand curves slopes downward to the right indicating that:
   a. inflation and output are inversely related.
   b. an increase in the price level leads to a decrease in the quantity of real GDP demanded.
   c. there is an inverse relationship between demand and the average level of prices.
   d. a greater quantity of real GDP will be demanded at higher price levels than at lower price levels.

2. Ceteris paribus, a decline in the domestic price level causes:
   a. an increase in exports, a decrease in imports, and an increase in the quantity of real GDP demanded.
   b. an increase in the purchasing power of a given money income.
   c. an increase in the interest rate and an increase in the real balances of households that save.
   d. all of the above are correct.
   e. only a. and b. are correct.

3. All of the following will increase aggregate demand ***except***:
   a. an increase in household wealth.
   b. an increase in expected future business sales and profits.
   c. a decrease in personal and business income taxes.
   d. a decrease in foreign real national income.

4. Ceteris paribus, an increase in aggregate demand when short-run aggregate supply is upward sloping causes the price level to ___________, real output to __________, and the unemployment rate to __________.
   a. increase; increase; increase
   b. decrease; decrease; decrease
   c. increase; increase; decrease
   d. increase; decrease; decrease
   e. increase; decrease; increase

5. An upward sloping short-run aggregate supply curve models the:
   a. direct relationship between the price level and the quantity of real GDP supplied.
   b. inverse relationship between the price level and the quantity of real GDP supplied.
   c. direct relationship between the price level and aggregate supply.
   d. inverse relationship between the price level and aggregate supply.

6. Higher wages and input prices lead to:
   a. increases in the cost of production and a decrease in short-run aggregate supply.
   b. increases in the cost of production and an increase in short-run aggregate supply.
   c. decreases in consumer confidence and a decrease in aggregate demand.
   d. decreases in consumer confidence and an increase in aggregate demand.

7. When the equilibrium (actual) level of real GDP is less than the natural level of real GDP, then:
   a. an inflationary gap exists and the unemployment rate is greater than the natural rate.
   b. a recessionary gap exists and the unemployment rate is greater than the natural rate.
   c. an inflationary gap exists and the unemployment rate is less than the natural rate.
   d. a recessionary gap exists and the unemployment rate is less than the natural rate.

8. In a self-correcting economy, inflationary gaps are eliminated by:
   a. lower wages and input prices leading to a decrease in costs of production which increases SRAS.
   b. lower wages and input prices leading to a decrease in costs of production which decreases SRAS.
   c. higher wages and input prices leading to an increase in costs of production which increases SRAS.
   d. higher wages and input prices leading to an increase in costs of production which decreases SRAS.

9. A laissez-faire policy with respect to the macroeconomy is associated with the:
   a. Classical view that the economy is self-correcting.
   b. Keynesian view that the economy is self-correcting.
   c. Classical view that the economy will not automatically move to equilibrium at full employment.
   d. Keynesian view that the economy will not automatically move to equilibrium at full employment.

10. The long-run aggregate supply curve (LRAS) curve is:
    a. horizontal at the economy's natural level of real GDP.
    b. vertical at the economy's natural level of real GDP.
    c. upward-sloping because firms respond to higher prices producing more output.
    d. upward-sloping because resources and technology are assumed to be fixed.

11. In the Classical model:
    a. aggregate demand determines the equilibrium level of output and income.
    b. flexible wages ensure that labor shortages and surpluses (unemployment) will be temporary.
    c. product prices will rise to eliminate shortages but are not likely to fall to eliminate surpluses.
    d. household saving is a function of personal disposable income.

12. Say's Law can be summarized as:
   a. markets are efficient.
   b. laissez-faire is appropriate.
   c. demand determines income and output.
   d. supply creates its own demand.

Use the graph below to answer the next two questions.

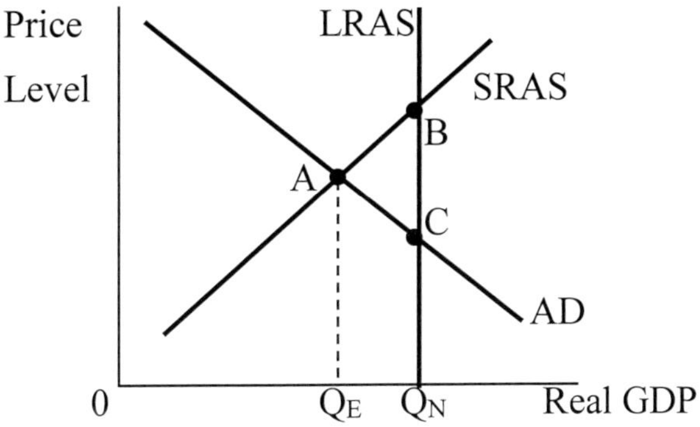

13. If the economy depicted in the graph above is currently in equilibrium at point A, then it is experiencing:
   a. a recessionary gap.
   b. an inflationary gap.
   c. a short-run equilibrium at full employment.
   d. long-run equilibrium.

14. If the economy depicted in the graph above is self-correcting, then:
   a. SRAS will increase and the economy will move to a new equilibrium at point B.
   b. AD will increase and the economy will move to a new equilibrium at point B.
   c. SRAS will increase and the economy will move to a new equilibrium at point C.
   d. AD will increase and the economy will move to a new equilibrium at point C.

15. The significance of Say's Law is that, if it holds true, government policy makers:
   a. do not have to implement policies designed to increase aggregate demand for the economy to move toward equilibrium at natural real GDP.
   b. must increase government spending in order to move the economy to an equilibrium at natural real GDP.
   c. will have to implement price ceilings to lower input prices in order to increase short-run aggregate supply.
   d. should continue to use fiscal policy to stimulate the demand-side of the economy.

16. When total production in the economy is less than total expenditures:
   a. people are not willing and able to buy all output, inventories increase, and firms decrease production and employment.
   b. people are willing and able to buy all output, inventories decrease, and firms increase production and employment.
   c. an inflationary gap will emerge and output will decrease.
   d. a recessionary gap will emerge and output will increase.

17. In *The General Theory of Employment, Interest and Money*, John Maynard Keynes argued that:
   a. a market economy may settle at an equilibrium below full employment in the short run.
   b. a market economy will automatically eliminate recessionary and inflationary gaps through shifts in AD and move toward equilibrium at full employment.
   c. the Great Depression was primarily a result of falling prices and wages.
   d. the Civil War illustrated that it is necessary for the national government to actively manage a market economy.

Use the information in the table below to answer the next four questions.

Disposable Income (Y_d)	Consumption Spending (C)
\$0	\$1,000
\$1,000	\$1,750
\$2,000	\$2,500
\$3,000	\$3,250
\$4,000	\$4,000

18. In the above example, autonomous consumption is:
   a. \$0.
   b. \$750.
   c. \$1,000.
   d. \$4,000.

19. The algebraic form of the consumption function for the above example is:
   a. $C = \$1,000 + .75(Y_d)$.
   b. $C = \$250 + .75(Y_d)$.
   c. $Y_d = C + S$.
   d. $MPC = 1 - MPS$.

20. In the above example, consumption spending at income equal to \$5,000 is:
   a. \$1,250.
   b. \$3,750.
   c. \$5,000.
   d. \$4,750.

21. In the above example, at disposable income of \$2,000, saving is equal to:
   a. \$0.
   b. \$500.
   c. –\$500.
   d. –\$250.

22. According to Keynes:
   a. equilibrium income and output are determined by available resources and technology in the short run.
   b. equilibrium income and output are determined by aggregate demand in the short run.
   c. the greatest macroeconomic concern during a recession is inflation.
   d. whatever is produced will be purchased.

23. In the Keynesian model of the macroeconomy, both consumption spending and personal saving increase in response to:
   a. lower interest rates.
   b. higher interest rates.
   c. higher disposable income.
   d. lower disposable income.

Use the following equations for a closed (no EX – IM) economy to answer the next four questions.

$C = \$300$ billion $+ 0.75(Y_D)$ $I = \$450$ billion $G = \$200$ billion $T = \$200$ billion

24. In equilibrium, output and income will equal _________ billion, and disposable income will equal _________ billion.
   a. $3,200; $3,000
   b. $3,200; $2,400
   c. $3,000; $2,400
   d. $3,000; $3,200

25. If full-employment (natural) real GDP in this economy is equal to $3,500 billion, then:
   a. the economy is at full-employment equilibrium.
   b. a recessionary gap exists.
   c. an inflationary gap exists.
   d. this economy can never achieve full employment.

26. If full-employment real GDP in this economy is $3,500 billion, how much of an increase in government spending would be necessary to achieve equilibrium at full employment, given the simplifying assumptions of the Keynesian model?
   a. $300 billion   c. $100 billion
   b. $450 billion   d. $75 billion

27. If full-employment real GDP in this economy is $3,500 billion, how much of a decrease in taxes would be necessary to achieve equilibrium at full employment, given the simplifying assumptions of the Keynesian model?
   a. $300 billion   c. $100 billion
   b. $450 billion   d. $75 billion

28. Keynes argued that, during the Great Depression, the economy may not automatically correct itself in the short run partly because:
   a. Say's Law was true.
   b. prices and wages were not flexible, especially downward.
   c. the economy was very competitive.
   d. aggregate supply was not able to increase as fast as aggregate demand.

29. The Keynesian approach to dealing with the massive unemployment during the Great Depression was to:
   a. allow market forces to initiate the changes in output and input prices necessary to move the economy toward full employment.
   b. argue in favor of government policies designed to stimulate total spending in the economy in order to increase aggregate demand.
   c. concentrate fiscal policy efforts on the supply side of the macroeconomy to increase long-run aggregate supply.
   d. use a mixture of expansionary and contractionary policies in order to achieve a balanced budget.

30. Changes in government spending or taxing policy for the purpose of influencing macroeconomic outcomes is:
   a. fiscal policy and is conducted by Congress.
   b. fiscal policy and is conducted by the Federal Reserve.
   c. currently unconstitutional but Congress is considering an amendment to make it legal.
   d. associated with the Classical model.

31. If equilibrium real GDP is equal to $5,000 billion and natural real GDP is equal to $5,450 billion and the MPC is 0.90, which of the following could move the economy to equilibrium at natural real GDP?
   a. A $45 billion increase in government spending
   b. A $50 billion decrease in taxes
   c. A $450 billion increase in government spending financed by a $450 billion increase in taxes
   d. All of the above
   e. Answers a. and b. only

32. When the marginal propensity to consume is 0.80, the spending multiplier is _______, the tax multiplier is _______, and the balanced-budget multiplier is ______.
   a. 8; -8; 1
   b. 8; -7; 5
   c. 5; -4; 1
   d. 4; -5; 5

33. What is the maximum change in equilibrium real GDP that could occur as result of a one-time $50 billion tax cut if the MPC is 0.75?
 a. $200 billion decrease.
 b. $200 billion increase
 c. $150 billion decrease.
 d. $150 billion increase.

34. An example of automatic fiscal policy is:
 a. an increase in the number of people receiving unemployment benefits during an economic downturn.
 b. Congress approving a government spending increase in order to stimulate aggregate demand when the economy is in a recession.
 c. lower interest rates leading to increases in private consumption and investment spending.
 d. the President issuing an executive order limiting the ability of people to become U.S. citizens.

35. Expansionary fiscal policy may not be an effective tool for increasing aggregate demand if:
 a. increases in government spending crowd out private sector (investment) activity.
 b. investors are very sensitive to changes in interest rates.
 c. there are no time lags associated with fiscal policy.
 d. businesses are very optimistic with respect to future economic conditions.

36. Which of the following is an example of supply-side fiscal policy?
 a. Increases in tax rates designed to increase government revenue, which will enable government to supply more social programs
 b. Increases in government spending that lead to multiple increases in equilibrium income and output
 c. Decreases in marginal tax rates designed to increase incentives to work and produce
 d. Decreases in government spending and taxing in order to decrease the impact of government on the supply-side of the economy

37. The relationship between tax rates and tax revenues is shown by the:
 a. aggregate demand curve.
 b. aggregate supply curve.
 c. Laffer Curve.
 d. Phillip's Curve.

Use the information in the table below to answer the next two questions.

Income	Tax Liability
$10,000	$0
$20,000	______
$30,000	$4,500
$40,000	$7,200

38. If the tax rate on $20,000 of taxable income is 12%, then the tax liability on the $20,000 will be _________.
    a. $1,200
    b. $1,667
    c. $2,000
    d. $2,400

39. The data in the above table indicate that the income tax structure is:
    a. proportional.
    b. progressive.
    c. regressive.
    d. categorical.

40. When government spending exceeds tax revenue in a given year:
    a. a budget deficit exists and the national debt increases.
    b. a budget deficit exists but the national debt stays the same.
    c. a budget surplus exists and the national debt decreases.
    d. the federal budget is in balance.

Answers to Practice Exam II

1. b	11. b	21. c	31. d
2. e	12. d	22. b	32. c
3. d	13. a	23. c	33. d
4. c	14. c	24. a	34. a
5. a	15. a	25. b	35. a
6. a	16. b	26. d	36. c
7. b	17. a	27. c	37. c
8. d	18. c	28. b	38. d
9. a	19. a	29. b	39. b
10. b	20. d	30. a	40. a

CHAPTER 10 Money and Banking

The Keynesian model presented the notion that government can use stabilization policy to shift AD and close a recessionary gap. One type of stabilization policy, fiscal policy, was addressed in the previous chapter. Before moving on to the other type of stabilization policy, monetary policy, the role of money in the economy and how banks affect the supply of money must be explained. The money and banking portion of this course is divided into three chapters, each with a distinct focus. This chapter defines many of the terms and presents the mathematics used to show the role of money in the modern U.S. economy. The next chapter (Chapter 11) introduces the Federal Reserve System, which is the central bank in the U.S. and is responsible for monetary policy in this country. It combines the mathematics of deposit creation with the tools of the Federal Reserve to give an overview of how monetary policy can be used to help stabilize the macroeconomy. Chapter 12 looks a several different theories regarding how monetary policy affects the economy.

The Nature of Money

Most people think of money simply as a medium of exchange: money is necessary for buying the goods and services people desire. Money, however, performs several other important functions that help facilitate exchange and aid in the smooth functioning of the financial side of the economy. One way to see the importance of money to the economy is to consider barter, which is the primary alternative to using money to conduct transactions. **Barter** is the direct exchange of goods and services. Barter transactions require that a **double coincidence of wants** be satisfied. For example, if I have a car that I am willing to trade for a boat, I have to find someone with a boat that I want, and that person has to want my car. In addition, we would both have to agree that it is a fair exchange. The transaction costs associated with barter are high because they are very time-consuming. Using money to conduct exchanges eliminates the need to satisfy a double coincidence of wants which reduces transaction costs and thereby facilitates exchange.

Money can take many physical forms and is considered money when it is generally accepted as a means of payment for goods and services and is the basis of a payments system. **Commodity money** is an item that serves a useful purpose other than acting as a medium of exchange. Salt, gold and other precious metals are examples of commodity moneys that have been used in the past. **Fiat money** is paper currency and coin that have been designated by government as legal tender (it must be accepted as payment for debts) but it is not convertible into a specific precious metal or other commodity. Modern payments systems make extensive use of checks, electronic payments, and e-money as forms of money. Advances in computer technology have decreased the need for people to carry around significant amounts of actual cash. Payments can be made over the phone, on the computer, with plastic cards, and by mail using checks, all of which reduce the need for currency. Not only that, many people have debit cards that let them access funds in a checking or savings account from an ATM (automatic teller machine) with the swipe of the card and an access code. Money can take many different physical forms and is considered money if it performs three primary functions for the economy: as a medium of exchange, as a unit of account, and as a store of value.

The Functions of Money

1) Medium of Exchange: a medium of exchange is something that is generally accepted in trade for goods and services and settlement of debts. People use money as a medium of exchange whenever they make purchases. The use of money as a medium of exchange allows us to avoid a barter economy and is considered beneficial because barter requires a double coincidence of wants and leads to inefficiency.

2) Unit of Account (Standard of Value): money acts a common denominator for comparing the relative values of goods and services. It is very convenient to be able to discuss the value of something, enter into a contract, or keep accounting records using money values. Money serves this function and increases efficiency because using money values to make decisions, communicate, and keep records reduces transactions costs.

3) Store of Value (Store of Wealth): money serves as a store of value, because it stores purchasing power over time and can be used for future purchases. People don't always want to spend all of their income as soon as it is received. Money is not unique as a store of value and its value actually depreciates during periods of inflation. For large sums over long periods of time, most people use stocks, bonds, or real assets to store value. However, it is necessary for money to serve as a store of value in order for it to be accepted as a medium of exchange; in an economy with hyperinflation (the inflation rate is greater than 50% per month), money loses value so quickly that people may refuse to accept it in exchange for goods and services.

Money is not necessarily the best store of value, but people still hold some of their wealth in the form of money because it is liquid. **Liquidity** is the ease with which an asset can be converted into a medium of exchange (cash) without loss of value. Money is the most liquid of all assets because it is already a medium of exchange. Other assets entail transactions costs when converted into money: there is either a time cost, such as the time required to sell stocks and bonds and receive the funds from the sale, or a money cost, such as a monetary penalty for early withdrawal from a time deposit.

Measures of the Money Supply

The Federal Reserve is the central bank of the U.S. and is responsible for controlling the nation's money supply. The Federal Reserve (the Fed) uses several **monetary aggregates** to measure and define the money supply. Until March 2006, the Fed tracked measures of money designated M1, M2, and M3. They no longer track and record the M3 measure because it has not revealed useful information not already contained in M1 or M2 in quite some time.

The narrowest definition, M1, includes liquid assets, such as cash and checking account deposits, that are directly and immediately spendable.

M1 = currency held by the public + demand and other checkable deposits + traveler's checks

In September, 2018, the value of the seasonally adjusted M1 money supply was \$3,731.1 billion. Currency comprised \$1,610.7 billion, traveler's checks were \$1.7 billion, demand deposits were \$1,486.4 billion and other checkable deposits were \$632.3 billion. Currency is currently the largest single component of the M1 money supply.

The broader measure of the money supply, M2, includes both liquid (spendable) assets that are contained in the M1 measure of money plus less liquid assets, or near-monies. Money market deposit accounts are included in savings deposits

M2 = M1 + savings deposits + small denomination time deposits + retail money funds

At the end of September, 2018, the value of the M2 money supply was \$14,253.7 billion, and it was nearly four times larger than M1. The Federal Reserve releases money supply data every Thursday at 4:30 p.m. To view this and other related topics, visit the Federal Reserve's website at www.federalreserve.gov.

Fractional Reserve Banking and Deposit Creation

In a **fractional reserve banking system**, depository institutions, which will be referred to as **banks** from this point on, are required to hold only a small fraction of their total deposits on reserve. In the U.S., **bank reserves** can legally be in the form of cash in a bank's vault or as deposits at a Federal Reserve Bank. The fraction of deposits that must be held as reserves is called **required reserves**. Required reserves are expressed as a percentage of total deposits and this percentage is called the **required reserve ratio**. Currently, the typical required reserve ratio for demand deposits is 10 percent. Reserves held beyond the minimum required are called **excess reserves**. Profit-maximizing banks may have an incentive to keep excess reserves close to zero because banks may earn more by putting funds into other interest-bearing assets such as loans and securities.

When the public makes deposits in a bank, the bank gains reserves. Since the bank must retain only a small fraction of these reserves, the rest (**excess reserves**) may be loaned out. Whenever banks make loans using excess reserves, money is created. For example, suppose you deposit \$100 cash into your checking account. If the required reserve ratio is 10 percent, then your bank must keep \$10 on reserve, but may now make a loan in the amount of \$90. The person who borrows the \$90 from the bank is now free to spend that amount, while you are still free to spend your \$100. Thus, money has been created. Furthermore, the \$90 that was borrowed and then spent will be deposited in another bank if we assume that there are no **currency leakages**. The bank that receives the \$90 deposit must keep 10 percent, or \$9, on reserve, and may now make a loan in the amount of \$81. This process, referred to as a **multiplier** process, will continue for some time, with a smaller amount being loaned (created) in each successive round. Rather than taking the time to calculate the change in the money supply with each of these successive rounds, a formula for the simple deposit multiplier will help easily estimate the eventual impact of an increase in reserves on the money supply. The process is referred to as **deposit creation.**

The amount of deposits that can be created as a result of an initial increase in bank reserves is illustrated using some very basic equations and t-accounts. The terms and equations are given below.

Actual or Total Bank Reserves (R) consist of cash in the bank's vault and deposits at the Federal Reserve Bank.

Required Reserves (RR) = the required reserve ratio x Total Deposits = (r)(D)

Excess Reserves (ER) = Total Bank Reserves – Required Reserves = R - RR

The model of deposit creation that follows is based on several simplifying assumptions:

1) there are no leakages into cash. This means that all new loans will show up as new deposits somewhere in the banking system.
2) banks will not hold idle excess reserves. This means that banks will continue to lend until excess reserves are equal to zero and all reserves are required reserves. When excess reserves are equal to zero, there are no available funds to lend and banks are said to be "fully loaned up." When banks are fully loaned up, the banking system is in equilibrium.
3) demand deposits are the only liabilities of a bank and reserves and loans are the only assets. This assumption will be relaxed in the next chapter to account for the fact that banks can use excess reserves to purchase government securities as well as make loans.
4) the required reserve ratio is 10%.

For convenience, the transactions associated with money creation or deposit expansion can be recorded in a simplified balance sheet called a t-account. A t-account may be drawn for either an individual bank or for the banking system as a whole. In this simplified t-account, only the assets and liabilities that are relevant to the money creation process are represented. Whenever someone makes a deposit, the bank records both an asset (reserves) and a liability (demand deposits).

Assets	Liabilities
Total Bank Reserves	Demand Deposits
Loans	

Assume you make that $100 cash deposit into your checking account at Your Bank. If the required reserve ratio is 10 percent, then Your Bank is required to keep only $10 in reserves to support the $100 deposit. The difference, excess reserves, may be loaned out. The bank retains a paper asset, or an IOU, representing a promise to repay the loan. This paper asset is recorded in the t-account as a loan. As a result of the bank's loan, $90 has been added to the money supply because the original depositor can still spend the $100 checking account balance, and now the borrower can spend the $90 provided by the bank in the form of a loan. The following t-account summarizes the transactions that occurred at Your Bank. Notice that the change in total assets is equal to the change in total liabilities, or that the t-account is in balance.

Your Bank Assets	Your Bank Liabilities
Bank Reserves = +$10	Demand Deposits = +$100
Loans = +$90	
Total Assets = +$100	Total Liabilities = +$100

The loan is very likely to be spent by the person who borrowed $90. The person who receives the funds will deposit these funds into another bank, so the money creation process will continue. Bank #2 receives a new deposit and new reserves of $90. Bank #2 is required to hold 10%, or $9, of the deposit as reserves and now has excess reserves of $81. Bank #2 lends the $81 and the transactions for Bank #2 are shown in the t-account below.

Bank #2 Assets	Bank #2 Liabilities
Bank Reserves = +$9	Demand Deposits = +$90
Loans = +$81	
Total Assets = +$90	Total Liabilities = +$90

The $81 is spent and deposited in yet another bank somewhere in the banking system. That bank then has $81 in new reserves, $8.10 of which must be held as reserves, and $72.90 in new excess reserves. The bank can lend the $72.90, which in turn, becomes a new deposit and new reserves, et cetera. Notice that the amount available for loans is getting smaller in each successive round. This is because each bank must hold 10% of the initial deposit as required reserves. The lending process continues until there are no excess reserves in the system and all reserves are required reserves.

Rather than go through numerous rounds of lending and illustrating each round in a t-account, a simple equation can be used to show the maximum amount of new deposits that can be created through lending. The **simple deposit multiplier** is equal to one divided by the required reserve ratio, or 1/r. This multiplier gives the number of deposit dollars that can be supported by $1 of reserves. If the required reserve ratio is 10%, the simple deposit multiplier is equal to 1/0.10 = 10. The maximum amount of total deposits that can be supported by $100 of reserves when the simple deposit multiplier is 10 is (10)($100) = $1,000. The **simple deposit multiplier** can be used to find the maximum possible amount of total bank deposits that can be created (deposit creation) when bank reserves increase and lending occurs until excess reserves are equal to zero for all banks. **Potential deposit creation** is equal to the change in excess reserves (ΔER) times the simple deposit multiplier (1/r).

This equation can be used to finish the example of the impact of your deposit of $100 into Your Bank. The initial increase in excess reserves was $90 in Your Bank. The $90 increase in excess reserves can be multiplied 10 times to become new loans and new deposits in the banking system. The result is that new deposits can be created through lending equal to:

$$\text{Potential Deposit Creation} = (\Delta ER)(1/r) = (\$90)(10) = \$900.$$

The maximum increase in the money supply as a result of deposit creation is $900. Combining all of the changes for banks within the system into one t-account shows the final impact on the system.

T-Account for the Banking System

Assets	Liabilities
Bank Reserves = +$100	Demand Deposits = +$100 from your initial deposit
Loans = +$900	Demand Deposits = +$900 created through lending
Total Assets = +$1,000	Total Liabilities = +$1,000

Double-check the outcome by using the simple deposit multiplier to determine the maximum number of deposit dollars that can be supported by bank reserves. If the required reserve ratio is 10%, the simple deposit multiplier is 10 and $100 in bank reserves can support, at most, (10)($100) = $1,000 in deposits. The banking system has total liabilities of $1,000 once banks are fully loaned up. The real world multiplier is less than 1/r because there are leakages into cash, banks may choose to hold excess reserves greater than zero, and banks have assets other than reserves and loans. The next chapter looks at how bank holdings of government securities affect the money creation process and how the Federal Reserve influences the amount of reserves and securities held by banks.

The Mathematics of the Simple Deposit Creation Model

Equations to remember:

(1) Required Reserves (RR) = Required Reserve Ratio (r) x Total Deposits (D)

OR: RR = (r)(D)

(2) Excess Reserves (ER) = Total Bank Reserves (R) – Required Reserves (RR)

OR: ER = R – RR

(3) Simple Deposit Multiplier = 1/Required-Reserve Ratio = 1/r

(4) Potential Deposit Creation = Excess Reserves x Deposit Multiplier = (ER)(1/r)

(5) When excess reserves are zero, total reserves times the deposit multiplier equals deposits.

OR: If ER = 0, then (R)(1/r) = D

EX 1: Calculate required reserves when total deposits are $80,000,000 and the required reserve ratio is 20%. Use equation (1).

RR = (r)(D) = (.20)($80,000,000) = $16,000,000

EX 2: What is the required reserve ratio if banks are required to hold $100 billion in reserves to support $400 billion in deposits? Rearrange equation (1).

r = RR/D = $100 billion/$400 billion = .25 or 25%

EX 3: Calculate deposits if required reserves are $150,000 and the required reserve ratio is 10%. Rearrange equation (1).

D = RR/r = $150,000/.10 = $1,500,000

EX 4: What are excess reserves if $75 billion of the $120 billion in total reserves held by banks are required reserves? Use equation (2).

ER = R – RR = $120 billion - $75 billion = $45 billion

EX 5: How much do banks have in excess reserves if total reserves are $400,000, deposits are $2,000,000, and the required reserve ratio is 10%?

Step 1: Use equation (1) to calculate RR. RR = (r)(D) = (.10)($2,000,000) = $200,000

Step 2: Use equation (2) to calculate ER. ER = $400,000 - $200,000 = $200,000

EX 6: What is potential deposit creation throughout the banking system from EX 5 on the previous page?

Step 1: Use equation (3) to calculate the deposit multiplier.

Simple Deposit Multiplier = $1/r = 1/.10 = 10$

Step 2: Use equation (4) to calculate potential deposit creation.

Deposit Creation = $(ER)(1/r) = (\$200{,}000)(10) = \$2{,}000{,}000$

OR: Use equation (5) to determine the maximum supportable deposits (D_2) and subtract current deposits (D_1) from the maximum to get the potential increase in deposits.

Maximum Deposits = $D_2 = (R)(1/r) = (\$400{,}000)(10) = \$4{,}000{,}000$

Potential Increase in Deposits = $D_2 - D_1 = \$4{,}000{,}000 - \$2{,}000{,}000 = \$2{,}000{,}000$

EX 7: By how much can the banking system expand deposits if total reserves are \$600,000, deposits are \$2,500,000, and the required reserve ratio is 20%?

Step 1: Use equation (1) to calculate RR.

$RR = (r)(D) = .20(\$2{,}500{,}000) = \$500{,}000$

Step 2: Use equation (2) to calculate ER.

$ER = R - RR = \$600{,}000 - \$500{,}000 = \$100{,}000$

Step 3: Use equation (3) to calculate the simple deposit multiplier.

Simple Deposit Multiplier = $1/r = 1/.20 = 5$

Step 4: Use equation (4) to calculate potential deposit creation.

Deposit Creation = $(ER)(1/r) = (\$100{,}000)(5) = \$500{,}000$

OR: Use equation (5) to get maximum potential deposits and subtract current deposits.

Maximum Deposits = $D_2 = (R)(1/r) = (\$600{,}000)(5) = \$3{,}000{,}000$

Potential Increase in Deposits = $D_2 - D_1 = \$3{,}000{,}000 - \$2{,}500{,}000 = \$500{,}000$

NAME____ SECTION #______________

Print Last Name, First Name

DEPOSIT AND RESERVE CALCULATIONS

Use the simple deposit creation model to fill in blanks 1 – 10. Assume no leakages into cash, and that the only assets of banks are reserves and loans, and the only liability is deposits.

1. A bank with $1,500,000 in deposits has required reserves of $____________________ if the required ratio is 10%.

2. If the bank in number 1 has total reserves of $200,000, then the bank has excess reserves of $____________________.

3. The required reserve ratio is __________ if banks are required to hold $60 billion in reserves to support $400 billion in deposits

4. If Bank A is holding $15 million in reserves, then Bank A has checkable deposits equal to $ ________________, if excess reserves are currently equal to zero and the required reserve ratio is 20%.

5. If the required reserve ratio is 10%, the value of the simple deposit multiplier is _______.

6. If the required reserve is 10%, then $2 million in bank reserves can support a maximum of $______________________ in deposits.

7. Required reserves are $_____________________ when total reserves are $800,000, the required reserve ratio is 20%, and total checkable deposits are $4,000,000.

8. Based on the information in number 7, excess reserves are $____________________.

9. The required reserve ratio is ____________ if banks are required to hold $125 billion in reserves to support $1,000 billion in deposits.

10. If the required reserve ratio is 10% and Bank C is holding $400,000 in reserves, then Bank C's checkable deposits are $__________________ if Bank C has excess reserves currently equal to zero.

NAME____ SECTION #______________
Print Last Name, First Name

T-ACCOUNTS

Use the simple deposit creation model to draw t-accounts based on the information given below. Assume no leakages into cash, that banks wish to be fully loaned up (excess reserves equal zero), and that reserves and loans are the only assets, and deposits are the only liability.

1 Draw a T-account for Bank A assuming it has $6,000,000 in checkable deposits and $5,250,000 in outstanding loans. What is the required reserve ratio if excess reserves are equal to zero?

2. Draw a T-account for Bank A assuming it has $5,000,000 in checkable deposits and $4,500,000 in outstanding loans. What is the required reserve ratio if Bank A's excess reserves are equal to zero?

NAME____ SECTION #_____________

Print Last Name, First Name

MONEY

1. Money is best defined as:
   a. a debt incurred when payment is deferred when making a purchase on credit.
   b. an asset that is generally accepted as a means of payment for goods and services.
   c. an asset that serves as the best possible store of value over time.
   d. anything you can trade in exchange for other goods and services.

2. Which of the following is **not** one of the three main functions of money?
   a. Medium of exchange
   b. Unit of account
   c. Protection against inflation
   d. Store of value

3. You are using money as a store of value when you:
   a. purchase an ice cream cone.
   b. save for a vacation.
   c. tell a friend how much you paid for your new car.
   d. buy something on sale and get good value for your money.

4. Money is more efficient than barter for conducting transactions because:
   a. using money requires satisfying a double coincidence of wants, which increases transaction times.
   b. using money does not require satisfying a double coincidence of wants, which reduces transaction times.
   c. most money is made of paper that is difficult to counterfeit.
   d. barter does not use any specific material so it cannot be counterfeited.

5. Since the U.S. government has decreed that U.S. currency is legal tender:
   a. people are more likely to accept the dollar as a medium of exchange.
   b. the government must hold enough gold to redeem all currency.
   c. it is illegal for people to make trades with anything else.
   d. All of the above are correct

6. When depositors move funds from their saving accounts into their checking accounts:
   a. M1 decreases, M2 stays the same, and the system becomes less liquid.
   b. M1 decreases, M2 increases, and the system becomes less liquid.
   c. M2 increases, M1 increases, and the system becomes more liquid.
   d. M2 stays the same, M1 increases, and the system becomes more liquid.

NAME____ SECTION #____________

Print Last Name, First Name

Use the data in the table below to answer questions 7 – 8:

Currency held by the public	**\$1,200 billion**
Demand and other checkable deposits	**\$2,000 billion**
Traveler's checks	**\$2 billion**
Small denomination time deposits	**\$500 billion**
Savings deposits*	**\$9,200 billion**
Retail money funds	**\$780 billion**

***money market deposit accounts are included in savings deposits**

7. The value of the M1 money supply is:
   a. \$3,200 billion.
   b. \$3,202 billion.
   c. \$2,205 billion.
   d. \$1,002 billion.

8. If the public deposits \$200 billion of currency into savings deposits, then the value of:
   a. M1 decreases by \$200 billion and the value of M2 increase by \$200 billion.
   b. M1 decrease by \$200 billion and the value of M2 remains \$13,682 billion.
   c. M1 stays the same and the value of M2 increases to \$13,882.
   d. M1 and M2 both increase by \$200 billion.

9. M1 is the most liquid measure of the money supply because its components:
   a. cannot be used to purchase goods and services directly.
   b. may be used to purchase goods and services directly.
   c. do not retain their real value over time and do not serve as a hedge against inflation.
   d. retain their real value over time and serve as a hedge against inflation.

10. The "liquidity" of an asset refers to:
   a. how well the asset serves as a store of value.
   b. the rate of return earned by the holder of the asset.
   c. the ease with which the asset may be converted into a medium of exchange without loss of value.
   d. how well the asset serves as a hedge against inflation.

NAME____ SECTION #____________

Print Last Name, First Name

BANKING

1. Who sets the required reserve ratio? How would lowering the required reserve ratio affect bank lending, the money supply, and the economy (output, employment, and prices)?

2. Complete the table below:

Required reserve ratio	Simple deposit multiplier	Maximum amount of deposits if reserves = \$2 billion
25%	______________	____________________
20%	______________	____________________
12.5%	______________	____________________
10%	______________	____________________
5%	______________	____________________

3. The simple deposit multiplier can be used to predict the effect of a change in total bank reserves (R) on total bank deposits (D) and the money supply (M1). What assumptions are necessary to conclude that $\Delta D/\Delta R = \Delta M1/\Delta R = 1/r$?

NAME____ SECTION #______________

Print Last Name, First Name

MONEY AND BANKING

Use the monetary aggregates below to fill in blanks 1 – 10.

Note: Monetary Aggregates provide values for ALL BANKS in the banking system

Currency held by the public = $180 billion
Total Checkable Deposits = $720 billion
Total Bank Reserves = $185 billion
Required Reserve Ratio = 25 percent

1. Currently, the M1 money supply is equal to $__________________ billion.

2. Required Reserves (for all banks combined) equal $________________ billion.

3. Excess Reserves (for all banks combined) equal $________________ billion.

4. The simple deposit multiplier is equal to ______________.

Assume that maximum deposit expansion occurs with **no currency leakages** (that is, currency held by the public remains equal to $180 billion).

5. Total Checkable Deposits can increase by a maximum of $________________ billion, for all banks combined) assuming that each bank is "fully loaned up" or holding zero excess reserves.

6. The new amount of Checkable Deposits is $________________ billion.

7. The new value for M1 is $____________________ billion.

Fill in the t-account for the banking system showing Total Bank Reserves, Total Checkable Deposits, and the value of loans held by all banks combined, assuming maximum deposit expansion has occurred as calculated above.

Assets (billions) *for all banks*	**Liabilities (billions)** *for all banks*
Total Bank Reserves = 8. _______________	**Checkable Deposits** = 10._______________
Loans = 9._______________	

NAME____ SECTION #____________

Print Last Name, First Name

BANKING AND DEPOSIT CREATION

1. In the U.S. banking system, banks are required to hold:
   a. a fraction of total deposits on reserve.
   b. a multiple of total deposits on reserve.
   c. whatever amount of cash they feel is prudent.
   d. enough cash to back every dollar of deposits.

2. In the U.S. banking system, depository institutions (banks) may hold required reserves:
   a. only as vault cash.
   b. only on deposit at a Federal Reserve Bank.
   c. as government bonds so they can be easily liquidated.
   d. as either vault cash or on deposit at a Federal Reserve Bank.

Use the information in the T-account for a single bank in the banking system to answer questions 3 - 5:

Assets		Liabilities	
Total Bank Reserves	**$50,000**	**Checkable Deposits**	**$400,000**
Loans	**$350,000**		

3. If the required reserve ratio is 10%, then required reserves are equal to:
   a. $400,000.
   b. $40,000.
   c. $50,000.
   d. $60,000.

4. If the required reserve ratio is 10%, then excess reserves are equal to:
   a. $0.
   b. $10,000.
   c. $15,000.
   d. $20,000.

5. If the required reserve ratio is 10%, then the maximum additional amount this bank can lend is:
   a. $0.
   b. $10,000.
   c. $15,000.
   d. $20,000.

NAME______________________________ SECTION #__________

Print Last Name, First Name

Use the information in the T-account for the Banking System to answer questions 6 – 9:

Assets (billions) *for all banks*		**Liabilities (billions)** *for all banks*	
Total Bank Reserves	**$65**	**Checkable Deposits**	**$500**
Loans	**$435**		

6. If the required reserve ratio is 12.5 percent, the banking system currently has excess reserves equal to:
   a. $12.5 billion.
   b. $50 billion.
   c. $2.5 billion.
   d. $0.

7. If the required reserve ratio is 12.5 percent, the simple deposit multiplier is equal to:
   a. 2. b. 4. c. 8. d. 12.5.

8. If every bank in the system with a 12.5 percent required reserve ratio continues to make new loans until excess reserves in the entire system are equal to zero and there are no currency leakages, then checkable deposits can increase *by* a maximum of:
   a. $8 billion.
   b. $10 billion.
   c. $12.5 billion.
   d. $20 billion.

9. If the M1 money supply was initially equal to $1,500 billion, and then checkable deposits increased by the amount indicated in the previous question, the new value of M1 will be:
   a. $2,000 billion.
   b. $1,520 billion.
   c. $2,500 billion.
   d. $1,600 billion.

10. In a fractional reserve banking system, money is created when:
    a. banks accept cash deposits.
    b. the Treasury Department prints new coins.
    c. banks make new loans.
    d. the U.S. Mint issues new paper money.

NAME____ SECTION #____________

Print Last Name, First Name

BANKING AND MONEY CREATION

1. Which of the following is ***correct***?
   a. Total bank reserves = excess reserves/required reserves
   b. Total bank reserves = excess reserves + required reserves
   c. Excess reserves = total bank reserves + required reserves
   d. Required reserves = (excess reserves) x (total bank reserves)

2. Mr. Jones deposited $5,000 cash into his account at Bank A. If the required reserve ratio is 10%, Bank A has to keep _____ in the form of required reserves and can make a loan equal to _____.
   a. $500; $4,500
   b. $1,000; $4,000
   c. $500; $5,000
   d. $5,000: $0

3. To support checkable deposits, banks are legally required to hold reserves equal to:
   a. total checkable deposits.
   b. vault cash.
   c. total checkable deposits multiplied by the required reserve ratio.
   d. total checkable deposits divided by the required reserve ratio.

4. If the required reserve ratio is 10%, the banking system has total reserves in the amount of $40 billion, there are no currency leakages, and each bank makes loans until excess reserves equal zero, then total checkable deposits for the banking system will equal:
   a. $10 billion.
   b. $40 billion.
   c. $200 billion.
   d. $400 billion.

5. If the required reserve ratio decreases from 10 percent to 8 percent:
   a. potential deposit expansion decreases.
   b. potential deposit expansion increases.
   c. the simple deposit multiplier decreases from 12.5 to 10.
   d. the simple deposit multiplier increases from 10 to 12.5.
   e. Both b. and d. are correct.

NAME____ SECTION #______________

Print Last Name, First Name

Use the information in the T-account for a single bank to answer questions 6 – 10:

Assets		Liabilities	
Total Bank Reserves	**$100,000**	**Checkable Deposits**	**$500,000**
Loans	**$400,000**		

6. If the required reserve ratio is 20%, then required reserves are equal to:
   a. $0.
   b. $5,000.
   c. $15,000.
   d. $100,000.

7. If the required reserve ratio is 20%, then excess reserves are equal to:
   a. $0.
   b. $5,000.
   c. $15,000.
   d. $115,000.

8. If the required reserve ratio is 20%, then the maximum additional amount this bank can lend is:
   a. $0.
   b. $5,000.
   c. $15,000.
   d. $115,000.

9. If the required reserve ratio is 20% and this bank is 'fully loaned up' (i.e., makes loans until excess reserves are equal to zero), then the bank's total loan assets will be equal to:
   a. $100,000.
   b. $400,000.
   c. $500,000.
   d. $1,000,000.

10. If the required reserve ratio is 20%, the simple deposit multiplier is equal to:
   a. 4.
   b. 5.
   c. 8.
   d. 12.5.

CHAPTER 11 The Federal Reserve System and Monetary Policy

The Federal Reserve System, which is the central bank of the U.S., was created by Congress in 1913, with the vision that the primary role of the central bank would be as lender of last resort to the banking community. The Federal Reserve (the Fed) would provide reserves in the form of discount loans to the banking system to avoid bank panics, which occurred with relative frequency in the late 1800s and early 1900s. A widespread panic in 1907 that caused bank failures and substantial losses to depositors helped convince a previously resistant nation to create a central bank. The role of the Fed has expanded and the Fed now serves several functions in addition to serving as lender of last resort. Several pieces of legislation in the 1930s gave the Fed more control over the tools of monetary policy.

Monetary policy refers to actions by a central bank, such as the Federal Reserve, to control the flow of money and credit through the economy in order to help promote national economic goals. The Fed uses three main tools of monetary policy – **reserve requirements, the discount rate, and open market operations** – to regulate and influence the lending activity (deposit creation) of depository institutions (banks) within the banking system. The Fed uses the three tools to influence the demand for, and supply of, reserve balances held by depository institutions at Federal Reserve Banks. Changes in reserves in the system affect the **federal funds rate,** which in turn impacts other rates and the flow of credit in the economy. Recent events in credit and other related markets have prompted Congress to expand the Fed's role to increase its lending and oversight activity to include some nonbank institutions.

The goals of the Fed in its conduct of monetary policy and oversight of the financial system are to provide stability to the financial sector of the economy, stabilize the price level, and foster full employment and economic growth. The three main entities within the Federal Reserve System that have the greatest impact on, and ability to influence, monetary policy are the Federal Reserve banks, the Board of Governors of the Federal Reserve System, and the Federal Open Market Committee.

The Structure of the Fed

The U.S. is divided into twelve separate Federal Reserve districts; each district has one main Federal Reserve Bank and one or more branches in other locations within the district. The largest Federal Reserve Bank is the Federal Reserve Bank of New York. Each Federal Reserve bank is a quasi-public institution (part private, part government) that is owned by member banks within the district that have bought stock in their district bank. National banks must be members of the system and state-chartered banks have the choice of whether or not to be a member. Federal Reserve district banks perform several functions, including:

1) **issuing new currency**
2) **providing check-clearing services**
3) **holding depository institutions' reserve accounts**
4) **making discount loans to banks**
5) **collecting data on business conditions within their district**
6) **researching topics related to monetary policy.**

The **Board of Governors** of the Federal Reserve System consists of seven members. Governors are appointed by the President (with Senate confirmation) to 14-year, nonrenewable, staggered terms and must come from different Federal Reserve districts to ensure that one area of the country will not be overrepresented. One member is chosen by the President every four years to serve as the Chair of the Board of Governors. Jerome Powell was appointed by President Trump and took office as the 16th Chairman of the Federal Reserve in February 2018. Powell previously served as a member of the Board of Governors under Chair Janet Yellen. Only four of the seven seats on the Board are filled as of September 2018. The Board of Governors is responsible for the discount rate and reserve requirements.

The **Federal Open Market Committee (FOMC)** holds eight regularly scheduled meetings a year in Washington, D.C., to make decisions regarding the conduct of open market operations, the main tool for conducting monetary policy. The FOMC holds additional meetings as needed. The voting members of the FOMC are the seven members of the Board of Governors, the President of the Federal Reserve Bank of New York, and four other Federal Reserve Bank Presidents who serve on a rotating basis. The chair of the Board of Governors also serves as chair of the FOMC. The presidents of the other seven district banks attend the meetings and participate in discussions but are not voting members of the committee. The minutes of the regularly scheduled FOMC meetings are made public on the Federal Reserve Board's website (www.federalreserve.gov/monetarypolicy/fomccalendars.htm) three weeks after the day of each meeting.

National banks, those chartered by the Office of the Comptroller of the Currency, are required to be members of the Federal Reserve System. State-chartered banks are not required to be members but can choose to join by purchasing stock in their district Federal Reserve bank. Prior to 1980, only member banks were required to comply with Fed reserve requirements, and only member banks had access to Federal Reserve services and facilities. The Depository Institutions Deregulation and Monetary Control Act of 1980 changed the rules: all depository institutions (banks) are subject to the same reserve requirements and have equal access to the Fed discount window and Fed services, such as check clearing.

<u>The Monetary Policy Tools of the Fed</u>

The Fed has three basic monetary tools it can use to directly control the money supply: **open market operations, discount loans, and reserve requirements**. The Fed can use both open market operations and discount loans to alter the monetary base and the money supply. The **monetary base (MB)**, also referred to as high-powered money, has two components: currency in circulation (C) and total reserves in the banking system (R). The monetary base is expressed as:

$$MB = C + R.$$

When a Federal Reserve action alters the amount of reserves (R) in the system, the monetary base changes.

Open Market Operations

The primary way the Fed causes changes in the monetary base and the money supply is through the use of **open market operations (OMO)**. Open Market Operations are the responsibility of the Federal Open Market Committee. When the Fed buys and sells government securities on the open market, it directly alters the reserves of the banking system and hence the system's ability to make loans. The FOMC issues an order to BUY bonds in the open market if an increase in the monetary base and the money supply is desired. The FOMC issues an order to SELL bonds in the open market as a means of slowing down monetary growth or even reducing the money supply.

The basic mechanics of deposit creation and t-accounts can be used to illustrate the impact of an **open market purchase of securities** from a bank. At this point, the model will be expanded to include U.S government treasury securities (bonds) as assets that can be held by banks. Suppose the Fed buys $1,000 worth of bonds from a bank and pays for the bonds with a check. The bank may deposit the check in its account at a Federal Reserve district bank or cash it and store the proceeds in its vault. Recall that bank reserves can be in the form of bank deposits at Federal Reserve district banks or as vault cash held by banks. Either way, bank reserves have increased by $1,000. All of the $1,000 in new reserves represents excess reserves because the bank did not receive a deposit and thus has no offsetting liability. The bank converted its securities, an asset, to reserves, another asset. The t-accounts below show the impact of the Federal Reserve open market purchase on the banking system and the Federal Reserve System.

Banking System

Assets	Liabilities
Securities: – $1,000	
Reserves: + $1,000	

The impact on the banking system is $1,000 in new reserves, all of which can become new loans.

Federal Reserve System

Assets	Liabilities
Securities: + $1,000	Bank Reserves: +$1,000

The impact on the Fed's balance sheet is an increase in Fed assets because the Fed now holds an additional $1,000 in securities. There is also an increase on the liabilities side of the Fed's balance sheet as a result of holding an additional $1,000 of reserves for banks.

If all of the new bank reserves are excess reserves, then additional loans of $1,000 can be made. These new loans become new deposits elsewhere in the system and there can be a multiple expansion of deposits (deposit creation through lending) by a maximum of the initial increase in excess reserves times the simple deposit multiplier. Assuming that the required reserve ratio is 10 percent, the banking system can expand loans and deposits by a maximum of:

$$\text{Potential Deposit Creation} = (\Delta ER)(1/r) = (\$1{,}000)(10) = \$10{,}000.$$

The initial $1,000 increase in reserves could lead to an increase in the money supply of as much as $10,000. **A Federal Reserve open market purchase of securities (the Fed buys bonds) is expansionary**. When the Federal Reserve buys securities from banks, the amount of reserves in the banking system and the monetary base both increase by the amount of the Fed transaction.

The Fed may also buy bonds from the public. When this occurs, banks experience an increase in reserves when the public deposits the proceeds from the sale of bonds into banks. Bank reserves increase but because the increase comes as a result of a new deposit, banks must hold 10 percent to meet reserve requirements. Only $900 will be excess reserves and subject to the lending multiplier and a maximum of ($900)(10) = $9,000 can be created by lending. However, the impact on the money supply is the same because the Fed purchase led to an increase of $1,000 in checkable deposits for the public plus the $9,000 of created deposits for an increase of $10,000 in the money supply. This assumes that there are no leakages into cash. If the public chooses to hold the proceeds from the Fed purchase in the form of currency, then the monetary base increases by the amount of the Fed purchase but reserves in the banking system will remain unchanged.

If the Federal Reserve conducts an **open market sale of securities**, the process is reversed. When the Fed sells bonds to banks, bank reserves and the monetary base decrease by the amount of the Fed transaction. When the Fed sells bonds to the public, the monetary base decreases by the amount of the Fed sale but the impact on reserves depends on how the public pays for the bonds. In either case, **a Federal Reserve open market sale of securities (the Fed sells bonds) is contractionary** because it decreases the monetary base and the potential for the system to support new deposits created through lending.

The Discount Rate

In the Fed's capacity as lender of last resort, it often makes short-term loans to banks with reserve deficiencies, called **discount loans**. Discount lending also affects the monetary base because bank reserves are altered when bank borrowings from the Fed change. The **discount rate** is the rate of interest the Fed charges banks on such loans. Changes in the discount rate send signals to the financial community as to the monetary policy leanings of the Fed. An increase in the discount rate signals the Fed's intent to either slow monetary growth or contract the money supply. A decrease in the discount rate is often interpreted as a signal of monetary expansion. Recall that the Fed is considered to be the lender of last resort by banks. Reserve-poor banks are more likely to borrow from reserve-rich banks than from the Fed.

Reports by the media frequently stress the Fed's announcements about changes in the **federal funds rate target**. When banks borrow reserves directly from the Fed, the rate of interest they pay is the discount rate. When banks borrow reserves from each other, the rate of interest they pay is the **federal funds rate**. Unlike the discount rate, which the Fed sets, the federal funds rate is determined by supply and demand in the federal funds market (the market for reserves). When many banks have excess reserves, the supply of funds in this market is high, leading to a low rate of interest. The Fed can influence the federal funds rate by altering the amount of reserves in the system, usually through open market operations. Financial markets normally react to an announcement by the Fed that the federal funds rate target has been raised or lowered by assuming that other interest rates, including bond yields, will move in the same direction as the federal funds rate.

Another important interest rate in the economy is the **prime rate**, which is the rate banks charge their best, most credit-worthy (prime) customers. The 'prime rate' quoted in the news is usually the Wall Street Journal Prime Rate (listed as WSJ Prime Rate), which is the consensus rate for the 30 largest banks. The WSJ surveys the 30 largest banks; when ¾ of those banks change their prime rate, the WSJ Prime Rate changes. While most consumers are not considered most-favored customers and are charged rates above prime, the prime rate affects them because other rates in the economy, such as mortgage and credit card rates, are often tied to the prime rate. In October of 2018, the prime rate was 5.25%, the federal funds rate was 1.02%, and the discount rate was 2.75%, all up 1%, or one basis point, from the previous year. This data shows the recent pattern in the relationship between the three rates: the federal funds rate is the lowest and the prime rate is the highest. The three rates also tend to move together. For information on these rates and other rates, go to www.federalreserve.gov and www.bankrate.com.

Reserve Requirements

The final tool at the Fed's disposal for influencing credit conditions and the money supply is reserve requirements. Changes in the **required reserve ratio** are infrequent because the effect is more powerful and less controlled than using open market operations. Even a small reduction in the required reserve ratio may have a large impact on bank reserves and potential lending activity, because each and every bank would have excess reserves. Changing the required reserve ratio also changes the simple deposit multiplier. If the required reserve ratio is 10 percent, the simple deposit multiplier is 1/.10 = 10 and $1 in reserves can support $10 in deposits. If the required reserve ratio was lowered to 8 percent, the simple deposit multiplier would increase to 1/.08 = 12.5; that same $1 in reserves could now support $12.50 in deposits.

A decrease in the required reserve ratio would have an expansionary effect on the money supply. An increase in the required reserve ratio is contractionary because it decreases the value of the simple deposit multiplier as well as the amount of deposits that can be supported by a given level of bank reserves. Currently, the required reserve ratio for demand deposits is 10 percent for most depository institutions. The Fed has not historically used changes in the reserve ratio as a tool of monetary policy because changes in the reserve ratio can cause too much uncertainty and instability.

Bond Prices and Bond Yields

The Federal Reserve cannot force banks or the public to buy or sell bonds. The Fed makes bonds more or less attractive to hold by changing the price of the bonds. When the Fed changes the price it is willing to pay for bonds, bond yields also change. To show this relationship, a rate called the **current yield** on a coupon bond can be used. The equations for calculating current yield are given below. The annual coupon payment is found by multiplying the face value of the bond (the amount the bond holder receives when the bond matures) by the coupon rate, which is the stated rate of interest on the bond. The annual coupon payment is the same regardless of the price paid for the bond.

$$\text{Current Yield} = \frac{\text{Annual Coupon Payment}}{\text{Price Paid for the Bond}}$$

$$\text{Annual Coupon Payment} = (\text{Coupon Rate})(\text{Face Value of Bond})$$

Suppose a $1,000 coupon bond that has a coupon rate of 10% is currently selling at par, or face value, so its price is $1,000. In this case, the current yield on the bond is:

$$\text{Current Yield} = \frac{(.10)(\$1{,}000)}{\$1{,}000} = 0.10 \text{ or } 10\%$$

If this same bond were to sell at a discount, then the price of the bond is less than its face value but the coupon payment remains the same. Suppose the $1,000 bond sells for $900. The current yield on the bond in this case is:

$$\text{Current Yield} = \frac{(.10)(\$1{,}000)}{\$900} = 0.111 = 11.1\%$$

If the bond were to sell at a premium, or at a price greater than its face value, then its yield would fall. If the $1,000 bond sells for $1,100, its yield will be 9.09%. **Bond prices and bond yields are inversely related.** When the Federal Reserve buys and sells bonds, it not only affects rates by altering the amount of loanable funds, it also affects the yields on bonds and other competing financial assets.

Monetary Policy Tools Summary and Recent Federal Reserve Actions

The simple model of deposit creation gives the impression that the Federal Reserve is able to exert precise control over the amount of deposits in the banking system by setting reserve requirements and controlling reserves and the monetary base. In reality, the behavior of banks and depositors influence the Fed's ability to exercise control over the money supply process. Depositors may shift away from deposits into currency, which will decrease bank reserves. The public may not take advantage of new lending capacity in the system. Banks may choose not to extend loans or buy bonds with excess reserves – banks may choose to hold excess reserves greater than zero. An infusion of reserves by the Fed into the banking system does not guarantee that there will be a multiple expansion of loans and deposits. Because the Fed is not the only entity that influences the process, it must try to take into account the behavior of banks and the public in determining the appropriate way to implement monetary policy.

Open market operations are the tool of choice and are the main tool used by the Fed for conducting monetary policy because open market operations are:

1) conducted by the Fed and the Fed does have control over the volume of open market purchases and sales.
2) flexible and precise. The Fed can generate small or large changes in the monetary base by using small or large purchases and sales.
3) easily reversed. If the Fed believes that a purchase or sale is too large, it can immediately reverse itself.
4) easy and quick to implement. The Fed does not need the approval of any other branch of government when it changes its policy so there are no administrative delays associated with monetary policy. If the Fed wants to increase the monetary base, it simply places a buy order with bond dealers and the trades occur immediately.

Expansionary Monetary Policy

If the Federal Reserve wants to increase the growth rate of the money supply and support a credit expansion, it will most likely do so by being a net purchaser of securities on the open market. It may also lower the discount rate and announce a lower federal funds rate target. The short-run impact of such a policy is generally lower short-term interest rates. The increase in reserves increases the supply of loanable funds, and, ceteris paribus, an increase in supply leads to a lower price. Interest is the price of using somebody else's money so an increase in the supply of loanable funds generally leads to a lower interest rate.

The Fed is most likely to pursue an expansionary monetary policy, also called easy money policy, if the economy is slowing down or in a recession. Expansionary monetary policy shifts aggregate demand to the right to help close a recessionary gap. The goal is to increase aggregate demand which may then lead to higher output and lower unemployment. The Fed could choose to lower the required reserve ratio but this is not likely.

The Fed has recently conducted some very large purchase transactions in an attempt to keep rates low and credit available. The very low inflation and relatively sluggish economic growth have decreased the concern of such actions causing inflation. The Fed's usual response to an economic downturn or contraction is to use OMO to decrease short-term interest rates in order to increase lending and spending. Rates were so low by 2008 that the strategy was no longer considered effective and the Fed opted to use an unconventional monetary tool called **quantitative easing** (QE) to stimulate the economy. This entails the Fed buying assets like long-term securities such as Treasuries and mortgage-backed securities from commercial banks and other financial institutions. This puts money in the economy and decreases long-term interest rates. Lower long-term rates increase the incentive for investors to spend rather than tie up funds in low-rate long-term assets.

In November 2008, the Fed started buying up mortgage-backed securities and Treasury bills and had acquired more than $2 trillion in assets by June 2010. This move is now referred to as QE1. Another round of buying, QE2, began in August 2010. In September 2012, the Fed announced a third round of quantitative easing, QE3, in a continued effort to stimulate the economy. The Fed stayed committed to continuing its monthly purchase of assets for a considerable amount of time after the recovery strengthened, and announced the end of QE3 in October 2014 but continued its policy of keeping rates low until December 2015.

Under former Chair of the Federal Reserve Janet Yellen, the Federal Reserve began a gradual increase in interest rates at the end of 2015 along with an orchestrated sell-off of some of the bonds the Fed purchased to prop up the economy after the 2008 financial crisis. Jerome Powell, current Chair of the Fed, agreed with the policy and has continued this approach, citing inflationary concerns associated with economic growth and very low rates of unemployment.

<u>Contractionary Monetary Policy</u>

The Federal Reserve is likely to pursue a contractionary monetary policy, or tight money policy, if it is concerned that aggregate demand is growing faster than aggregate supply which leads to inflation. To close an inflationary gap, the Fed will most likely be a net seller of securities on the open market. It may also raise the discount rate and announce a higher federal funds rate target. The short-run impact of tight money policy is an increase in interest rates. Higher interest rates generally lead to less borrowing and decreases in aggregate demand. Contractionary monetary policy shifts aggregate demand to the left which decreases inflationary pressures. The Fed could choose to raise the required reserve ratio but this is not likely.

Monetary Policy Tools of the Fed

<u>Expansionary Monetary Policy</u>	**<u>Contractionary Monetary Policy</u>**
Buying bonds in the open market	**Selling bonds in the open market**
Lowering the discount rate	**Raising the discount rate**
Decreasing the fed funds rate target	**Increasing the fed funds rate target**
Lowering the required reserve ratio	**Raising the required reserve ratio**

NAME____ SECTION #____________

Print Last Name, First Name

THE FEDERAL RESERVE

1. The ***primary*** responsibility of the Federal Reserve System is to:
   a. make loans to businesses and consumers.
   b. provide currency to banks and automated teller machines (ATMs).
   c. control the nation's money supply and add stability to the financial system.
   d. issue government bonds to finance the government budget deficit.

2. The Federal Reserve:
   a. determines U.S. fiscal policy.
   b. cannot legally provide loans to banks.
   c. is responsible for monetary policy in the United States.
   d. is responsible for tax policy in the United States.

3. The Federal Reserve System consists of _______ Federal Reserve Districts.
   a. 12
   b. 14
   c. 24
   d. 50

4. All of the following are functions of the Federal Reserve District Banks ***except***:
   a. clearing checks.
   b. providing currency to banks.
   c. making loans to banks.
   d. accepting deposits from individuals.

5. The Federal Reserve Board of Governors consists of:
   a. 7 members elected by Congress to lifetime terms.
   b. 7 members appointed by the U.S. President to 14-year terms.
   c. 12 members appointed by the U.S. President to 14-year terms.
   d. 12 members appointed by the Senate to lifetime terms.

6. The Federal Open Market Committee (FOMC) members include:
   a. 7 Federal Reserve Governors plus 5 Federal Reserve Bank Presidents.
   b. 5 Federal Reserve Governors plus 7 Federal Reserve Bank Presidents.
   c. one banker from each Congressional district.
   d. one banker from each of the 10 Federal Reserve Districts.

7. The Federal Reserve controls the creation of money and the money supply by:
   a. setting the interest rate for new bank loans to the public.
   b. influencing the amount of reserves in the banking system.
   c. altering the required reserve ratio in order to change interest rates.
   d. raising and lowering the prime rate.

8. ______________________________became Chair of the Board of Governors of the Federal Reserve System in February 2018.
   a. Steve Mnuchin
   b. Mitch McConnell
   c. Jerome Powell
   d. Janet Yellen

9. When it was first created by Congress in 1913, the primary role of the Federal Reserve System was to:
   a. make loans to small businesses and farmers in the agricultural sector of the economy.
   b. act as lender of last resort to the banking community.
   c. regulate business practices by granting loans only to those businesses that met federal competitive guidelines.
   d. provide a safe bank for the government to store the tax revenue it collected as a result of the establishment of a permanent federal income tax.

10. A bank is likely to charge its biggest and most important, or most-favored, customers the ________________ rate.
   a. discount
   b. federal funds
   c. prime
   d. required reserve

NAME____ SECTION #____________

Print Last Name, First Name

MONEY, BANKING, AND THE FED

1. If the banking system holds $50 billion in total reserves and the required reserve ratio is 10%, then the maximum amount of checkable deposits the system can legally support is:
   a. $10 billion.
   b. $50 billion.
   c. $250 billion.
   d. $500 billion.

2. Ceteris paribus, a decrease in the required reserve ratio will:
   a. increase the value of the simple deposit multiplier.
   b. decrease the value of the simple deposit multiplier.
   c. have no impact on the value of the simple deposit multiplier.
   d. nullify the value of the simple deposit multiplier.

3. Total checkable deposits in the banking system will equal total bank reserves times the simple deposit multiplier as long as:
   a. there are no currency leakages and each bank holds zero excess reserves.
   b. there are no currency leakages and each bank holds positive excess reserves.
   c. banks are not profit-maximizers.
   d. the public holds at least part of all newly-created money in the form of cash.

4. If Sue Jones deposits $1,000 of previously circulating currency into her checking account and the required reserve ratio is 10%, the money supply:
   a. does not change immediately, but can potentially increase by as much as $10,000.
   b. does not change immediately, but can potentially increase by as much as $9,000.
   c. increases by $900.
   d. increases by $1,000.

5. When the Fed buys bonds in the open market, ceteris paribus:
   a. the monetary base, bank loans, and the money supply increase.
   b. the monetary base and bank loans increase, but the money supply decreases.
   c. bank loans are not affected, but the monetary base and the money supply increase.
   d. nothing happens to the monetary base, bank loans, or the money supply.

6. Suppose the Board of Governors has determined that continued increases in consumption and investment spending are likely to be inflationary. To control inflation, the Fed would most likely pursue policies that promote:
   a. lower interest rates and a contraction of bank lending activity.
   b. lower interest rates and an expansion of bank lending activity.
   c. higher interest rates and a contraction of bank lending activity.
   d. higher interest rates and an expansion of bank lending activity.

NAME____ SECTION #____________
Print Last Name, First Name

7. Banks pay the ________________ rate to borrow reserves from the Federal Reserve. Banks pay the ________________ rate to borrow reserves from other banks.
   a. federal funds; prime
   b. federal funds; discount
   c. discount; prime
   d. discount; federal funds

Use the information in the T-account for the Banking System to answer questions 8 – 10:

Assets *for all banks*		**Liabilities** *for all banks*	
Total Bank Reserves	**$200 billion**	**Checkable Deposits**	**$1,000 billion**
Securities	**$100 billion**		
Loans	**$700 billion**		

8. The banking system is currently fully loaned up (in equilibrium) if the required reserve ratio is:
   a. 10 percent.
   b. 12.5 percent.
   c. 20 percent.
   d. 25 percent.

9. The $700 billion in Loans currently held by the banking system:
   a. are funds that have been invested in the stock market by bankers.
   b. do not earn interest for the banks because these are sterile assets.
   c. are held as vault cash or on deposit at the Federal Reserve Bank.
   d. are interest-bearing assets that help earn profits for the banks over time.

10. Suppose the Fed buys $20 billion worth of government bonds (securities) from banks (assume the required reserve ratio is as calculated in question 8). If all banks proceed to make new loans until excess reserves are equal to zero and there are no cash leakages, then checkable deposits will grow to:
   a. $1,000 billion.
   b. $1,100 billion.
   c. $1,200 billion.
   d. $2,000 billion.

NAME____ SECTION #___________

Print Last Name, First Name

THE FEDERAL RESERVE AND MONETARY POLICY

1. The discount rate is the rate of interest that:
   a. a bank pays to the Fed for an overnight loan of reserves.
   b. one bank pays another for an overnight loan of reserves.
   c. the best corporate customers pay on short-term business loans.
   d. depositors earn on Eurodollars.

2. The federal funds rate is the rate of interest that:
   a. a bank pays to the Fed for an overnight loan of reserves.
   b. one bank pays another bank for an overnight loan of reserves.
   c. the best corporate customers pay on short-term business loans.
   d. depositors earns on Eurodollars.

3. Suppose the Fed desires to ***decrease*** the growth rate of the money supply. This would likely involve:
   a. an announcement of an increase in the federal funds rate target.
   b. a tightening of credit conditions by decreasing the required reserve ratio.
   c. an announcement that interest rates in the open market are likely to decrease.
   d. the purchase of government bonds by the Fed.

4. Which of the following would likely to an ***increase*** in the money supply?
   a. An open market bond sale by the Fed
   b. An increase in the federal funds rate target
   c. An increase in the amount of excess reserves in the banking system
   d. A decision on the part of the public to decrease their holdings of checkable deposits

5. The monetary tool of the Fed that has been used ***least*** often in recent years is:
   a. changing the discount rate.
   b. changing the federal funds rate target.
   c. changing the required reserve ratio.
   d. buying or selling government bonds in the open market.

6. The most important and most frequently used tool of the Fed for controlling the money supply is:
   a. open market operations.
   b. the prime rate.
   c. the required reserve ratio.
   d. the discount rate.

7. The Federal Reserve uses open market operations to control the money supply when it:
   a. issues government bonds to finance the federal government's deficit.
   b. purchases government bonds to decrease the money supply.
   c. purchases government bonds to increase the money supply.
   d. sells government bonds to increase the money supply.

8. If a bond with a face value of $10,000 and coupon rate of 4.5% sells for $9,000, the current yield on the bond:
   a. is 4.5%.
   b. is 6.25%.
   c. is 5%.
   d. cannot be calculated from the information given.

9. If the Fed's goal is to increase the growth rate of the money supply, the ***most likely*** action it will take is to:
   a. lower the required reserve ratio.
   b. raise the federal funds rate target.
   c. raise the discount rate.
   d. buy government bonds in the open market.

10. Ceteris paribus, if bond prices increase, then:
   a. there is no effect on bond yields (interest rates).
   b. bond yields (interest rates) will increase.
   c. bond yields (interest rates) will decrease.
   d. the Federal Reserve must be pursuing contractionary monetary policy.

NAME______________________________ SECTION #__________

Print Last Name, First Name

MONETARY AND FISCAL POLICIES

Use the graph below to answer questions 1 – 5:

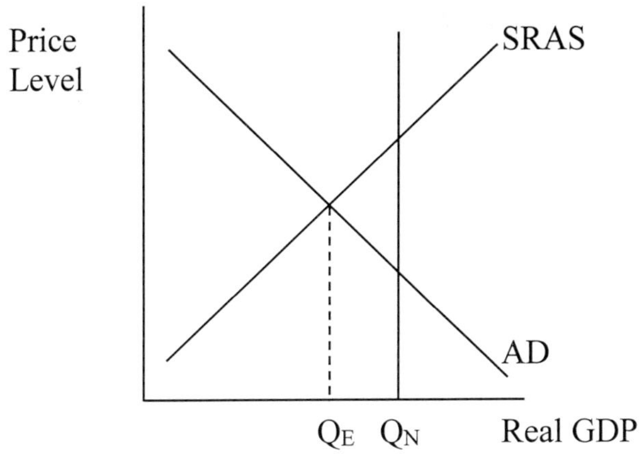

1. The economy represented by the above graph is experiencing a(n):
   a. monetary gap.
   b. structural gap.
   c. recessionary gap.
   d. inflationary gap.

2. A *fiscal* policy solution to this problem might include:
   a. increasing taxes.
   b. increasing government expenditures.
   c. decreasing the federal funds rate target.
   d. decreasing the discount rate.

3. A *monetary* policy solution to this problem might include:
   a. decreasing taxes.
   b. increasing government expenditures.
   c. increasing the federal funds rate target.
   d. decreasing the discount rate.

4. To help alleviate this situation, the President and Congress might:
   a. raise tax rates for each income tax bracket.
   b. increase the amount of time an unemployed worker can collect benefits.
   c. decrease the standard deduction to increase income taxes for many families.
   d. postpone plans to build and improve interstate highways.

5. To help alleviate this situation, the Federal Reserve might:
   a. lower the discount rate.
   b. lower the federal funds rate target.
   c. conduct an open market purchase of government bonds.
   d. do all of the above.

NAME____ SECTION #____________
Print Last Name, First Name

Use the graph below to answer questions 6 – 10:

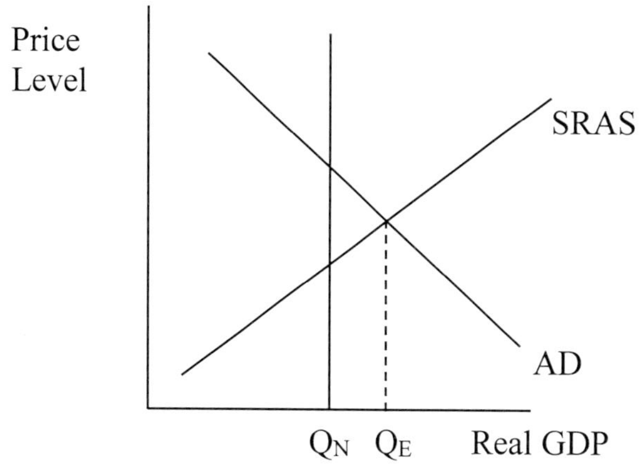

6. The economy represented by the above graph is experiencing a(n):
   a. monetary gap.
   b. structural gap.
   c. recessionary gap.
   d. inflationary gap.

7. A *fiscal* policy solution to this problem might include:
   a. increasing taxes.
   b. increasing government expenditures.
   c. decreasing the federal funds rate target.
   d. decreasing the discount rate.

8. A *monetary* policy solution to this problem might include:
   a. increasing taxes.
   b. increasing government expenditures.
   c. increasing the federal funds rate target.
   d. decreasing the discount rate.

9. To help alleviate this situation, the President and Congress might:
   a. decrease tax rates for each income tax bracket.
   b. increase the amount of time an unemployed worker can collect benefits.
   c. decrease the number and amount of tax deductions that can be taken by the wealthy.
   d. increase funding to build and improve interstate highways.

10. To help alleviate this situation, the Federal Reserve would ***most*** likely:
    a. raise the required reserve ratio.
    b. lower the federal funds rate target.
    c. conduct an open market purchase of government bonds.
    d. conduct an open market sale of government bonds.

CHAPTER 12 Monetary Theory

The Keynesian model emphasizes the potential for government policy to improve the economy's performance, causing us to expect policymakers to succeed in their pursuit of full employment, price stability, and growth. Out of this culture of high expectations, another school of thought, **Monetarism**, has evolved based on the work of Nobel laureate Milton Friedman.

The Monetarist model develops a modern version of *laissez-faire* in which government policymakers, rather than doing nothing, implement policy rules designed to promote long-term economic stability. Monetarists believe that monetary policy is more powerful than fiscal policy for stabilizing the economy. Fiscal policy, which involves changing the amount of government spending and taxing as a means of influencing aggregate spending, is considered the most powerful tool for correcting an economic downturn by Keynesian theorists. Monetary policy, which involves adjusting the rate of growth in the money supply and, in turn, affecting interest rates, is believed to be the best way to keep the economy on a stable path by Monetarists. The problem with fiscal policy, Monetarists argue, is that it takes too long to implement and the economy may begin to self-correct before the policy takes full effect. Furthermore, during a downturn or recession, increasing government spending or lowering taxes in order to increase private spending usually requires deficit spending, which may lead to higher interest rates and crowding out of investment spending. To the extent that the initial increases in spending brought about by fiscal policy are accompanied by reductions in investment spending, the overall effectiveness of the policy is limited.

The Monetarist model concludes that stable money growth is the key to a stable economy. Taxation and spending by government are necessary to provide for national defense and other programs, but should not be used in an attempt to manipulate the economy. The Monetarists advocate policy rules over policy discretion to promote stability.

The Quantity Theory of Money

The Monetarist view uses the Classical equation of exchange as the cornerstone of its theory. The **equation of exchange** gives the relationship between the money supply and the number of times per year the money supply must "turn over" in order to purchase all of GDP and is written as:

$$\mathbf{MV = PQ}$$

where **M** is the money supply, **V** is the velocity of money, **P** is the price level, and **Q** is the quantity of goods and services (real GDP). A very simple version of the theory assumes that both V and Q are constant, which implies that the money growth rate will equal the inflation rate. However, in the modern **Quantity Theory of Money**, Monetarists assume that real GDP is determined by supply-side factors, such as resource productivity and technology, so Q increases each year. Although forecasting is not exact, they assume that the economy's rate of growth can be accurately predicted. They also assume that velocity is very stable because it is determined by institutional forces, such as the frequency with which people are paid, that tend to change very slowly over time. The numerical example on the next page demonstrates why "inflation is always and everywhere a monetary phenomenon" according to economist Milton Friedman.

Suppose the money supply (M) is equal to \$400 and velocity is equal to 5, so that MV = (\$400)(5) = \$2,000 = PQ = nominal GDP. With total spending equal to \$2,000, if real GDP (Q) is equal to 2,000, then the price level (P) is equal to 1.

Next, suppose that the economy grows, so that real GDP increases to \$2,400 (this is a 20 percent rate of growth) and, at the same time, the money supply is increased from \$400 to \$504 (a 26 percent increase in the money supply). Assuming velocity remains equal to 5, the increase in the money supply causes total spending to increase from \$2,000 to \$2,520. Using the equation of exchange to solve for the unknown variable (the price level, P), shows that MV = PQ, (\$504)(5) = P(\$2,400), so P = \$2,520/\$2,400 = 1.05. Since the price level increased from 1 to 1.05, the inflation rate is equal to 5 percent.

The above example illustrates that when velocity is fixed, the percentage change in the money supply is approximately equal to the percentage change in the price level plus the percentage change in real GDP (or the inflation rate plus the growth rate). The significance of this relationship is that, if policymakers seek to keep the inflation rate low, they should set the money growth rate equal to the (expected) percentage change in real GDP. This result, developed by Monetarists, is referred to as **the monetary rule**.

<u>The Money Market</u>

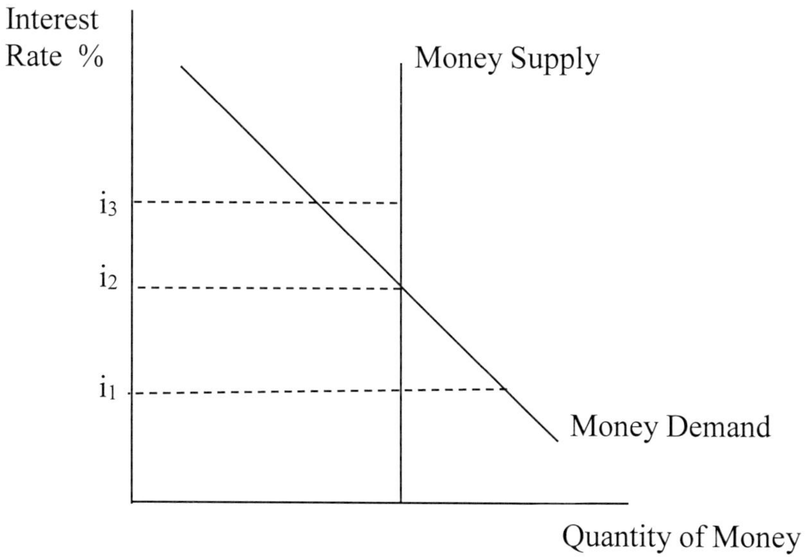

A money market graph is usually drawn with the interest rate on the vertical axis and the quantity of money on the horizontal axis. People "demand" money when they choose to hold their assets in the form of money. Using the M1 measure of money, holding assets in the form of money means holding cash, checkable deposits, or traveler's checks. The demand for money slopes downward and to the right because many people prefer to hold bonds or other interest-earning assets when interest rates are relatively high. As interest rates fall, the opportunity cost of holding money falls, and people choose to hold more money and less in the form of bonds or other interest-earning assets. The money supply is drawn as a vertical line because we assume that the Fed simply fixes some quantity of money to supply and that this quantity is the same regardless of the interest rate. The money market adjusts like any other market. If the interest rate is i_3, it is above the equilibrium rate, which is denoted as i_2. At the rate above the equilibrium rate, there is a surplus of money balances and the interest rate will fall. People do not desire to hold as much money and are likely to decrease their holdings of cash and increase their holdings of interest bearing assets such as bonds. There will be a shortage of money balances if the interest rate is below the equilibrium rate, such as i_1. The shortage will cause the interest rate to rise. People are holding fewer money balances than they desire and are likely to move out of interest bearing assets such as bonds and into money.

The interest rates determined in the graph on the previous page are called **nominal interest rates**. Firms and individuals base many financial decisions on the **real interest rate**, which differs from the nominal interest rate when there is inflation. For example, if the bonds you held last year earned a 10% return, but prices rose 6%, then your purchasing power rose only 4%. Looking back, you can calculate the actual real interest rate as the nominal interest rate minus the actual inflation rate. Looking forward, subtract the expected inflation rate from the nominal interest rate to get the expected real rate of interest. When you are trying to decide if the rate of return you can earn on a financial asset justifies the fact that you must sacrifice present consumption to acquire the asset, it is the expected real interest rate that matters most. It is more difficult to make this decision when inflation is very unpredictable, which is one of the reasons that price stability is an important macroeconomic goal.

If the Federal Reserve pursues an expansionary monetary policy, there is an increase in the money supply. In the money market graph presented below, MS_1 shifts to the right to MS_2. The short run impact of the increase in the money supply when the money demand curve is downward sloping, is a lower interest rate. In this case, the interest rate falls from i_1 to i_2.

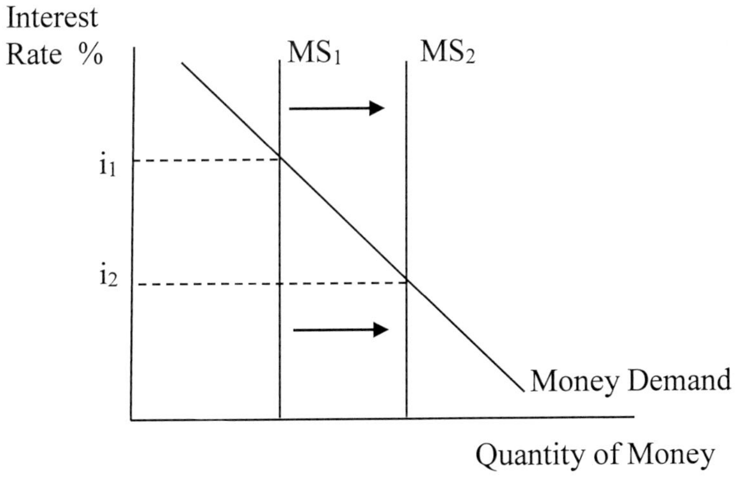

If the Federal Reserve pursues a contractionary monetary policy, the growth of the money supply will decrease and the money supply curve will shift left. The short run impact of the decrease in the money supply when the money demand curve is downward sloping is a higher interest rate. Shifts in the money demand function will also change short-term interest rates. An increase in the money demand curve, ceteris paribus, will increase the interest rate. A decrease in the money demand curve will decrease the interest rate, assuming the money supply is fixed.

The Keynesian View

The Keynesian view uses the money market model to predict the effect of monetary policy on the interest rate. In the Keynesian model, investment spending as well as some consumer spending is tied to the current rate of interest. Therefore, changing the interest rate may alter the level of aggregate spending and aggregate demand in the economy.

Keynes did not believe that relying solely on monetary policy to pull the economy out of a recession would be wise. He argued that an expansionary monetary policy could fail to stimulate aggregate spending due to the possibility of either a liquidity trap or pessimistic business expectations. The **liquidity trap** is an economic theory put forth by Keynes to illustrate why investment spending may not increase even at very low real rates of interest. If all participants in the money market hold the expectation that interest rates have bottomed out and must eventually rise, they will prefer to hold money, or remain liquid, to avoid locking in a low rate of return on their savings. In this situation, the money demand curve becomes horizontal, such as at i_0, and the economy experiences a "liquidity trap".

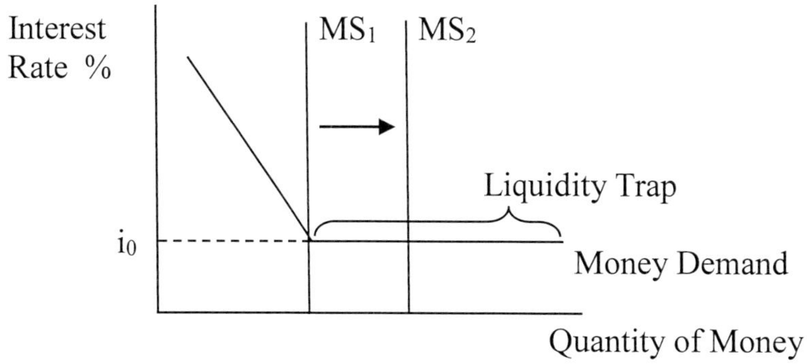

If the economy is in a liquidity trap, increases in the money supply will not reduce interest rates, so no increase in aggregate spending will be forthcoming. The graph above shows that an increase in the money supply in the horizontal portion of the money demand curve, i.e., the liquidity trap, leads to no change in the interest rate. People that sell bonds prefer to stay liquid and will "hoard" cash.

Another potential hazard associated with relying on monetary policy to stimulate the economy during recessions is the Keynesian view that expectations play an important role in determining the position of the investment demand function, or the amount of investment spending that businesses are willing to undertake at different interest rates. If **pessimistic business expectations** cause the investment demand function to shift leftward, then lower interest rates may not result in higher investment spending. In this case, monetary policy will again prove ineffective.

Keynes used these arguments to show that monetary policy is uncertain and ineffective for curing recession and to help make his case for using expansionary fiscal policy to stimulate aggregate demand when the economy is in a slump.

NAME____ SECTION #______________

Print Last Name, First Name

THE MONETARIST MODEL

1. The equation of exchange can be expressed algebraically as:
   a. MV = PQ.
   b. M/V = P/Q.
   c. M/V = PQ.
   d. MQ = PV.

2. According to Monetarists, the most important determinant of inflation in U.S. history has been:
   a. decisions by Congress to raise income tax rates.
   b. decisions by the Fed to allow the money supply to grow too quickly.
   c. supply shocks such as OPEC activity leading to higher energy prices.
   d. attempts by labor unions to raise wages.

3. Monetarists argue that continual increases in the growth rate of the money supply that are greater than the growth rate of real GDP will:
   a. increase real GDP in the short run and in the long run.
   b. increase real GDP without affecting the price level in the long run.
   c. decrease real GDP in the short run but increase real GDP in the long run.
   d. increase the price level in the long run.

4. According to Monetarists, sustainable and long-term economic growth is the result of:
   a. improvements in resource productivity and technology.
   b. contractionary fiscal and monetary policies.
   c. only policies that are designed to reduce the economy's rate of unemployment.
   d. expansionary fiscal and monetary policies.

5. The notion that the Fed should adhere to a policy of steady and predictable expansion of the money supply represents:
   a. the monetary rule put forth by Monetarists.
   b. the fiscal rule put forth by Monetarists.
   c. the monetary rule put forth by Keynesians.
   d. the fiscal rule put forth by Keynesians.

6. The Monetarists argue that one of the keys to economic stability is:
   a. stable money growth.
   b. continual adjustment of nominal interest rates to keep the real interest rate equal to zero.
   c. requiring the Federal Reserve to use the equation of exchange to determine the appropriate required reserve ratio.
   d. using discretionary fiscal policy to fine-tune the economy.

NAME____ SECTION #______________
Print Last Name, First Name

Use the data below to answer questions 7 – 10:

Year	Money Supply	Real GDP	Price Level
1	$1,600 billion	$7,845 billion	1.02
2	$1,620 billion	$8,021 billion	1.03

7. In year 2, the velocity of money is approximately _____.
   a. 4.8
   b. 4.9
   c. 5.0
   d. 5.1

8. In year 1, aggregate spending or nominal GDP is approximately:
   a. $1,600 billion.
   b. $7,845 billion.
   c. $8,002 billion.
   d. $9,445 billion.

9. In year 2, aggregate spending or nominal GDP is approximately:
   a. $1,620 billion.
   b. $8,021 billion.
   c. $8,261.6 billion.
   d. $9,641 billion.

10. Between year 1 and year 2, the money supply __________ and the economy __________.
    a. grew; grew
    b. grew; contracted
    c. contracted; grew
    d. contracted; contracted

NAME____ SECTION #____________

Print Last Name, First Name

MONETARY THEORY

Use the following information to fill in blanks 1 – 5.

In year 1, the money supply (M) is equal to $450, the velocity of money (V) is 6, and the price level is 1.0. In year 2, the money supply is increased to $495 and velocity remains unchanged.

1. Real GDP in year 1 is equal to $______________
2. Nominal GDP in year 1 is equal to $________________
3. If the economy grew at a rate of 5%, real GDP in year 2 is equal to $______________
4. What happened to the price level from year 1 to year 2? __________________________
5. The rate of inflation between year 1 and year 2 is equal to ____________

Use the following information to fill in blanks 6 – 10.

In year one, the money supply (M) is equal to $780, the velocity of money (V) is 4.5, and the price level is 1.0. In year 2, the money supply is increased to $820, velocity remains unchanged, and the economy grew at a rate of 2.6%..

	Year 1	**Year 2**
Money Supply (M)	$780	$820
Velocity (V)	4.5	4.5
Price Level (P)	1.0	8.________
Real GDP (Q)	6.________	9.________
Nominal GDP (PQ)	7.________	10.________

NAME____ SECTION #____________

Print Last Name, First Name

MONETARY POLICY IN THE KEYNESIAN MODEL

1. Use a money market graph to show the effect of an increase in the money supply on the equilibrium rate of interest.

2. Sketch a graph depicting investment demand and show the effect on investment spending of an interest rate decrease.

3. Use an AD/AS (short-run) graph to show the effect of higher spending on the equilibrium price level and real GDP.

NAME____ SECTION #_____________

Print Last Name, First Name

INTEREST RATES AND THE MONEY MARKET

1. Suppose the money market is initially in equilibrium. If the Fed raises the discount rate and sells bonds on the open market, then, ceteris paribus:
   a. the money supply will increase and interest rates will rise.
   b. the money supply will increase and interest rates will fall.
   c. the money supply will decrease and interest rates will rise.
   d. the money supply will decrease and interest rates will fall.

2. Ceteris paribus, the short-run impact of the Fed pursuing an expansionary monetary policy is:
   a. an increase in interest rates and an increase in spending.
   b. an increase in interest rates and a decrease in spending.
   c. a decrease in interest rates and an increase in spending.
   d. a decrease in interest rates and a decrease in spending.

3. Ceteris paribus, the short-run impact of the Fed pursuing a contractionary monetary policy is:
   a. an increase in interest rates and an increase in spending.
   b. an increase in interest rates and a decrease in spending.
   c. a decrease in interest rates and an increase in spending.
   d. a decrease in interest rates and a decrease in spending.

4. The nominal rate of interest is equal to the expected or desired real rate of interest:
   a. divided by the expected inflation rate.
   b. multiplied by the expected inflation rate.
   c. minus the expected inflation rate.
   d. plus the expected inflation rate.

5. If the nominal rate of interest is 2.5 percent and the inflation rate is 2.5 percent, then the actual real rate of interest is equal to:
   a. 2.5 percent.
   b. 6.25 percent.
   c. 5 percent.
   d. 0 percent.

6. A lender that expects a 4 percent real interest rate will charge a nominal interest rate of _________ if the expected rate of inflation is 2 percent.
   a. 2 percent
   b. 4 percent
   c. 6 percent
   d. 8 percent

NAME____ SECTION #____________

Print Last Name, First Name

7. If the nominal interest rate was 8 percent, expected inflation was 2 percent, and actual inflation was 4 percent, then:
   a. lenders expected to earn a 6 percent real rate of interest, but they actually earned a 4 percent real rate of interest.
   b. lenders expected to earn a 4 percent real rate of interest, but they actually earned a 2 percent real rate of interest.
   c. lenders earned a 6 percent real rate of interest, as expected.
   d. lenders earned a 4 percent real rate of interest, as expected.

8. If interest rates rise, ceteris paribus:
   a. the demand for money will shift to the right.
   b. the demand for money will shift to the left.
   c. the opportunity cost of holding money as an asset increases and people will want to hold more interest-earning assets, like bonds.
   d. the opportunity cost of holding money as an asset decreases so people are likely to move out of interest-earning assets in order to hold greater money balances.

9. If the Fed sells government bonds in the open market, ceteris paribus:
   a. money demand will shift to the right, causing interest rates to rise.
   b. money demand will shift to the left, causing interest rates to fall.
   c. money supply will shift to the right, causing interest rates to fall.
   d. money supply will shift to the left, causing interest rates to rise.

10. If the Fed announces a lower federal funds rate target, this most likely means that the Fed will act to:
    a. decrease bank reserves, which will likely increase borrowing and spending.
    b. decrease bank reserves, which will likely decrease borrowing and spending.
    c. increase bank reserves, which will likely increase borrowing and spending.
    d. increase bank reserves, which will likely decrease borrowing and spending.

NAME____ SECTION #____________

Print Last Name, First Name

KEYNESIAN MONETARY THEORY

1. The Keynesian view argues that:
   a. investment spending and some consumer spending depend on the current interest rate, which means a decrease in the interest rate may lead to an increase in aggregate demand.
   b. investment and consumer spending depend on disposable income, which means businesses and consumers do not alter their borrowing and spending in response to changes in the interest rate.
   c. investment spending is likely to increase in the current period if businesses develop pessimistic expectations regarding future economic conditions.
   d. investment and consumer spending vary directly with the interest rate, so raising the interest rate is likely to lead to an increase in business and consumer borrowing and spending.

2. The investment demand function is assumed to be:
   a. upward sloping because firms will likely undertake more investment projects when the cost of borrowing is lower.
   b. upward sloping because firms will likely undertake fewer investment projects when the cost of borrowing is lower.
   c. downward sloping because firms will likely undertake more investment projects when the cost of borrowing is lower.
   d. downward sloping because firms will likely undertake fewer investment projects when the cost of borrowing is lower.

3. The investment demand function would most likely shift to the right as a result of:
   a. more optimistic business expectations.
   b. more pessimistic business expectations.
   c. an increase in interest rates.
   d. a decrease in interest rates.

4. Ceteris paribus, a decrease in money demand would cause:
   a. an increase in the interest rate and a decrease in investment spending.
   b. an increase in the interest rate and an increase in investment spending.
   c. a decrease in the interest rate and an increase in investment spending.
   d. a decrease in the interest rate and a decrease in investment spending.

5. If investment spending is not sensitive to changes in interest rates, then:
   a. contractionary monetary policy will be more effective than contractionary fiscal policy for closing a recessionary gap.
   b. the investment demand function will be a horizontal line.
   c. the Fed will increase interest rates so that savers will earn higher rates of interest.
   d. expansionary monetary policy may not lead to an increase in aggregate demand.

NAME____ SECTION #______________
Print Last Name, First Name

6. Which of the following best describes the Keynesian perspective on how contractionary monetary policy affects the economy?
   a. Lower interest rates, lower investment and consumption expenditures, and a lower price level
   b. Lower interest rates, higher investment and consumption expenditures, and a higher price level
   c. Higher interest rates, lower investment and consumption expenditures, and a lower price level
   d. Higher interest rates, higher investment and consumption expenditures, and a higher price level

7. Which of the following best describes the Keynesian perspective on how expansionary monetary policy affects the economy?
   a. Lower interest rates, lower investment and consumption expenditures, and lower real GDP
   b. Lower interest rates, higher investment and consumption expenditures, and higher real GDP
   c. Higher interest rates, lower investment and consumption expenditures, and lower real GDP
   d. Higher interest rates, higher investment and consumption expenditures, and higher real GDP

8. According to Keynesian monetary theory:
   a. monetary policy is ineffective if the economy is in a liquidity trap.
   b. the effectiveness of monetary policy depends on the sensitivity of interest rates to changes in the money supply.
   c. the effectiveness of monetary policy depends on the sensitivity of investment spending to changes in the interest rate.
   d. All of the above are correct
   e. Only (b) and (c) are correct

9. The liquidity trap is:
   a. the horizontal portion of the investment demand curve.
   b. the vertical portion of the investment demand curve.
   c. the horizontal portion of the money demand curve.
   d. the vertical portion of the money demand curve.

10. If the Fed increases the money supply but the economy is in a liquidity trap, then:
   a. there will be no change in interest rates or aggregate expenditures.
   b. money demand will shift and cancel out the change in the money supply.
   c. interest rates will fall and aggregate expenditures will rise.
   d. interest rates will rise and aggregate expenditures will fall.

Practice Exam III

The answers to this practice exam are on page 255.

1. Which of the following is most likely to be studied in a macroeconomics course?
   a. The profit potential of firms servicing large industries, such as oil and transportation
   b. The national unemployment rate during severe economic downturns compared to the rate during periods of substantial economic growth
   c. The impact of a price increase on the quantity demanded of airline tickets
   d. Environmental Protection Agency regulation of auto emissions

2. The fundamental economic problem society faces, forcing it to decide how to allocate resources and distribute output, is:
   a. unemployment.
   b. recession.
   c. scarcity.
   d. scarce wants and needs.

Use the graph below to answer the next question.

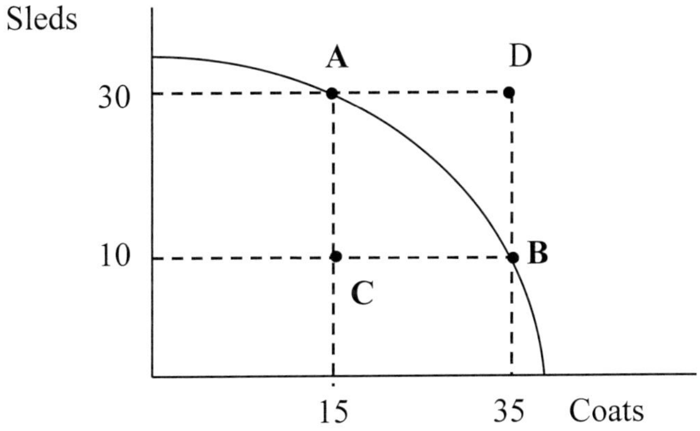

3. All of the following statements regarding the above production possibilities curve are true ***except***:
   a. A movement from point A to point D requires an increase in the resources or technology to produce both sleds and coats.
   b. All resources are used fully and efficiently in producing point A.
   c. The opportunity cost of moving from point A to point B is 30 sleds.
   d. Producing at point C means this economy is inefficient.

4. Which of the following is an example of **capital** as the term is used by economists?
   a. Forests and minerals
   b. College teachers
   c. A share of IBM stock
   d. A General Motors factory

Use the graph below to answer the next two questions.

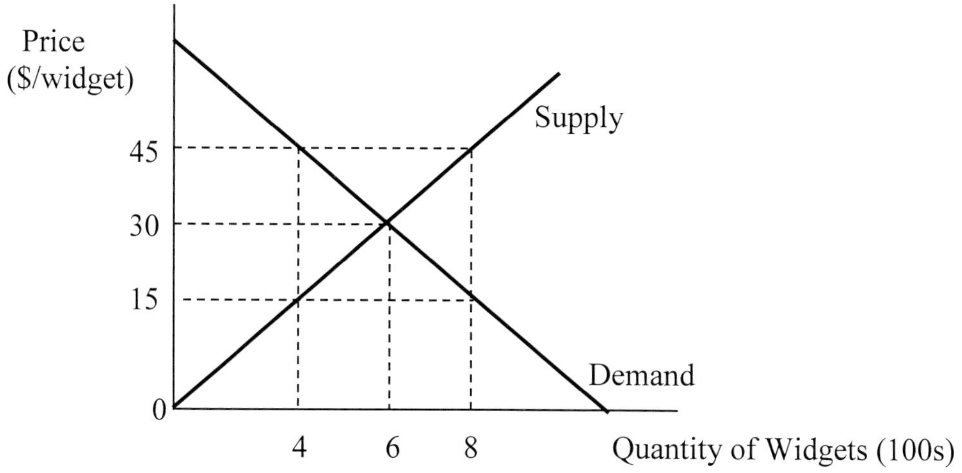

5. The market is in equilibrium at a price of ____ per ticket and a quantity of _____ tickets.
   a. $30; 400
   b. $15; 400
   c. $45; 800
   d. $30; 600

6. At a price of $45, there is a:
   a. shortage of 200 widgets.
   b. surplus of 200 widgets.
   c. shortage of 400 widgets.
   d. surplus of 400 widgets.

7. Which of the following is ***not*** a characteristic of capitalism?
   a. Limited government
   b. Government-ownership and control of resources
   c. Private property
   d. A market or price system

8. The major economic policy goals of most industrialized nations are:
   a. an equal distribution of income, full employment, and price stability.
   b. economic growth, price stability, and an equal distribution of income.
   c. full employment, price stability, and economic growth.
   d. price stability, economic growth, and wage protection.

9. According to the law of supply, a decrease in the price of corn, ceteris paribus, leads to:
   a. a decrease in the supply of corn.
   b. an increase in the supply of corn.
   c. a decrease in the quantity supplied of corn.
   d. an increase in the quantity supplied of corn.

10. Suppose there is an increase in the number of buyers of jeans and a decrease in the cost of manufacturing them. We would expect:
    a. equilibrium price to increase, but equilibrium quantity cannot be determined without additional information.
    b. equilibrium price to decrease, but equilibrium quantity cannot be determined without additional information.
    c. equilibrium quantity to decrease, but equilibrium price cannot be determined without additional information.
    d. equilibrium quantity to increase, but equilibrium price cannot be determined without additional information.

11. An auto worker whose skills are obsolete, leaving the worker without adequate skills to fill his/her job is _______________ unemployed, while an autoworker who is laid off due to recession is ___________________ unemployed.
    a. frictionally; structurally
    b. cyclically; naturally
    c. structurally; cyclically
    d. seasonally; frictionally

12. Inflation is:
    a. an increase in the average level of prices of goods and services over time.
    b. not an economic problem because each individual's income rises in proportion to the increase in the price level.
    c. a one-time increase in the price of all goods and services.
    d. an increase in the purchasing power of the dollar over time.

13. Suppose the consumer price index was 150 in year 11 and 157.5 in year 12. The rate of inflation in year 12 is:
    a. 7.5 percent.
    b. 4.76 percent.
    c. 5 percent.
    d. impossible to calculate from the information given.

14. The total market value of all final goods and services produced by resources within a nation's borders in a given time period is:
    a. Gross Domestic Product.
    b. National Income.
    c. Gross National Product.
    d. Net National Product.

Use the following table to answer the next question.

Exhibit: NATIONAL INCOME DATA--EXPENDITURE VIEWPOINT
(billions of dollars)

Consumption Expenditures	$920
Government Expenditures	140
Depreciation	80
Investment expenditures	130
Exports	40
Personal saving	30
Imports	50

15. Gross Domestic Product (GDP) is _______ billion; NDP is ________ billion.
    a. $1,230; $1,180
    b. $1,180; $1,100
    c. $1,280; $1,230
    d. $1,390; $1,280

16. The increase in the purchasing power of a given sum of money that occurs when the domestic price level decreases refers to the:
    a. real balance effect.
    b. interest rate effect.
    c. foreign trade effect.
    d. multiplier effect.

Use the graph below to answer the next question.

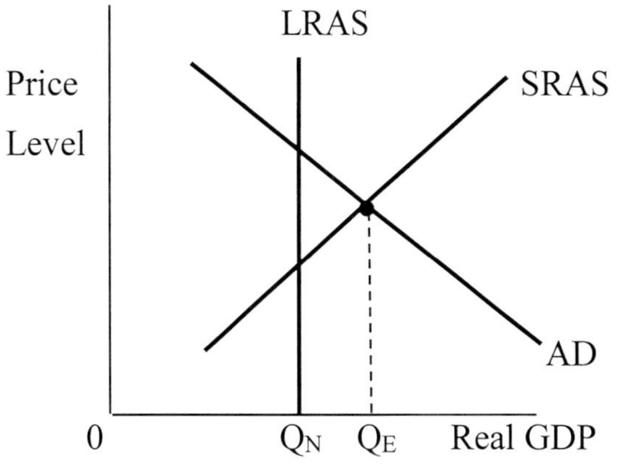

17. If the economy depicted in the graph above is self-regulating, then:
    a. SRAS will decrease to close the inflationary gap.
    b. AD will decrease to close the inflationary gap.
    c. SRAS will increase to close the recessionary gap.
    d. AD will increase to close the recessionary gap.

18. The long-run aggregate supply curve (LRAS) curve is:
 a. vertical at the economy's natural level of real GDP.
 b. horizontal at the economy's natural level of real GDP.
 c. upward-sloping because firms respond to higher prices by producing more output.
 d. upward-sloping because resources and technology are assumed to be fixed.

19. Ceteris paribus, if consumers become more pessimistic with respect to the future and short-run aggregate supply is upward sloping, then the price level will __________, real output will __________, and the unemployment rate will __________.
 a. increase; increase; increase
 b. decrease; decrease; increase
 c. increase; increase; decrease
 d. decrease; decrease; decrease

20. If Say's Law is true, then:
 a. aggregate demand determines equilibrium income and output.
 b. supply creates its own demand.
 c. government must actively manage the economy.
 d. the economy cannot self-correct.

21. The Classical model concludes that government should:
 a. take active steps to increase the price level to close an inflationary gap.
 b. take active steps to decrease the price level to close a recessionary gap.
 c. take a laissez-faire approach to macroeconomic policy only when the economy will not correct itself.
 d. take a laissez-faire approach to macroeconomic policy because a market economy is self-correcting.

Use the information in the table below to answer the next two questions.

Disposable Income (Y_d)	Consumption Spending (C)
\$0	\$200
\$500	\$650
\$1,000	\$1,100
\$1,500	\$1,550
\$2,000	\$2,000
\$2,500	\$2,450

22. The algebraic form of the consumption function for the above example is:
 a. $Y_d = \$500 + .75(C)$.
 b. $C = \$500 + .9(Y_d)$.
 c. $C = \$200 + .75(Y_d)$.
 d. $C = \$200 + .9(Y_d)$.

23. In the above example, at disposable income of \$3,000, saving is equal to:
 a. –\$100.
 b. \$0.
 c. –\$400.
 d. \$100.

24. Changes in government spending or taxing policy for the purpose of influencing macroeconomic outcomes refers to:
   a. a currently unconstitutional situation but Congress is considering an amendment to make it legal.
   b. the Classical model which is consistent with Keynesian economics.
   c. fiscal policy which is conducted by Congress.
   d. fiscal policy which is conducted by the Federal Reserve.

25. When the marginal propensity to consume is 0.75, the spending multiplier is _______, the tax multiplier is _______, and the balanced-budget multiplier is ______.

a. 7.5; -2.5; 1		c. 4; -3; 1	
b. 7.5; -2.5; 4		d. 4; -4; 1	

Use the graph below to answer the next two questions.

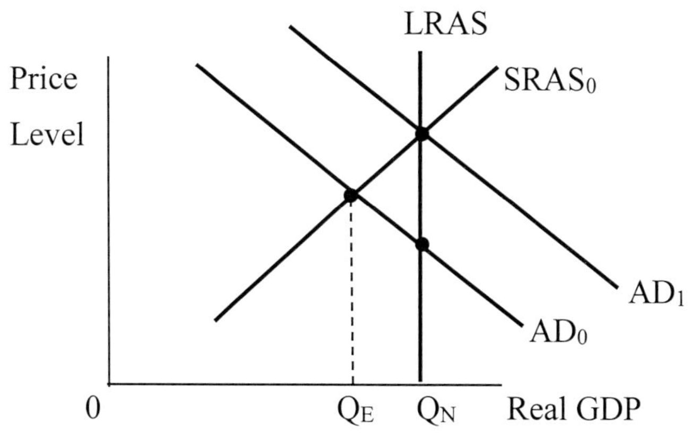

26. If the economy depicted in the graph above is currently in equilibrium on AD_0 and $SRAS_0$, then it is experiencing:
   a. a recessionary gap.
   b. an inflationary gap.
   c. a short-run equilibrium at full employment.
   d. long-run equilibrium.

27. AD_0 might shift right to AD_1 to close the gap if:
   a. the President raises taxes on businesses and households.
   b. Congress uses expansionary discretionary fiscal policy.
   c. input prices decline causing decreases in costs of production.
   d. the money supply decreases.

28. What is the maximum change in equilibrium real GDP that could occur as result of a $20 billion decrease in investment spending if the MPC is 0.90?
   a. $200 billion increase
   b. $200 billion decrease
   c. $180 billion increase
   d. $180 billion decrease

29. Suppose short-run equilibrium real GDP is $5,000 billion, full-employment (natural) real GDP is $5,200 billion, and the MPC is 0.80. What fiscal policy action could put the economy at full-employment equilibrium, according to the simple Keynesian model?
    a. Increase government spending by $40 billion
    b. Decrease taxes by $50 billion
    c. Increase both government spending and taxes by $200 billion
    d. All of the above are possible actions that could put the economy at full-employment equilibrium

30. According to Keynes, recessions are a result of:
    a. insufficient aggregate demand.
    b. insufficient aggregate supply.
    c. flexible prices, wages, and interest rates.
    d. flexible income, output, and employment.

31. Keeping money in a savings account as a safety measure against possible future income declines or job loss represents money functioning as a:
    a. store of value (store of wealth).
    b. unit of account.
    c. medium of exchange.
    d. standard of value.

32. The use of money is more efficient than barter for conducting exchanges because:
    a. the government has complete control over the use of money.
    b. using money increases transactions times and decreases specialization.
    c. barter makes it easier to compare the relative values of goods and services which helps consumers make better buying decisions.
    d. money does not require satisfying a double coincidence of wants which reduces transactions times.

33. In a fractional reserve banking system, banks create money by:
    a. purchasing securities from the Federal Reserve.
    b. printing money to lend to the public.
    c. making loans from their required reserves.
    d. making loans from their excess reserves.

34. A bank with $120 million in deposits has required reserves of __________ if the required reserve ratio is 10%.
    a. $1.2 million
    b. $10 million
    c. $12 million
    d. $120 million

35. What is the maximum amount of deposits that can be supported by total bank reserves of \$50 billion when the required reserve ratio is 10%?
   a. \$5 billion
   b. \$10 billion
   c. \$50 billion
   d. \$500 billion

Use the data in the table below to answer the next three questions. Assume the value of any item not listed is zero.

Currency held by the public	**\$200 billion**
Checkable deposits	**\$700 billion**
Traveler's checks	**\$10 billion**
Small denomination time deposits	**\$300 billion**
Savings deposits	**\$200 billion**
Retail money funds	**\$200 billion**
Total bank reserves	**\$87.5 billion**
Excess reserves	**\$0**

36. The value of the M1 money supply is:
   a. \$210 billion.
   b. \$700 billion.
   c. \$910 billion.
   d. \$1,830 billion.

37. If depositors move \$50 billion from savings deposits into checkable deposits, then the value of M1:
   a. increases by \$50 billion, the value of M2 decreases to \$1,560 billion, and the system becomes more liquid.
   b. increases by \$50 billion, the value of M2 stays \$1,610 billion, and the system becomes more liquid.
   c. stays \$900 billion, the value of M2 decreases by \$50 billion, and the system becomes more liquid.
   d. increases to \$750 billion, the value of M2 stays the same, and the system becomes less liquid.

38. A decrease in the required-reserve ratio will:
   a. decrease the value of the simple deposit multiplier.
   b. increase the value of the simple deposit multiplier.
   c. have no impact on the value of the simple deposit multiplier.
   d. negate the value of the simple deposit multiplier.

Use the information for Better Bank below to answer the next two questions.

Assets		Liabilities	
Total Bank Reserves	**$80,000**	**Checkable Deposits**	**$800,000**
Loans	**$720,000**		

39. If the required-reserve ratio is 10%, Better Bank must hold required reserves equal to:
    a. $10,000.
    b. $80,000.
    c. $72,000.
    d. $720,000.

40. If the required-reserve ratio is 10%, then Better Bank can make new loans equal to:
    a. $0.
    b. $10,000.
    c. $72,000.
    d. $720,000.

41. The Federal Reserve:
    a. determines U.S. fiscal policy by influencing the amount of available credit in the economy.
    b. cannot legally provide loans to banks but can ease bank liquidity problems through purchasing government securities from banks.
    c. is responsible for both fiscal and monetary policy in the United States.
    d. controls the flow of money and credit in the economy through its conduct of monetary policy.

42 . The voting members of the Federal Open Market Committee (FOMC) are:
    a. all 7 Federal Reserve Governors plus 5 Federal Reserve Bank Presidents.
    b. 5 Federal Reserve Governors plus 7 Federal Reserve Bank Presidents.
    c. all of the regional Federal Reserve Bank Presidents.
    d. one member from each of the 12 Federal Reserve Districts.

43. The rate one bank pays another for an overnight loan of reserves is called the:
    a. discount rate.
    b. prime rate.
    c. federal funds rate.
    d. federal reserve rate.

44. If the Fed is pursuing an expansionary monetary policy, it would ***not***:
   a. buy bonds in the open market.
   b. raise the federal funds rate target.
   c. lower the discount rate.
   d. increase the money supply.

Use the information for the banking system below to answer the next three questions.

Assets		**Liabilities**	
Total Bank Reserves	**$20 billion**	**Checkable Deposits**	**$100 billion**
Loans	**$70 billion**		
Securities (Bonds)	**$10 billion**		

45. The banking system is currently fully loaned up (in equilibrium) if the required-reserve ratio is:
   a. 25%.
   b. 20%.
   c. 10%.
   d. 5%.

46. Using the required-reserve ratio found in the previous question, if the Fed buys $5 billion worth of government bonds from banks, assuming no leakages into cash, total bank reserves will equal _____ billion, and excess reserves will equal _____ billion.
   a. $5; $4
   b. $25; $5
   c. $25; $10
   d. $24; $4

47. After a $5 billion purchase of securities (government bonds) from banks by the Fed, if all banks make loans until excess reserves equal zero and there are no cash leakages, checkable deposits can expand as a result of new lending by a maximum of (using the reserve ratio found above) _______ billion.
   a. $5
   b. $10
   c. $20
   d. $25

48. Suppose the Federal Reserve Board of Governors has determined that tighter credit conditions and higher interest rates will help control inflation. To accomplish this goal, they will ***most*** likely do which of the following?
   a. Announce a lower federal funds rate target
   b. Raise the required-reserve ratio
   c. Announce a lower discount rate
   d. Sell government securities (bonds) in the open market

49. The primary way the Fed alters the amount of reserves and lending capacity in the banking system is:
   a. changes in the discount rate.
   b. changes in the required-reserve ratio.
   c. by printing money.
   d. open market operations.

50. If the economy is in a recession, Federal Reserve policy will most likely be:
   a. expansionary and tax rates will be kept low by the Fed.
   b. expansionary and interest rates will be kept low by the Fed.
   c. contractionary and tax rates will be kept high by the Fed.
   d. contractionary and interest rates will be kept high by the Fed.

51. If the nominal rate of interest is 7.5 percent and the expected real rate of interest is 5 percent, then the expected inflation rate is equal to:
   a. 2.5 percent.
   b. 7.5 percent.
   c. 5 percent.
   d. 12.5 percent.

52. If the Fed sells government bonds in the open market, the:
   a. money demand will shift to the right, causing interest rates to rise.
   b. money demand will shift to the left, causing interest rates to fall.
   c. money supply will shift to the left, causing interest rates to rise.
   d. money supply will shift to the right, causing interest rates to fall.

53. Suppose the money market is initially in equilibrium. If the Fed lowers the discount rate and buys more bonds on the open market, then:
   a. the money supply will increase and the interest rate will rise.
   b. the money supply will increase and the interest rate will fall.
   c. the money supply will decrease and the interest rate will rise.
   d. the money supply will decrease and the interest rate will fall.

54. Which of the following best describes the Keynesian perspective of how expansionary monetary policy affects the economy?
   a. Lower interest rates, higher investment and consumption expenditure, and higher real GDP
   b. Lower interest rates, lower investment and consumption expenditure, and lower real GDP
   c. Higher interest rates, lower investment and consumption expenditure, and lower real GDP
   d. Higher interest rates, higher investment and consumption expenditure, and higher real GDP

55. According to Keynesian monetary theory, monetary policy is ineffective:
a. when the money demand curve slopes downward to the right.
b. if interest rates are very sensitive to changes in the money supply.
c. if the money market is in a liquidity trap.
d. when investment spending responds significantly to changes in the interest rate.

56. Bond prices and the market rate of interest (yields) are:
a. always equal.
b. negatively (inversely) related.
c. positively (directly) related.
d. unrelated to the money supply.

57. The cause of continued increases in aggregate demand and continued inflation is:
a. continued increases in the money supply.
b. continued increases in the tax rate.
c. adverse supply shocks, such as an increase in the price of oil.
d. beneficial supply shocks, such as unseasonably good weather.

Use the graph below to answer the next question.

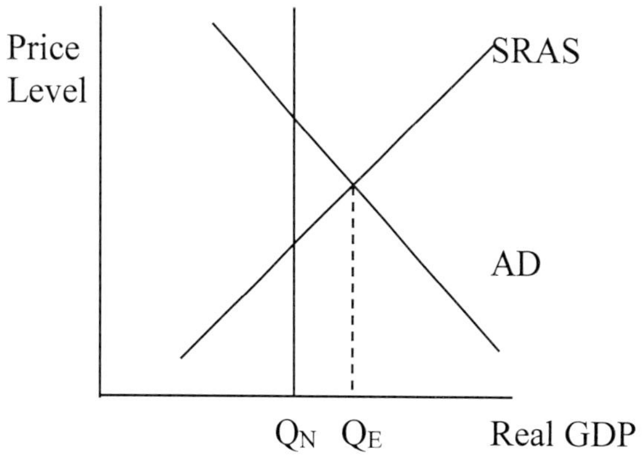

58. An appropriate *monetary* policy approach to the situation in this economy might include:
a. the Federal Reserve increasing taxes.
b. Congress reducing government spending.
c. a Federal Reserve open market sale of securities (government bonds).
d. Congress decreasing the discount rate.

59. The notion that the Fed should adhere to a policy of steady and predictable expansion of the money supply represents:
   a. the monetary rule put forth by the Monetarists.
   b. the fiscal rule put forth by the Monetarists.
   c. the monetary rule put forth by the Keynesians.
   d. the fiscal rule put forth by the Keynesians.

Use the information below to answer the next question.

Velocity = 4   Real GDP = \$4 billion   Price Level = 1.25

60. According to the equation of exchange, the value of the money supply is:
   a. \$5 billion
   b. \$1.25 billion
   c. \$12.8 billion
   d. impossible to determine from the information given.

Answers to Practice Exam III

1. b	16. a	31. a	46. b
2. c	17. a	32. d	47. d
3. c	18. a	33. d	48. d
4. d	19. b	34. c	49. d
5. d	20. b	35. d	50. b
6. d	21. d	36. c	51. a
7. b	22. d	37. b	52. c
8. c	23. d	38. b	53. b
9. c	24. c	39. b	54. a
10. d	25. c	40. a	55. c
11. c	26. a	41. d	56. b
12. a	27. b	42. a	57. a
13. c	28 b	43. c	58. c
14. a	29. d	44. b	59. a
15. b	30. a	45. b	60. b